The Quality
Audit Handbook

Also available from ASQ Quality Press

After the Quality Audit: Closing the Loop on the Audit Process
J. P. Russell and Terry Regel

Fundamentals of Quality Auditing
B. Scott Parsowith

The Quality Audit: A Management Evaluation Tool
Charles A. Mills

Quality Audits for Improved Performance, Second Edition
Dennis R. Arter

Quality Management Benchmark Assessment, Second Edition
J. P. Russell

How to Plan an Audit
ASQ Quality Audit Technical Committee; Charles B. Robinson, editor

To request a complimentary catalog of publications, call 1-800-248-1946
or visit our Website at qualitypress.asq.org.

The Quality Audit Handbook

Principles, Implementation and Use

Second Edition

ASQ Quality Audit Division

J. P. Russell, Editor

ASQ Quality Press
Milwaukee, Wisconsin

The Quality Audit Handbook, Second Edition
J.P. Russell

The quality audit handbook / ASQC Quality Audit Division; J.P. Russell, editing
director.—2nd ed.
     p.   cm.
   Includes bibliographical references and index.
   ISBN 0-87389-460-X (alk. paper)
   1. Auditing—Handbooks, annuals, etc. I. Russell, J. P. (James P.),
   1945- II. American Society for Quality Control. Quality Audit Division.
   HF5667 .Q35 1999
   657'.45 21—dc21   99-044972

10 9 8 7 6 5 4 3 2

ISBN 0-87389-460-X

Acquisitions Editor: Ken Zielske
Project Editor: Annemieke Koudstaal
Production Administrator: Shawn Dohogne

ASQ Mission: The American Society for Quality advances individual and organizational
performance excellence worldwide by providing opportunities for learning, quality
improvement, and knowledge exchange.

Attention: Bookstores, Wholesalers, Schools and Corporations:
ASQ Quality Press books, videotapes, audiotapes, and software are available at quantity
discounts with bulk purchases for business, educational, or instructional use. For
information, please contact ASQ Quality Press at 800-248-1946, or write to ASQ Quality
Press, P.O. Box 3005, Milwaukee, WI 53201-3005.

To place orders or to request a free copy of the ASQ Quality Press Publications Catalog,
including ASQ membership information, call 800-248-1946. Visit our web site at
www.asq.org. or qualitypress.asq.org.

Printed in the United States of America

Printed on acid-free paper

American Society for Quality

Quality Press
611 East Wisconsin Avenue
Milwaukee, Wisconsin 53202
Call toll free 800-248-1946
qualitypress.asq.org

Contents

Foreword

The quality audit profession has grown remarkably in the two years since the handbook was first published. ISO 9000, ISO 14000, QS-9000, and a myriad of other recent standards call for the certification of audit personnel and the performance of audits. This growth has been international in scope and has given new opportunities to every quality auditor. It has given rise to new job opportunities, new companies, and even new business sectors. We have witnessed a transition from stated quality to verified quality for many businesses. We have witnessed a renaissance of the quality audit profession and its recognition as an integral part of doing business.

The second edition of the handbook has recognized the transition and transformation of the audit profession. In addition, we have all learned a lot since the first edition was published in 1997. Some of what we have learned has been added to this second edition of *The Quality Audit Handbook*. Some must wait while we develop more information, develop transferable techniques, and develop a consensus among auditors before including it in the handbook.

This edition has been expanded to include more information on the softer sides of auditing, including ethics, liability, and sampling considerations. Each chapter has been revisited and, where necessary, revised to address our current knowledge of quality auditing. Some chapters have had extensive revision; some have had little revision. We anticipate more changes, revisions, and additions as we move into the new millennium.

A journey of a thousand miles begins with the first step. Our first step was the first edition of *The Quality Audit Handbook* published in 1997.

This second edition represents the second step of our journey. The handbook has been reorganized to parallel the revised ASQ Certified Quality Auditor Body of Knowledge.

Regardless of the updating, reorganization, and new material added, the handbook will always be a work-in progress because auditing is a vital, changing, growing profession seeking continuous improvement. In keeping with the aim of continuous improvement, we invite each member, organization, and industry with information to share on subjects related to the BoK, to submit their new knowledge, new perspectives, or new practices to the editor.

I want to thank J. P. Russell for his patient efforts at coordinating the second edition of the handbook. His efforts at bringing some form of consensus to each chapter are recognized by all who participated in the second edition. I also want to recognize Wendy Finnerty, Chairperson for the Quality Audit Division, who authorized the second edition and worked with us to ensure that we met the various deadlines for publishing.

Norman C. Frank
Vice Chairperson, Technical
ASQ Quality Audit Division

Notes to the Reader

This handbook supports the quality auditor Body of Knowledge (BoK) developed for the ASQ Certified Quality Auditor (CQA) program. The quality audit Body of Knowledge was revised in August 1997. The second edition addresses the new Body of Knowledge topics and the new arrangement. The body of knowledge was re-arranged from V Parts to VII Parts and (27 percent of the topics in the new BoK were not specifically addressed in the old BoK). The fundamental quality audit principles have not changed, but additional topics were added to address ethics, alignment with organization objectives, audit program management activities, and corrective action of audit findings. The second edition also contains additional information on sampling in an appendix.

The text is aligned with the Body of Knowledge for easy cross-referencing. Through use of this handbook, we hope to increase your understanding of the quality audit Body of Knowledge.

The Use. The handbook can be used by new auditors to gain an understanding of quality auditing. Experienced auditors will find it to be a useful reference. Audit managers and quality managers will use the handbook as a guide for leading their auditing programs.

The handbook will also be used by trainers and educators as source material for teaching the fundamentals of quality auditing. It is not designed as a stand-alone text to prepare for the ASQ Certified Quality Auditor (CQA) exam. As for all ASQ certification activities, you are encouraged to work with your local section for preparation. *The Quality*

Audit Handbook, when used in conjunction with other published materials, is appropriate for refresher courses, and we hope that trainers will use it in that manner.

The handbook contains information to support all aspects of the quality audit Body of Knowledge and is not limited to what only new auditors need to know. Hence, the amount of material in each part of the handbook is not directly proportional to exam emphasis. The CQA exam is designed to test a candidate's basic knowledge of quality auditing. All the information in the handbook is important, but those preparing for the CQA exam should spend more time in their weakest areas and the BoK parts receiving more emphasis on the exam. The number of questions and percentage of CQA exam questions is indicated at the start of each part of the handbook.

The Contents. The handbook is organized to be in alignment with the quality auditor Body of Knowledge. We have included this Body of Knowledge in back of the handbook as an appendix. Since many concepts and practices of quality auditing are still evolving, the Body of Knowledge will be revised from time to time. As changes occur, the handbook must also be revised to keep current.

Terms and definitions are addressed throughout the text and especially in Part VII, Chapter A and in the glossary. The glossary is based on the definitions in ANSI/ISO/ASQ A8402-1994. ANSI/ISO/ASQ A8402-1994 definitions have undergone extensive peer review and are accepted worldwide. However, even the definition of audit terms continues to evolve in order to meet the needs of standard users.

The Quality Audit Handbook represents generally accepted quality audit practices for both internal and external applications. As such, it may not depict the best practice for all situations.

The handbook uses generic terms to support broad principles. For clarity, specific industry examples and stories from CQA's are sometimes used to explain a topic in the Body of Knowledge. The stories, depicted as side bars, are a way to share the experiences of other quality auditors. Industry examples incorporated into the text are not intended to be all inclusive and representative of all industries. Needless to say, this work cannot address the most appropriate practice for every industry or organization.

This publication, which describes audit methods and their application, is not intended to be used as a national or international standard, although it references many existing standards. The conventions for writing standards and using the term *shall* to mean a requirement and *should* to mean a guideline *do not* apply to the quality audit handbook.

Who Wrote It. The Certified Quality Auditors who supplied information for the handbook represent a broad spectrum of organizations in the United States and around the world. About 70 individuals contributed material for the first edition and another 40 for the second edition. Input from members and a number of published texts were also used to create and develop *The Quality Audit Handbook.* It represents internal and external audits in a variety of product and service industries, regulated and nonregulated.

To avoid the perception of bias toward any particular approach, for the first edition we chose a unique way to develop the handbook. A professional writer from outside the quality field conducted telephone interviews to supplement the information provided in contributed papers and published texts. Significant issues relating to the principles and intent of quality auditing were referred to a tie-breaker committee for resolution. Extensive peer review further strengthened the manuscript. We followed a similar (though less extensive) approach for the second edition. The handbook committee members were the writers; reviewers provided feedback on the revised text; and the editor sorted, culled, and refined the manuscript.

Why the Handbook. The ASQ Quality Audit Division sponsored the development of this handbook to promote the use of quality auditing as a management tool our primary mission. We believe that the Quality Audit Division's members possess the greatest concentration of theoretical and practical quality auditing knowledge in the world. In *The Quality Audit Handbook,* we tried to give you the benefits of this collective expertise.

J. P. Russell, Editor

Acknowledgments

ASQ Quality Audit Division members contributed to both the first and second editions of *The Quality Audit Handbook.* For the first edition, some wrote topical papers specifically for use in the handbook, and others provided input through a series of telephone interviews. A professional writer prepared a manuscript, and a team of reviewers provided feedback. For the really difficult areas, a tie-breaker committee made the final decisions concerning the technical content. Over 70 Quality Audit Division members participated. The initial effort resulted in the first edition, published in January 1997, which became the basis for the second edition. Where possible the exact wording of the first edition was retained for the second edition except for when additional clarification was needed and when apparent conflicts existed within the handbook.

For the second edition, members of a handbook committee provided text and examples to fill in the gaps created by the quality audit body of knowledge issued in August 1997. A team of reviewers provided feedback to the editor who revised and refined the second edition. The evolution and development of the handbook has continued to be a team effort. In all, over 40 QAD members participated in the second edition.

The acknowledgments for the first and second editions are in chronological order of involvement of project by teams and do not reflect the significance of individual contributions.

EARLY PROJECT PARTICIPATION (OUR VISIONARIES)

Norman C. Frank

Barbara Houlihan

John C. Dronkers

FIRST EDITION

Topical Paper Contributions

Early in the development of the handbook, division members provided new or existing papers for consideration for the proposed handbook. Some papers were not selected because they simply did not fit our needs. Putting together a creditable paper is very difficult, and the importance of the contributions cannot be overstated. We wish to thank all those who prepared and submitted papers to support the development of the handbook. Here are the authors whose papers were used.

Glena G. Anger and co-authors Robert Cofer, Tom Feyerabend, Joyce Ford, Marti Levy, Patti McGuire, and Betty Wims

Shyam Banik

Rudolph C. Hirzel

Kathryn E. Jackson and Thomas B. Tucker

Joseph H. Maday, Jr.

Larry McArthur

Jerry Nation

Writer Organization

Dorinda Clippinger (owner of Penworthy, Inc., of Cincinnati) and Janice Smith (writer) worked well with the members of the Quality Audit Division. Their professional approach and can-do attitude made the development of the handbook run smoothly. They provided us with a great first edition of the handbook.

Interviews with the Writer

Some of the necessary material was not initially available. Additionally, some of the material from the referenced texts was conflicting. We therefore found it necessary to query some of our members by telephone about certain topics within the quality audit Body of Knowledge. They provided supplemental information and examples for us to use. They helped fill in the missing pieces of information needed to complete the work. The members who participated in the interviews and their credentials at that time are:

Dennis R. Arter, PE, FASQ, ASQ CQA

John Barrett, ASQ CQA, ASQ CRE, RAB QSA

Don Beckwith, ASQ CQA, Ball State University CTC

Mary Carter Berrios, ASQ CQA, ASQ CQE, ASQ CQM

Cheryl A. Boyce, ASQ CQA and RAB QSLA

John J. Boyle, ASQ CQA

Bruce H. Campbell, PE, FASQ, ASQ CQA, ASQ CQE

Mike Coughlin, ASQ CQA, ASQ CQE

Traci V. A. Edwards, ASQ CQA, ASQ CQE, ASQ CQM

Norman C. Frank, PE, ASQ CQA, ASQ CQE

Marvin C. Gabalski, ASQ CQA, ASQ CQE, ASQ CRE, RAB QSLA

David A. Kelly, Ph.D., ASQ CQA, ASQ CQE, RAB QSLA

Judith Ann Malsbury, ASQ CQA, ASQ CQE, ASQ CQM

George Mouradian, PE, FASQ, ASQ CQA, ASQ CQE, ASQ CRE

Robert J. Nash, Ph.D., ASQ CQA, ASQ CQM

Terry Regel, ASQ CQA, ASQ CQE, RAB QSLA, IRCA LA

Charles Robinson, FASQ, ASQ CQA, RAB QSLA

Haakon Rud, DnV Certified Lead Auditor

Douglas Stimson, ASQ CQE, RAB QSLA

Steven Wilson, ASQ CQA

Manuscript Reviewers

It was the job of the reviewers to review text for technical correctness. The many reviewers provided feedback, ideas for developing the work, and provided examples for inclusion into the handbook.

United States Reviewers

Ronald L. Ackers, PE, FASQ, ASQ CQA, ASQ CQE, ASQ CRE, ASQ CQM, IIE-CST, RAB QSLA

Douglas G. Anderson, ASQ CQA

Richard M. Baehr, ASQ CQA, RAB QALA

Lon L. Barrett, ASQ CQA

Jimmy Bell, ASQ CQA

Bernard Carpenter, ASQ CQA, ASQ CQM, MSQA

Ariel Castro, ASQ CQA

Robert G. Chadwick, FASQ, ASQ CQA, ASQ CQE, ASQ CMI

Robert G. Chisholm, Sr., ASQ CQA, ASQ CQE, ASQ CMI, RAB QSLA, QS-9000 Auditor

Jim Coley, ASQ CQA

Peter R. Corradi, ASQ CQA, ASQ CQE, RAB QSA

Harold Crotts, ASQ CQA, ASQ CQE, ASQ CMI, AAS, Ind. Eng.

Jeffrey A. Deeds, ASQ CQA

Kathleen L. Eaves, ASQ CQA

Cheryl A. Hadley, ASQ CQA

Rudolph C. Hirzel, ASQ CQA, ASQ CQE, ASQ CQM

David Kildahl, ASQ CQA

Ramesh Konda, ASQ CQA, ASQ CQE

Jim Lamar, ASQ CQA

James (Rusty) Lusk, ASQ CQA, ASQ CQE, ASQ CQM, RAB QSLA

Donald Mason, ASQ CQA

Jerry T. Nation, PE, ASQ CQA, ASQ CQE, ASQ CQM, RAB QSLA

Chris Newcomer, ASQ CQA

Martin F. Patton, ASQ CQA, RAB QSLA, IRCA LA

Steven L. Pearson, ASQ CQA, RAB QSLA, AIAG Cert, QS-9000 LA

David Prins, ASQ CQA, ASQ CMI, ASQ CQE, ASQ CQT, ASQ CRE, NAPM-CPM

Terry Regel, ASQ CQA, ASQ CQE, RAB QSLA, IRCA LA

John Rinaldi, ASQ CQA

Gwen E. Sampson, ASQ CQA

Stephen Sheng, ASQ CQA, RAB QSLA

Ron Spring, ASQ CQA

David L. Thibault, ASQ CQA, ASQ CQE

Alfred F. Wales, ASQ CQA, ASQ CQE

Stoney F. Walker, ASQ CQA

Worldwide Reviewers

Steven Britton (Canada), PE, ASQC CQE, ASQC CQA

Chui Karson (Hong Kong), ASQC CQA, ASQC CQE

Darren Kent (Canada), ASQC CQA

Ian A. MacNab (Canada),

Akhilesh Singh (India), IRCA LA

Peter Wright (Canada), ASQC CQA, IRC A, AOQ CQT

Jorge Xavier (Brazil)

Roger Zigmond (Canada), ASQC CQA, ASQC CQE

Tie-Breaker Committee

The tie-breaker committee resolved differences that surfaced in the review process. They provided guidance to the editor and writer. The tie-breaker committee helped to ensure that various views were considered. It also kept the project focused on the quality audit Body of Knowledge.

Norman C. Frank, PE, ASQ CQA, ASQ CQE

Linda Reinhart, ASQ CQA

Gerry Sherman, ASQ CQA, ASQ CQE, ASQ CQM

SECOND EDITION

For the second edition, a group of ASQ Quality Audit Division members formed the handbook subcommittee and volunteered to be responsible for updating one part of the quality audit Body of Knowledge. Updating included adding examples and addressing new topics introduced by the August 1997 revised Body of Knowledge. Committee contributors and their assigned part of the Body of Knowledge were as follows.

Richard M. Baehr, Part VI: Audit Program Management

Wallace (Chuck) Carlson, Jr., Part IV: Audit Reporting

Bernie Carpenter, Part II: Audit Preparation

Norman C. Frank, Part I: Ethics, Professional Conduct, and Liability; Audit Sampling Appendix

Rudolph C. Hirzel, Part VII: General Knowledge and Skills

Baskar Kotte, Part III: Audit Performance

Jim Maiden, Part VI: Audit Program Management

Terry Regel, Part V: Corrective Action Follow-up and Closure

J. P. Russell, Handbook Committe Chair

Second Edition Manuscript Reviewers

The reviewers provided feedback on the updated information from the committee members and the editor. It is obvious from the quality of the review comments and the examples provided that many reviewers spent long hours carefully reviewing the manuscript.

Rober A. Abbott, FASQ, ASQ CQE, RAB QSLA

Judith J. Akers, RAB QSLA

Ron Akers, PE, FASQ, ASQ CQE, ASQ CQA, ASQ CRE, ASQ CQM, IIE-CSI, RAB QSLA

Ralph W. Arnott, Principal, ASQ CQA, ASQ CQE

Dennis R. Arter, PE, FASQ, ASQ CQA

Richard M. Baehr, ASQ CQA, RAB QSLA

Shyam Banik, ASQ CQA, ASQ CQE, RAB QSLA

John Barrett, ASQ CQA, ASQ CQE, ASQ CRE, ASQ CQM, RAB QSA

John J. Boyle, Principal Quality Eng. ASQ CQA

James M. Coley, ASQ CQA, RAB QSPA

Linda L. Feaster, ASQ CQA

Wendy Finnerty, ASQ CQA

Norman C. Frank, ASQ CQA, ASQ CQE

Peter J. Gauthier, ASQ CQA

Milad R. Matthias, Ph.D., PE

A. B. (Gus) Mundel, Chair of TAG 69, FASQ, ASQ Edwards Medallist

Jay Michael Pratt, RAB QSLA, Institution of Nuclear Engineers Fellow

Alfred F. Wales, ASQ CQA, ASQ CQE

Daniel S. Whelan, ASQ CQA, ASQ CQM

The final acknowledgment is for the QAD officers, especially Norman Frank (Vice Chair Technical) and Terry Regel (Technical Publications Chair), for their help and leadership. Many times they were asked for their assistance on certain topics and the direction the handbook needed to take.

J. P. Russell, Editor

Overview

This Second Edition of the Quality Audit Division handbook starts with Part I and ends with Part VII of the quality audit Body of Knowledge. Although this has a distinct logic and value to the reader, it can also be confusing to readers who are not familiar with auditing terms. This chapter is an overview of quality auditing to better prepare readers for Part I of the handbook. It is not meant to be an explanation of the Body of Knowledge. If after reading the overview, you would like additional background information, turn to Part VII, chapter A.

The word *audit* is associated with formal or methodical examining, reviewing, and investigating. Professional groups such as the American Society for Quality and the Institute of Internal Auditors define preferred methods for conducting examinations and investigations. For *quality audits,* the Quality Audit Division of the American Society for Quality has developed a Body of Knowledge for quality auditing. The American Society for Quality also certifies individuals who meet the criteria for Certified Quality Auditor. This handbook explains the topics listed in the Body of Knowledge issued by the American Society for Quality.

Quality auditing is a prescribed work practice or process. There is a preferred sequential order of activities that should be performed to conduct a proper quality audit. Part II (Audit Preparation) through Part V (Corrective Action Follow-up and Closure) of the Body of Knowledge follows the same preferred order. Quality audits must be prepared for (planning ahead), performed (conducting the audit), have the results reported (let everyone know what was found), and then have the results responded to (feedback on what is going to happen next) from the organization that was audited. It is common to refer to these as phases of an audit: preparation phase, performance phase, report phase, and follow-up and closure phase. As with most service jobs, the way the service provider goes about performing the job may influence the outcome. That is why Part I of the handbook is about ethics and conduct. Auditing is considered a profession; therefore, individual auditors need to know how to conduct themselves in a professional manner.

We can start with one of the many definitions of an audit (see Part VII, chapter A for a detailed discussion of audit terms). The ASQC Quality Auditing Technical Committee (now the Quality Audit Division of American Society for Quality) defined *audit* as "A planned, independent, and documented assessment to determine whether agreed-upon requirements are being met."

For now, let us think of a quality audit as an assessment to determine whether agreed-upon *quality* requirements are being met (whereas an environmental audit may be related to environmental requirements or a financial audit to financial or accounting requirements). A distinguishing attribute of an audit, compared to an inspection, is independence. The individual performing an audit must be independent of the area being audited. The degree of independence varies depending on the situation and the type of audit. For example, one cannot achieve total independence when auditing departments within his/her own organization.

There are several groupings or classifications of audits depending on the relationships (external and internal), need for independence, and reason for the audit (verification of product, process, or system). In the following diagram, the circle represents an organization. Outside the circle is the organization's customers and suppliers. All organizations have customer-supplier relationships. Any audits done inside the circle are *internal* audits, and audits done outside the circle are *external* audits. We further classify the audits as first-party, second-party, and third-party audits based on relationships. *First-party audits* take place within the organization itself (the same as *internal* audits) and are inside the circle. *Second-party audits* are audits of suppliers or of customers crossing into the circle to audit the organization (their supplier). *Third-party audits* are totally independent of the customer-supplier relationship and off to the right in the diagram. Third-party audits may result in independent certification of a product, process, or system.

Types of audits.

Source: J. P. Russell & Associates training materials. Used with permission.

Auditors can focus the audit (examination and investigation) on different areas, depending on the needs. A product or service audit determines if product or service requirements (tangible characteristics or attributes) are being met. The process audit determines if process requirements (methods, procedures) are being met. A system audit determines if system requirements (manual, policy, standards, regulations) are being met. The handbook discusses all types of quality audits, but most of the discussion is focused on quality system audits (which are the most complex and have the greatest potential influence). A system can be thought of as a group of processes providing a product or service.

When auditors are auditing, they are making observations and collecting objective evidence (data). They are seeking to verify that requirements are being met. They must do this by collecting hard evidence, not hearsay or promises. Evidence produced as a result of the activity may be tangible objects, records, or eyewitnesses. Auditors must be familiar with auditing techniques and the standards they are auditing against. What auditors observe is not always straightforward or obvious, so they must be able to judge whether the intent (reason for the requirement) is being met or addressed. The objective evidence and the method of collecting the evidence will form the basis of the audit report.

The primary participants needed for conducting an audit are auditor, auditee, and client. The person conducting the audit is called the auditor, lead auditor, or audit team leader. The organization being audited or investigated is called the auditee. There is also a client, the person or organization that has requested the audit. Audits are only conducted when someone requests one; they do not happen by accident. There has to be a sponsor or client with authority to call for a quality audit.

Any type of organization can be audited against a set of standard requirements. The organization can produce a product or provide a service. An organization can be audited against almost any type of standards or set of requirements. The requirements or performance standards can be government regulations, ANSI/ISO/ASQ Q9001-1994 or Q9004-1994 requirements, QS-9000, Malcolm Baldrige National Quality Award criteria, and so on. If there is a set of rules, auditors can compare actual practice to the rules.

While auditors are comparing actual practice to the rules or standards (determining compliance to requirements), they may also observe that certain practices and trends are not in the best interest of the organization being audited. Hence, in some cases, areas that are not effective or areas that can be improved are reported as input for management review.

Findings are the results of the investigation. Findings of the audit may be reported as nonconformances, findings, noncompliances, defects, concerns, and so forth. It is important for everyone to agree on the terminology that will be used in the audit report.

Recently there has been more emphasis on looking beyond conducting the audit steps to management of the audit process. It is important to understand the objectives of the audit function and the potential benefits to the organization. This understanding and clarification has resulted in some audit programs being strictly limited to auditing for compliance and other audit programs seeking management input on the effectiveness of compliant systems.

Auditing is a management tool. Used internally, its purpose is to verify that systems are compliant and suitable to achieve objectives. Externally, it may be used to determine compliance to a set of rules. For additional background information on quality auditing, turn to Part VII, chapter A.

Part I

Ethics, Professional Conduct, and Liability Issues

[5 of the CQA exam questions or 3%]

Part I covers three areas of prime importance to the professionalism of an auditor and the quality audit profession. Ethics affect professional conduct, and professional conduct affects liability.

Ethics are basic philosophical conclusions about whether conduct and behavior is right or wrong. Ethics are also moral principles by which an individual is guided. It is imperative that quality auditors be ethical (i.e., honest and impartial) and behave appropriately (i.e., with professional conduct) in carrying out their responsibilities.

Professional conduct is the manner in which the auditor conducts him/herself. Objectivity, courtesy, honesty, and many other character attributes combine to make up the particular conduct of any auditor during an audit.

Liability is the degree of legal responsibility an individual or company has in a given situation. Liability issues are beginning to surface with the increase in third-party auditing and certification/registration. The effect of the ISO registration program has yet to be fully felt in the legal arena, but several issues important to the auditor will be discussed in this part of the book.

Chapter A
ASQ Code of Ethics

The American Society for Quality (ASQ) developed a code of ethics that each ASQ Certified Quality Auditor must understand and follow. The content of the ASQ code of ethics is included in the examination for Certified Quality Auditor. Acceptance of the code of ethics by the examinee is required prior to certification.

Audit ethics is perhaps the area that demands the most skill from an auditor. Training is available for enhancing skills in checklist development, interviewing techniques, audit documentation, follow-up methods, and almost all other phases of an audit. Very little information, on the other hand, is available on the topic of audit ethics. An auditor's use of questionable or unethical methods during or following an audit can quickly erase any favorable impressions and be detrimental to the auditor and the auditing organization as a whole.

A code of ethics is a standard for conduct. An auditor's ethical and moral principles should be compatible with a formal set of ethical standards. ASQ's code of ethics[1] for members is shown in Figure 1.

Many companies and professional organizations have developed a code of ethics to guide them in the performance of their work. The Institute of Internal Auditors (IIA), the professional society for financial auditors, developed their code of ethics in 1974. The IIA took a slightly different approach in the content of their code of ethics than ASQ. Although these codes of ethics represent different perspectives, they both have the same basic principles described in their standards of conduct. Figure 2 presents the IIA Code of Ethics.

To uphold and advance the honor and dignity of the profession, and in keeping with high standards of ethical conduct, I acknowledge that I:

Fundamental Principles

  I.   Will be honest and impartial; will serve with devotion my employer, my clients, and the public.

 II.   Will strive to increase the competence and prestige of the profession.

III.   Will use my knowledge and skill for the advancement of human welfare and in promoting the safety and reliability of products for public use.

IV.   Will earnestly endeavor to aid the work of the Society.

Relations With the Public

1.1   Will do whatever I can to promote the reliability and safety of all products that come within my jurisdiction.

1.2   Will endeavor to extend public knowledge of the work of the Society and its members that relates to the public welfare.

1.3   Will be dignified and modest in explaining my work and merit.

1.4   Will preface any public statements that I may issue by clearly indicating on whose behalf they are made.

Relations With Employers and Clients

2.1   Will act in professional matters as a faithful agent or trustee for each employer or client.

2.2   Will inform each client or employer of any business connections, interests, or affiliations that might influence my judgment or impair the equitable character of my services.

2.3   Will indicate to my employer the adverse consequences to be expected if my professional judgment is overruled.

2.4   Will not disclose information concerning the business affairs or technical processes of any present or former employer or client without his or her consent.

2.5   Will not accept compensation from more than one party for the same service without the consent of all parties. If employed, I will engage in supplementary employment of consulting practice only with the consent of my employer.

Figure 1. ASQ code of ethics.

Relations With Peers

3.1   Will take care that credit for the work of others is given to those to whom it is due.

3.2   Will endeavor to aid the professional development and advancement of those in my employ or under my supervision.

3.3   Will not compete unfairly with others; will extend my friendship and confidence to all associates and those with whom I have business relations.

Figure 1. *Continued.*

The Institute of Internal Auditors Code of Ethics

PURPOSE: A distinguishing mark of a profession is acceptance by its members of responsibility to the interests of those it serves. Members of The Institute of Internal Auditors (Members) and Certified Internal Auditors (CIAs) must maintain high standards of conduct in order to effectively discharge this responsibility. The Institute of Internal Auditors (Institute) adopts this *Code of Ethics* for Members and CIAs.

APPLICABILITY: This *Code of Ethics* is applicable to all Members and CIAs. Membership in The Institute and acceptance of the "Certified Internal Auditor" designation are voluntary actions. By acceptance, Members and CIAs assume an obligation of self-discipline above and beyond the requirements of laws and regulations.

The standards of conduct set forth in this *Code of Ethics* provide basic principles in the practice of internal auditing. Members and CIAs should realize that their individual judgment is required in the application of these principles.

CIAs shall use the "Certified Internal Auditor" designation with discretion and in a dignified manner, fully aware of what the designation denotes. The designation shall also be used in a manner consistent with all statutory requirements.

Members who are judged by the Board of Directors of The Institute to be in violation of the standards of conduct of the *Code of Ethics* shall be subject to forfeiture of their membership in The Institute. CIAs who are similarly judged also shall be subject to forfeiture of the "Certified Internal Auditor" designation.

(continued)

Figure 2. IIA code of ethics.

Standards of Conduct

   I. Members and CIAs shall exercise honesty, objectivity, and diligence in the performance of their duties and responsibilities.

  II. Members and CIAs shall exhibit loyalty in all matters pertaining to the affairs of their organization or to whomever they may be rendering a service. However, Members and CIAs shall not knowingly be a party to any illegal or improper activity.

 III. Members and CIAs shall not knowingly engage in acts or activities which are discreditable to the profession of internal auditing or to their organization.

 IV. Members and CIAs shall refrain from entering into any activity which may be in conflict with the interest of their organization or which would prejudice their ability to carry out objectively their duties and responsibilities.

  V. Members and CIAs shall not accept anything of value from an employee, client, customer, supplier, or business associate of their organization which would impair or be presumed to impair their professional judgment.

 VI. Members and CIAs shall undertake only those services which they can reasonably expect to complete with professional competence.

 VII. Members and CIAs shall adopt suitable means to comply with the *Standards for the Professional Practice of Internal Auditing.*

VIII. Members and CIAs shall be prudent in the use of information acquired in the course of their duties. They shall not use confidential information for any personal gain nor in any manner which would be contrary to law or detrimental to the welfare of their organization.

 IX. Members and CIAs, when reporting on the results of their work, shall reveal all material facts known to them which, if not revealed, could either distort reports of operations under review or conceal unlawful practices.

  X. Members and CIAs shall continually strive for improvement in their proficiency, and in the effectiveness and quality of their service.

 XI. Members and CIAs, in the practice of their profession, shall be ever mindful of their obligation to maintain the high standards of competence, morality, and dignity promulgated by The Institute. Members shall abide by the *Bylaws* and uphold the objectives of The Institute.

Figure 2. *Continued.*

According to Charles A. Mills:

"A formal code of ethics allows quality auditors to approach audit performance uniformly. A formal code provides a benchmark against which an auditee and client can measure an auditor's activities, establish an auditor's independence, and recognize potential conflicts of interest."[2]

Ethical standards serve as a general behavioral guide for auditors. Auditors often rely on personal judgments and past experiences to determine ethical conduct in specific situations, however. Auditor's personalities, temperaments, auditing styles, and basic perceptions can vary tremendously. By incorporating a set of ethical principles into their daily audit activities, auditors can maintain the high standards of conduct, honor, and character needed for audit results to be received as an unbiased and accurate product.

1. CONFLICT OF INTEREST

The subject of conflict of interest often arises during audits. Conflict-of-interest situations sometimes encountered prior to and during audits include:

- Previous employment of the auditor (or close relative) by the auditee or a major competitor of the auditee, regardless of the reason for separation

- Holding of significant amounts of stocks or bonds in the auditee's business or that of a major competitor by the auditor

- Previous or current close working relationship (e.g., teaming partner, major supplier) with the organization

- Prior involvement by the auditor in developing the quality program or procedures used by the group being audited

- Desire to be hired by the group being audited

- Close friendships within the group being audited

- Offer by auditee of money, goods, or services in the nature of a bribe, kickback, or secret commission

- Acceptance of a gift (money, gratuity, or other thing of value) with more than a nominal value, or involvement in auditee-sponsored sales promotions or other activities that may represent or be construed as a conflict of interest

- Performance of outside work for the auditee that might adversely affect the auditor's performance or judgment on the job

The auditor should be aware of the different types of conflicts of interest. Prior to accepting an audit, the auditor should examine his/her activities and relationship with the auditee and determine whether an actual or potential conflict of interest exists.

When a Conflict of Interest Exists

When there is an actual or potential conflict of interest with the organization or people being audited, the auditor must relay this information to management or decline to conduct the audit, whichever is more appropriate. Actions that management and the audit team leader can take include:

- Ensuring that sufficient time has passed to eliminate the conflict

- Assigning a different auditor to cover the specific area of conflict

- Removing the auditor or the audit team leader from the team

SIDEBAR

For example, during an internal audit, the auditor may face a situation where the auditor was involved in the development of the quality system under evaluation. If the auditor developed the process or wrote the procedure, it would be difficult for him/her to maintain objectivity when the process or procedure is audited for acceptability against a reference standard.

By avoiding conflicts of interest, an auditor upholds the standards of independence, fairness, and objectivity.

2. CONFIDENTIALITY

With processes, formulas, and equipment being developed by individual companies, the question of confidentiality of proprietary information has become a major concern during audits. Businesses could suffer great financial loss if customers or competitors were to gain access to proprietary processing knowledge, formulas, and trade secrets. The auditor must maintain confidentiality, but not to the point of performing an inadequate audit. Each auditor needs to be prepared to sign agreements or utilize techniques for working around a proprietary area.

Confidentiality and Security Concerns

Auditees can use a confidentiality agreement or nondisclosure agreement to protect their interests. Both serve the same purpose—to keep proprietary information within the control of the auditee.

Confidentiality Agreement. An auditor often is expected to sign a confidentiality or nondisclosure agreement before an audit begins. In general, these agreements require that the auditor not disclose any proprietary information gained during the audit. They may be extended to the auditor's company, family, assigns, etc., through legal language. Some confidentiality agreements that auditees expect the auditor to sign before being allowed to perform an audit of proprietary areas have become particularly onerous. Often these are written in legal language and are understandable only by someone familiar with the legal definitions of the words used. Auditors are normally not authorized to obligate their organizations. Agreements should contain a release that takes effect if proprietary information becomes public. An auditor should receive the agreement in advance so that it can be reviewed and approved by the auditing organization's legal counsel or designated authority before the auditor signs it.

SIDEBAR

I was recently asked to sign a four-page confidentiality agreement before being allowed to perform an audit of a supplier. The agreement was written in legal language and obligated me, my heirs, my assigns, and my company to pay for any damages that might come about if the information was obtained by their competitors. There was no time frame to the agreement, so if the information was disclosed at any time and by anybody, we were all liable for the damages. Our company attorney advised against signing this agreement, and the audit team used alternate techniques to determine whether the process was adequate.

Conduct. Discussing proprietary information with others destroys the integrity of the audit function. While it is acceptable for an auditor to discuss actual audit experiences with other auditors, the discussion should be generic so that the auditee cannot be identified. Proprietary information should never be divulged in a sharing situation with other auditors.

Even body language could disclose proprietary information. For example, when asked a question about a proprietary process, an auditor's shrug, rolled eyes, or raised eyebrows could signal the answer even if no words were spoken.

Techniques. Several techniques are available to the auditor to ensure that proprietary information remains proprietary. When auditing in a nondisclosure area, the auditor can rely on memory and not write audit notes. Any notes could become accessible to the public and would be discoverable in litigation.

An auditor can "audit around" an undisclosed area. The auditor needs to be very flexible to be able to accomplish audit objectives even when the auditee erects barriers. At times, a company may be in the process of getting a patent on a new method, for example, and may flatly refuse to allow the auditor to view a certain portion of that system. In these instances, the auditor must respect the auditee's wishes and "audit around" the undisclosed area. If the inputs going into the undisclosed area appear to be correct and the outputs are likewise acceptable, then the auditor can assume that the undisclosed process is doing its job correctly.

The auditor can view parts of a document or have the auditee certify it. A company sometimes will refuse to allow an auditor to look at the procedure for a certain process even though a written procedure is required. To verify that the procedure exists, the auditor can ask the auditee to certify that the procedure does exist and that it covers the relevant process. The auditee may allow the auditor to view nonconfidential sections of the document. The auditor may never actually view all the details, but can assume that a procedure does exist and is approved for use.

Such situations often resolve themselves on subsequent audits involving the same parties. As an auditee becomes more comfortable with the audit team and places greater trust in the ethics of the team members, the need to limit access to certain areas often becomes nonexistent.

Security. Companies in certain highly sensitive industries, such as those involved in national defense, may require that auditors have or obtain security clearances. This requirement should be determined well in advance of the audit to permit sufficient time for processing the request. Without the proper security clearance, an auditor may be restricted to certain areas of a company.

SIDEBAR

One way to work through this without having a security clearance is to be constantly escorted, with classified areas, equipment, and activities shielded from view. This way, the auditor can evaluate part of the process and interview the people on the line.

Chapter B

Professional Conduct and Responsibilities

1. AUDITOR CONDUCT

Professionalism is defined as the aims and qualities that characterize a profession or a professional person. Auditors must comply with high standards of honesty, integrity, work ethic, diligence, loyalty, and commitment.[3] Auditing is a profession that requires individuals to conform to certain behaviors for maximum job proficiency.

The Institute of Internal Auditors developed a set of *Standards for the Professional Practice of Internal Auditing.*[4] This document defines and amplifies five general standards:

1. **Independence**—Internal auditors should be independent of the activities they audit.

2. **Professional Proficiency**—Internal audits should be performed with proficiency and due professional care.

3. **Scope of Work**—The scope of the internal audit should encompass the examination and evaluation of the adequacy and effectiveness of the organization's system of internal control and the quality of performance in carrying out assigned responsibilities.

4. **Performance of Audit Work**—Audit work should include planning the audit, examining and evaluating information, conducting interviews, communicating results, and following up.

5. **Management of the Internal Auditing Department**—The director of internal auditing should properly manage the internal auditing department.

These general standards could also apply to quality auditing. People in the auditing field should be aware of standards of performance of other professions. A broader knowledge allows the auditor to quickly understand different and difficult situations as they arise.

Communicating with the Auditee

An auditor's temperament is often key to making an audit a success. A sullen or unfriendly manner could lead to resistance or malicious compliance. Overly friendly or garrulous behavior could lead to the impression that the audit is not serious. The auditor should be able to find an acceptable balance.

By approaching an auditee in a diplomatic and objective manner, an auditor can set a tone of success for an audit. An auditor must be aware that each auditee views the audit process differently, on the basis of individual management style, culture, personality, and opinions. Many auditees are reluctant to welcome auditors into their world. Resentment, fear, and anxiety are obstacles that must be overcome. By diplomatically presenting and maintaining the audit program, an auditor can influence the auditee's perception of the audit function as well as the overall success of individual audits.

An auditor can establish good rapport with an auditee early in the audit by being respectful, courteous, and appreciative of any special arrangements made for the auditor's comfort and convenience. By demonstrating that the audit has been adequately planned and prepared for and by making every effort to maintain the audit schedule, the auditor projects an image of efficiency and professionalism.

Maintaining open communication channels throughout an audit is essential. An auditor must listen attentively during interviews, allow the interviewee adequate response time, and refrain from asking leading questions. Frequent and timely communication of findings, questions, and concerns gives both the auditor and the auditee opportunities to request clarifications, address corrective action, examine the scope of the situation, and discuss the progress of the audit.

The audit team should also try to gain a sense of management's attitude about sharing information with auditors. In some situations, members of the auditee organization have been punished for providing information to the auditor (e.g., performance appraisal was significantly lowered). Auditors should avoid "naming names" and should emphasize the purpose of the assessment of the process or system.

Additionally, an auditor can set a positive tone for an audit by highlighting commendable findings and observations. The auditor's ability to communicate effectively with management sets the tone for the entire audit and may influence the auditee's response to the audit findings.

However, exemplary conduct by an auditor does not prevent an auditee from making false claims of theft, discrimination, sexual misconduct or other forms of unprofessionalism. No one is immune from false accusations, but disgruntled auditees may target auditors who issue unfavorable reports. Grievance procedures can be abused by the auditee to "get even" with the auditor for finding problems in their area of responsibility.

While performing an audit, the auditor found several points where a specific auditee was not following procedures. The auditee was informed during the interview that these would show up in the audit report. Unknown to the auditor, the auditee immediately filed a formal, written complaint against the auditor claiming "unprofessional conduct and lack of objectivity." After an extensive investigation, that was not kept confidential and that damaged the auditor's professional reputation, the end result was that the complaint was dismissed because there was no basis for the complaint. Because of this investigation, none of the auditor's concerns were allowed to be included in the audit report.

All audit organizations should have grievance or complaint procedures. The procedures should include the protection of the rights of the accuser and the accused. For audits that represent a high risk of false claims or when the auditor feels uncomfortable with a situation, a second person should be scheduled to work with the auditor, recording devices (tape recorders, camcorders) should be used, or escorts should be present during interviews.

2. AUDITOR RESPONSIBILITIES

The auditee must be confident that the auditor will conduct the audit professionally and that the auditor possesses the integrity and technical knowledge to successfully complete the audit. Auditors are expected to exercise *due care* during the performance of their activities. This means that an auditor should be sufficiently competent to arrive at conclusions similar to those that another auditor would reach in the same or similar circumstance.

Since an audit only samples a particular product, process, or system at a particular point in time, an auditor cannot be held responsible if an audit fails to recognize all deficiencies or irregularities in a system, as long as that auditor has used theoretically sound sampling techniques, has complied with applicable standards, and has adhered to the code of ethics.

In addition to the usual responsibilities, an auditor may need to address difficult situations that require careful handling for successful resolution. Possible conflicts of interest should be recognized and reconciled before an audit begins. The detection of unsafe, unethical, or even illegal practices during an audit may rapidly change the planned course of the audit. Other less obvious, but equally challenging, situations may include antagonism, coercion, and even time-wasting techniques employed by the auditee to slow down or stop the audit process.

Difficult Situations May Arise

At times, an auditor may encounter difficult situations that are counterproductive to the auditing process. For example, an auditee may be antagonistic or coercive. Interviewing may be made ineffective by an interviewee who talks too much or not at all. An auditee may also use time-wasting tactics by deviating from the audit plan. In any difficult situation, the auditor should remain polite but firm, maintaining self-control and complete control of the audit.

Diffusing Antagonistic Situations. Sometimes employees may be openly hostile to an auditor. The reasons for such reactions may be totally unrelated to an audit, or the employees may be reacting to what they feel is a personal attack by the auditor on their abilities to do their work. An employee may have been part of the team that developed a process or a particular system, or may have just gone through a six-month-long endeavor to improve something that the auditor is now picking apart. When an auditee gets defensive, the auditor should separate people or suggest a break to defuse the situation. If the conversation must be continued, the auditor should do so later, when everyone is calm again.

Combating Time-Wasting Techniques. An experienced auditor will immediately recognize most time-wasting tactics employed by an auditee. An auditor needs to lead an audit and not allow the auditee to take control. If an auditee attempts a lengthy presentation at the opening meeting or an extended plant tour, for example, the lead auditor should call a halt to these activities or limit the time spent on them. Often, a lead auditor can eliminate wasted time by making specific requests during the audit plan-

The Problem	One Solution
Requested personnel are unavailable to the audit team.	Auditor could politely state that absence of key personnel may prolong the audit or that the audit's scope may have to be modified.
Escort is repeatedly late in the mornings.	Auditor could ask the escort for suggestions on how to start the meeting on time and make the necessary changes to the schedule.
Auditee makes the auditor wait repeatedly for needed supplies or requested documents and records.	Auditor should request needed supplies during the audit planning stage and anticipate document and record needs in advance.
Constant distractions occur during interviews (area is noisy, constant phone ringing, or other interruptions).	Auditor could suggest that they move away from area or close doors if possible; phones should be set to call forwarding or should be answered by someone else.
Interviewees state that they were not informed of the audit and are not prepared.	Auditor should confirm that employees are aware that an audit is taking place and should ask auditee management about the state of readiness of the quality system to be audited.

Figure 3. Common time-wasting ploys and possible solutions.

ning stage. For example, many audit teams prefer a catered lunch to going off-premises for several hours. Of course, auditee management and the client should be notified when an audit team repeatedly encounters delay tactics or if the audit schedule is severely compromised by such delays.

Figure 3 lists some common time-wasting ploys and suggests possible solutions that an auditor may use when faced with each problem. An auditor adjusting to specific situations could likely think of equally effective solutions.

3. DISCOVERY OF ILLEGAL OR UNSAFE CONDITIONS OR ACTIVITIES

Quality auditors are in a unique position to observe illegal or unsafe conditions during the course of an audit because of their access to almost any area necessary for successful completion of the audit. Each auditor must know what to do when these activities are detected.

When Unsafe Activities Are Detected

In some industries, an auditor may need to access potentially hazardous areas in a company during the course of an audit. Usually auditors are provided with proper safety equipment, such as goggles or hard hats. Normally, auditors face no physical danger as long as regulations are enforced and the process is functioning properly. Sometimes, however, negligence or inexperience on the part of the auditee's employees, a deficiency or malfunction of equipment or a process, or a combination of these may result in potentially dangerous situations.

When an unsafe practice—such as open containers of hazardous chemicals near work areas or flammable materials near a welding station—is detected, whether within or outside the scope of an audit, an auditor must not ignore it. In an internal audit, an auditor should immediately inform an auditee representative and the audit team leader, who will inform the auditee manager, so that the problem can be worked up the internal chain until it is resolved. In an external audit (second- or third-party audit), the auditor must immediately inform the auditee and create a record of the situation. If anyone on the audit team is endangered, the audit must be stopped and the auditors returned to a safe area. In most situations, management welcomes information about liability risks or other potential danger.

When Illegal or Unethical Activities Are Detected

An auditor finding evidence of wrongdoing, whether within or outside the scope of an audit assignment, has an ethical duty to bring the matter to the attention of the client and appropriate management for action. The auditor should keep a record of such matters, safeguard the evidence, and obtain copies of pertinent documents and records (if necessary). The auditor must be aware of and apply the ethics of the profession and the law in this regard. An auditor may ask the client about the company's ethics policy and ethics department prior to accepting the audit. If an ethics department exists, they may be a valuable resource if potentially unethical situations surface before, during, or after an audit.

Management will take appropriate action on illegal or unethical activities within the company. This may involve legal action of some type and the involvement of the auditor. Auditors should be aware of their legal responsibilities and rights under the law, including whistle-blower laws (see Figure 4).

If management sponsors allegedly illegal activities, either internally or externally, the auditor's employment may be threatened. An auditor should

Examples of federal whistle-blower laws.

Code of Federal Regulations

Title 5, Administrative Personnel, Chapter II—Merit Systems Protection Board, Parts 1200–1210

Title 10, Energy, Chapter III—Department of Energy, Parts 708.1–708.15

Title 29, Labor, Subtitle A–Office of the Secretary of Labor, Part 24—Procedures for the Handling of Discrimination Complaints Under Federal Employee Protection Statues, Parts 24.1–24.9

Figure 4. Examples of federal whistle-blower laws.

Source: Copyright © 1998 The Law Office of Bradley Scott Weiss (http://www.bsw-law.com/whistleb.htm).

have access to legal counsel to resolve questionable issues. Often that legal counsel is best if it comes from outside the company. The U.S. Congress and various states, listed in Figure 5, have passed laws protecting people who report incidents of wrongdoing, including waste, fraud, and abuse. These whistle-blower statutes protect auditors and others. Questions about specific laws should be directed to the appropriate federal, state, or local authorities (see Figure 6 for an example of a local regulation).

SIDEBAR

The 1863 False Claims Act was enacted by Congress to protect the government from the fraudulent suppliers of faulty war equipment during the Civil War. This law remained in effect until 1974, when it was narrowed in scope. It was expanded and strengthened in 1986. The 1986 amendment brought new attention to the whistle-blower as a key to enforcement. There is a current effort within Congress to issue an anti-gag statute, that further strengthens whistle-blower laws. The anti-gag statute will protect employees who signed a secrecy pact prior to government employment, agreeing to never discuss certain subjects, usually related to national defense issues. In the past, these whistle-blowers would be stripped of their clearances and, in most cases, their jobs based on their violation of the secrecy pact. The anti-gag statute allows such whistle-blowers to go around their management if management does not respond when given the information.

States with whistle-blower statutes.

The following states have enacted laws that provide protections for both private and public employees:

Connecticut	Hawaii	Louisiana
Maine	Michigan	Minnesota
New Hampshire	New Jersey	New York
Ohio	Rhode Island	

The following states have enacted laws that protect only state and local government employees:

Alaska	Arizona	California
Colorado	Delaware	Florida
Illinois	Indiana	Iowa
Kansas	Kentucky	Maryland
Missouri	New Hampshire	North Carolina
Oklahoma	Oregon	Pennsylvania
South Carolina	Tennessee	Texas
Utah	Washington	West Virginia
Wisconsin		

Figure 5. States with whistle-blower statutes.

Source: Copyright © 1998 The Law Office of Bradley Scott Weiss (http://www.bsw-law.com/whistleb.htm).

Examples of other whistle-blower laws.

University of California Business and Finance Bulletin G-29, Procedures for Investigating Misuse of University Resources, Appendix C, Whistle Blower Policy

Figure 6. Examples of other whistle-blower laws.

An auditor may encounter illegal or unethical situations during the course of an audit, such as when an auditee is deliberately shipping defective products. The auditor should verify the situation and then inform the audit team leader, who will inform the auditee. If the problem is caused by an oversight, it should be corrected immediately. However, an auditee who knowingly ships defective product may be unwilling to correct the problem. In this case, the auditing organization should refuse to return to that company or internal group. If a third-party audit is being performed, the auditor should immediately report the situation to the client. If the auditee is a supplier, the auditing organization may delay or stop shipments (if given the authority to do so) until the appropriate management function can resolve the issue. The auditing organization may advise its management to cancel any existing contracts or agreements and find more reputable sources for the item or service.

> ### SIDEBAR
>
> One auditor reported that one of the most blatantly unethical activities he observed was by a supplier who knowingly shipped empty outer casings for a particular device. The casings had a sticker over the edge of the casing stating, "Warranty void if sticker broken." The sticker would be broken if the customer opened the casing to look inside. After verifying what he had discovered, he discussed the situation with the audit manager, who in turn discussed it with auditee management. The auditor's company ended up pulling their order from the supplier.

An auditor who detects illegal or unethical activities within the auditing organization must tell the audit team leader, who will inform the manager. If the same or similar situation recurs often, the auditor's principles are probably not compatible with those of the organization, and new employment should be considered. Unethical activity that is in violation of internal company policy should be reported directly to management, whether it is unethical behavior of another employee, a customer, or a supplier. Illegal or unethical behavior on the part of an ASQ member that violates the ASQ code of ethics should be reported to the local section of ASQ for investigation and possible reporting to the ASQ Ethics Committee.

Although not commonplace, bribery is another example of an illegal or unethical situation that an auditor may encounter. An auditor encountering obvious bribery should flatly refuse the offer and stop the audit. The client and auditing organization management must be alerted and give the matter immediate attention. Gift-giving could be a less obvious form of bribery. Many public agencies and private companies have specific regulations and policies on ethical behavior. For example, a limited dollar amount, usually about $25, may be specified for gifts that the auditor may accept ethically. An auditor has an obligation to refuse or return any gift that exceeds the stated amount and has the option of refusing any item. Many auditors will accept an offer of an inexpensive meal since they feel that both parties benefit from the rapport established in a casual setting, while others will refuse even the offer of a soft drink.

SIDEBAR

During the course of an audit, an auditor happened to mention that she was an avid tennis player. Several weeks later she received a case of tennis balls from the auditee. She wrote a polite note and sent it to the auditee, along with the case of tennis balls.

In the international auditing arena, an auditor must be familiar with local customs so that potentially unethical situations can be interpreted correctly and responded to appropriately. For example, in the United States it is considered a breech of ethics for an auditor to accept a gift or favor from a person in the audited organization, but in Japan gift-giving is often part of doing business, and it would be rude for the auditor to decline. As quality auditing becomes increasingly global, organizations and individuals must be aware of such differences in order to prevent serious cultural misunderstandings from undermining the audit process.

The need to be familiar with different cultures and norms is not limited to international auditing. Auditors should also be aware of cultural differences and expectations in each individual workplace where the audit is being conducted. The auditor's awareness and willingness to work with different cultures will help avoid misunderstandings and ensure the effectiveness of the audit.

Overcoming Language and Literacy Barriers. Audit personnel must either (1) be fluent in the agreed-upon language of the audit or (2) have available at all times personnel with the necessary technical language skills.[5] When necessary, an auditing organization should employ a skilled interpreter to assist with an audit.

Even if all primary participants in an audit speak the same language, the auditor may encounter language or literacy barriers when attempting to interview individual employees. These same barriers may prevent the employee from understanding or performing assigned tasks. A written procedure may solve the problem; but if the employees are unable to read or understand the procedure, then the problem has not been addressed. If an auditor understands the physical process before going into an audit and then focuses on the work, some of the literacy issues may be overcome with the aid of flowcharts and other simple diagrams. At times, an auditor may need to ask extremely simple questions to overcome a lack of language skills.

Avoiding Other Problems. Selecting an auditor from within an organization (for a first-party audit) can cause problems, especially in the case of a one site operation. The objectivity of an auditor working in an area of previous employment may be questioned. Former peers may be intimidated, uncooperative, or use the auditor as a sounding board for complaints, making it difficult for the auditor to obtain objective information. They also may think that the auditor will not report procedural violations. Furthermore, the auditor's knowledge of how a product, process, or system functions may be outdated, and time may be wasted as the auditor follows the wrong paths using incorrect criteria.

Ideally, an auditor will not be assigned to an area of previous employment. For internal audits, though, such assignments cannot always be avoided. The negative effects must be weighed against the benefits that selecting an auditor from within the organization may offer. Such benefits may include a superior understanding of the organization's product or service and the processes involved in production, and a strong familiarity with the applicable quality requirements or standards. Negative effects may include hidden agendas, perceived bias on the part of the auditee, and the possibility that the auditors will try to solve problems using past knowledge rather than auditing.

During an audit, some auditees will request to be notified of potential nonconformances/findings so that they can take immediate action. In many cases, immediate action would be remedial action (also called containment action) and not corrective action. Remedial action only addresses the symptom and does not eliminate the underlying cause of the problem. The auditor may discuss the pitfalls of taking remedial action with the auditee. The auditor should also explain that even though remedial action was taken, it would be unethical not to include the observed nonconformance in the final report.

Besides looking and acting professionally at all times, the auditor must assume other responsibilities in external audits, such as maintaining the confidence of the auditing organization by never divulging proprietary information to the auditee, refraining from speaking negatively about the auditing organization or previous auditees, and refraining from discussing the performance of previous auditees with people in the organization currently being audited. When facing one of the above problems or other more difficult ones, the auditor must remain focused and in control of the audit function.

Chapter C
Liability Issues

This is not a primer on law as applied to quality auditing and should not be considered to be providing legal advice. If questions arise, auditors must consult their own lawyers for information.

Liability issues have become more apparent with the advent of the quality system and environmental system registration schemes. Each company and each auditor is accepting liability for the decisions made regarding whether to grant registration. There are appeal processes that are used, but in the end, a court of law could be called in for the final decision. A key liability consideration is whether a company relies on audit information as the basis for making a decision.

1. PERSONAL AND CORPORATE

Illegal Activities

As an auditor collects information throughout the audit process, the auditee may disclose certain kinds of information. This information can lead to illegal activities by the auditor, unless the auditor is aware that use of this information is illegal. Figure 7 provides a general explanation of each type of information and the illegal activity that the auditor can inadvertently take.

The Auditor as an Agent

As a representative of a company, an individual auditor can unknowingly acquire legal liability in several areas. First, the auditor might make statements that an auditee uses to make decisions. If these statements are later shown to be untrue, the auditee might have recourse against the auditor's company for damages. For example, if a third-party

Liability	Explanation	Auditor Example
Violation of securities laws	If someone learns information that is important to investors but not available to the public and proceeds to act on it or tells someone who then acts on it, it is a violation of securities laws.	During an audit interview, a senior manager accidentally reveals acquisition plans to an auditor. The auditor uses the information to make personal investments in the stock market.
Violation of antitrust laws	If someone learns information and uses it to restrict competition in a particular market, it is a violation of antitrust laws.	An auditor comments to the auditee that another supplier with the same quality system realizes far fewer gains. The auditee uses the information to produce negative advertisements against the supplier.
Violation of due care	If someone fails to exercise reasonable care or competency in the course of providing guidance for others in their business transactions, it is a violation of due care.	An auditor grants a supplier ISO 9001 certification despite the audit team's failure to follow correct accrediting procedure [not exercising "due care"] during the audit. Based on the certification, a company purchases faulty product from the supplier for commercial distribution.
Aiding and abetting	If someone willfully causes an act to be done and the same act would be an offense against the United States if directly performed by him or her, it constitutes aiding and abetting.	An auditor discovers that an auditee is using materials against contractual requirements but does not include the information in the final audit report.

Figure 7. Illegal auditor activities.

Source: ASQ's Foundations in Quality: Certified Quality Auditor, Module 1: Ethics, Professional Conduct, and Liability Issues (Milwaukee, WI: ASQ Quality Press, 1998), pp. 1–16.

auditor told the auditee that the auditee's company would get a discount on insurance by obtaining ISO registration, and the auditee used that information as a reason for deciding to obtain ISO registration, then the auditee might recover damages if no discount was forthcoming.

SIDEBAR

There is a myth pushed by some registrars that third-party registration is a strong defense in the event of a product liability lawsuit. This is not necessarily true. It apparently began when some insurance companies in the United Kingdom offered discounts of 20 percent to 40 percent to companies that achieved ISO 9001/2/3 registration. Unfortunately, these discounts have not made it to the United States. No lawsuit involving ISO 9001/2/3 has been publicized in U.S. media. The first lawsuit that comes to court will test the ability of third-party registration to limit liability based on good management practices and a quality management system. Until then, it appears that U.S. insurance companies are waiting to decide whether to give discounts.[6]

An auditor also has to be careful not to tell the auditee how to do their work or what decisions to make. If an auditee relies on the auditor's words and subsequently fails to provide a good product or service or obtain registration, the auditee might recover damages. Also, if an auditor provides guidance, even if the guidance fixes the problem, the auditor still owns the solution. If the recommended solution is not the best, there may be malicious compliance that will reflect back on the auditor.

SIDEBAR

An auditor discovers that the auditee is shipping defective products. After verifying and investigating the incident, the auditor records 10 product deficiencies that should be corrected before shipping resumes. The audit team ranks the deficiencies in priority order and includes them in the final report along with its findings.[7]

The fact that the audit team prioritized the deficiencies means that they accepted partial responsibility for the solution. This makes the audit team and their company at least partially liable should a problem surface in the future involving the defective products.

Registrar organizations and their auditors face a special liability during the audit and after registration. An organization certifying that others meet a set of standards must use reasonable care or competency in certifying.[8] The auditor must follow the procedures of the registrar during the audit process and base the registration decision on the results of the audit. The registrar must have specific procedures and requirements for registration and these must be applied equally to all companies. Registrars accredited in the United States must meet requirements of the Registrar Accreditation Board. The Registrar Accreditation Board requires adherence to ISO Guide 62 and interpretive guidance of the International Accreditation Forum.

Proprietary Information

An earlier section discussed proprietary information and techniques of working around a process or other information that the auditor was not allowed to view directly. Disclosure of proprietary information can come about inadvertently because of the legal process itself. An auditor completes audit checklists, makes notes of the results of the audit, and often makes copies of information supporting the findings of the audit. These notes, completed checklists, and copies find their way into the audit record and are kept for a specified period of time. If, during that time, a lawsuit is initiated, the contents of the file may become available for "discovery" by the parties to the lawsuit.

Records of both internal and external audits are subject to discovery by parties in a lawsuit. For example, if a supplier to your organization is party to a lawsuit and your organization conducted an audit (external) of the supplier, your records are subject to discovery. The same rights of discovery are true for both civil and criminal legal proceedings.

Through discovery, these records can become public. This is one of the main reasons an auditor should not make copies of or take notes on proprietary information when auditing a company. It is also a major reason for keeping extraneous comments out of the audit record. Such extraneous comments can come back to haunt an auditor at the most inappropriate time.

SIDEBAR

During one audit, the regulators asked to review the completed audit checklists. On one checklist, an auditor had written "this procedure is terrible" in the margin. The auditor and lead auditor spent the next three hours explaining why the comment was on the checklist even though the auditor evaluated the procedure as satisfactory.

2. AUDIT RECORD DISCLOSURE

Because the quality system requires records that each step is performed by following documented procedures or methods, there are many documents and records available for both the defense and the prosecution in the event of a lawsuit. Each record and document is made available to both the defense and to the prosecution.

SIDEBAR

> Discovery is a pretrial device used by one party to obtain facts and information about the case from the other party in order to help pre pare for trial. Under federal rules of civil procedure and in states that have adopted similar rules, tools of discovery include deposition to oral and written questions, written interrogatories, production of documents, permission to enter land or other property, physical and mental examinations, and requests for admission. In *criminal* proceedings, discovery emphasizes the right of the defense to obtain access to evidence necessary to prepare its own case.[9]

Copies of the audit report must be sent to the client, and almost always are sent to the auditee. Clients either designate other organizations and individuals to receive copies or make the distribution themselves.

The audit records should be treated as confidential information and not disclosed to internal or outside entities without prior approval of the client and the auditee. Accidental or deliberate disclosure of negative audit information that other companies use as a basis for making decisions that adversely affect the auditee may make the auditor and the auditor's company liable for damages. These damages can be considerable if a major contract is canceled or awarded to another company on the basis of the negative information.

Part II

Audit Preparation

[32 of the CQA exam questions or 21%]

Audit preparation consists of everything that is done in advance by interested parties, such as the auditor, lead auditor, client and audit program manager, to ensure the audit complies with the client's objective. The preparation stage of an audit begins with the decision to conduct the audit. For our purposes, preparation ends when the audit itself begins.

For a third-party audit—or when an outside organization is being used to conduct a first or second-party audit—the client selects and contracts with an auditing organization. For a first or second-party audit, the client and/or employer of the auditing organization usually initiate the audit either by request or by approval of an audit schedule. The client and/or the employer of the auditing organization should define the purpose and scope of the audit as well as the standard against which the audit is to be conducted. The auditing organization personnel, in return, prepare the audit plan and other working papers, select or participate in the selection of the audit team members, and notify the auditee in writing of the impending audit. For a contracted audit, the client should notify the auditee.

For a first-party internal audit that is not contracted out, the preparation stage may be less formal. Since internal audits often are scheduled on a regular or continuous basis, such as quarterly, an interoffice memo may suffice for notification. In some companies, a phone call followed by an e-mail message or memo might be acceptable because the lead auditor and manager of the area to be audited are likely to have greater contact prior to the actual audit.

An auditing organization must prepare carefully for an audit. A well-planned audit is more likely than an unplanned or poorly planned audit to progress according to schedule, earn respect for the auditor, get the full cooperation of the auditee, efficiently utilize the time and other resources of the auditee and auditor, and produce results that can be used by management in guiding the organization.

When preparing to be audited, an auditee organization has certain responsibilities, such as ensuring that the audit team will have adequate working space and that necessary personnel will be made available as needed. The auditee often assigns an escort to the audit team to function as a liaison with employees, management, and the audit team.

If preparation for an audit has been inadequate, the audit team risks wasting time during the performance stage of the audit or performing a mechanical audit on the basis of a "canned" checklist. An unprepared auditor may focus on trivial matters or personal areas of interest or knowledge [pet peeves], or spend more time in a conference room than in work areas. Such an audit is of limited value, since it fails to properly assess the quality system and wastes resources.

Chapter A
Audit Definition and Plan

Upon receiving an audit assignment from a client, an audit manager usually assigns a lead auditor who will be responsible for all phases of that audit. The lead auditor is responsible for preparing an *audit plan,* generally a one- to two-page document (see Figure 8 in Part II, chapter D) that serves as a link between audit planning and audit execution. An audit plan identifies:

- The purpose and scope of the audit
- The auditee and organizational units to be audited
- The audit team members
- The standard being audited against (specific sections of the standard may be included)
- Logistical issues such as the date and place of the audit, the expected duration of the audit, and the expected date of issue of the audit report

In addition, when applicable, the audit plan may list confidentiality requirements, transportation requirements, or required health and safety permits or security clearances.

During the audit preparation phase, the auditing organization must determine the audit's purpose and scope (defined by the client) and identify the needed resources and applicable reference standard. Based on these criteria, the audit team is selected. The lead auditor then secures the appropriate documentation, prepares (or ensures that other members of the audit team prepare) applicable checklists and other working papers, and determines the proper data collection methods. The written audit plan should be signed by the lead auditor and approved by the audit program manager, or the client, or the auditee.

The six areas discussed in this chapter are:

1. Identification of authority (internal and external)

2. Determination of audit purpose

3. Determination of audit type and scope

4. Determination of resources required

5. Team selection and identification of roles

6. Requirements to audit against

Each will be discussed in detail in the sections that follow. Logistics, which is also part of planning, will be discussed in the next chapter.

1. IDENTIFICATION OF AUTHORITY (INTERNAL AND EXTERNAL)

As soon as an audit team is selected, the team must verify its authority to perform the audit. By identifying the authority for the audit to all involved parties, an auditor confers legitimacy on the audit and removes or minimizes the adverse feelings the auditee may experience when informed of the forthcoming audit. Also, this step keeps the auditor from wasting time preparing for an audit that has not been authorized.[10]

The authority to perform an audit may come from a single source or a combination of sources. The important thing is not where the authority comes from but that it does indeed exist. Without a specific authority source that permits an audit, an auditor has no right to perform one.

Audit Authority

The authority to perform an audit can come from inside or outside the auditee organization. Internally, authority may come from an organization's quality program or from the chain of command. Externally, authority may reside in purchase agreements, industry standards, or government regulations.

Internal Sources. Internal sources of authority are either organizational or hierarchical. The term *organization* describes functions or groups but does not rank them. The word *hierarchy* refers to status, particularly among individuals. Internal audit authority can come from either source or a combination, depending on the company's structure.

Organization. The source of authority for the performance of internal audits usually resides in a document, often called a quality manual, that describes the organization's quality program. This document should define the authority of certain groups or individuals to perform audits.

At other times, a company's quality policy defines and authorizes audits. If an organization agrees to meet certain industry standards voluntarily, for example, then the quality policy specifies that those standards will be met. In this case, an audit is a planned group of activities to assure management that the organization is meeting those industry standards, which are usually promoted as voluntary, but which are often required of organizations to be competitive in the industry.

Sometimes an organization decides to adopt or adapt certain criteria even though not required to do so. For example, an organization may elect to meet ISO 9001 or ISO 9004 standards even though it has no intention of applying for registration to ISO 9001. Likewise, criteria for the Malcolm Baldrige National Quality Award may be used as a basis for quality improvement even when an organization has no intention of applying for the award.

Hierarchy. Hierarchy is the chain of command that controls how work is delegated and how responsibilities are assigned within an organization. Rather than being driven by written procedures, as in the case of organizational authority, an audit is driven by the people who have authority. The audit authority must be higher in the organizational structure than the functions being audited. For example, it would be extremely difficult for a division or department of a company to commission an audit of corporate headquarters. But the Vice President of Operations might request a quality audit of department operations. This kind of audit is not normally defined or required by the organization's policies and procedures, and it is usually requested at a higher level to address a specific need. The client in this case would be the Vice President of Operations.

External Sources. At times the authority for an audit is external to the auditee organization, as in the case of authority specified by a contract, standard, or regulatory body.

Contract. The authority to perform external second-party audits should reside in the purchasing agreement—a contract or purchase order—between an organization and its suppliers. Sometimes this authority is not readily visible; it may be included in a section on rights of access. A rights of access clause gives a customer or regulation body the right to inspect or audit a supplier facility, product, or service. The clause usually specifies reasonable access during normal business hours. Federal acquisition regulations require federal agencies to include this authority in most procurement documents.

A contractual audit source is common in second-party audits. The source of authority is the signed contract between two parties, a supplier and a customer. Proprietary processes, such as research and development projects or processes that are being conducted for a competitor, are defined and are excluded from the concern of the auditor. Access to plant locations is restricted in these circumstances, but should be defined in advance.

Standards. National and international standards include the ANSI/ISO/ASQ Q9001 and Q9004 series for quality management. These standards may be followed voluntarily or may be imposed by contract or regulation.

Industry standards are written to clarify, amplify, and, in some cases, limit federal regulations. For example, in the pharmaceutical industry, voluntary industry associations such as the Health Industry Manufacturers Association have developed standards that may be used as the basis for internal audits. After an industry has demonstrated that voluntary standards are working, the best practices may be incorporated into federal regulations. However, industry standards are not regulatory documents.

Normally, the requirements of the standards are incorporated or interpreted by the company's internal documentation. The quality manual or policy might include the authority to audit the organization and a reminder to managers that they are to cooperate with the auditors. Also, procedures implemented as a result of a national/international standard may provide guidance on how the audit program will be conducted.

Regulatory. These are primarily used by third-party auditors. International, federal, or state law may be the source of authority in certain regulated industries. Within the United States, these regulations derive from laws passed by Congress and interpreted by the code of federal regulations promulgated by the authorized agency. The courts have enforced and reinforced the rights of regulatory bodies to conduct inspections and audits of organizations to monitor their compliance with the law. Regulatory bodies include organizations that oversee safety, health, and environmental laws such as the FDA, EPA, and OSHA.

2. DETERMINATION OF AUDIT PURPOSE

It is the client's responsibility to determine the purpose of an audit. Usually this statement is specific; however, a client may state the purpose in general terms with the understanding that the lead auditor will specify the particulars to fit the situation. In the case of an audit performed on a regular basis, the purpose may have been defined and known by all parties well in advance of the audit.

First-party audits may be performed to assure management that the audited area is in compliance with particular quality standards and that the goals and strategies of an organization are being met. Several sample purpose statements for first-party audits follow.

The purpose of this first-party audit is

- To assure continued implementation of the management system, to evaluate the effectiveness of the system in meeting the stated goals and objectives, and to identify opportunities for continuous improvement in product, process, and system
- To review the mechanical assembly area's compliance with procedures and to evaluate the procedures for opportunities for improvement
- To confirm that project engineering, document control, and procurement activities being performed in support of basic design are being accomplished in accordance with the Quality Assurance Manual, selected integrated execution procedures, and governing project procedures, including, as appropriate, client requirements
- To assess the progress of the quality system toward meeting the requirements of ISO 9001: as outlined in the current Quality Manual

For a second-party audit, an auditor's quality assurance department or the purchasing department normally determines the purpose of the audit and communicates it to the auditee. The primary purpose of a second-party audit is to assess a supplier to verify that contract requirements are being followed or to assess a potential supplier's capability of meeting specific requirements for a product or service. By determining that the supplier is meeting the requirements specified in a contract, the purchaser gains confidence in the quality of goods and services being delivered.[11] Examples of purpose statements for second-party audits follow.

The purpose of this second-party audit is

- To assess the capability of XYZ Company to meet contract requirements by a review of the available resources and by obtaining objective evidence of management's commitment to the quality requirements of our product
- To verify that the materials, equipment, and work being performed under Contract 12345–P–001 are in accordance with the procurement

documents, as specified in Section 6 of this contract, and that the work is being executed by qualified personnel
- To identify the possible cause of recent nonconformities by conducting a comprehensive assessment of the tasks, procedures, records, and system documentation related to the production of the wireless widget

Most third-party audits are performed by auditing organizations to determine the compliance of the auditee's systems with agreed-upon criteria. In the case of an audit for registration, an auditor examines an auditee's systems for compliance with a specific standard—for example, ANSI/ISO/ASQ Q9001 or current good manufacturing practices. The purpose statement for most third-party audits is very specific.

The purpose of this third-party audit is

- To determine the degree of compliance to the requirements of ANSI/ISO/ASQ Q9001 for the purposes of registration of the company system
- To assess the compliance of the quality system to all requirements of ANSI/ISO/ASQ Q9001: for the purpose of recommending the organization for registration to the standard
- To assess the compliance of the organization to all requirements of Regulation 123 for the purpose of recommending approval or disapproval as a supplier

Third-party audits performed for regulatory purposes determine the compliance of the auditee's systems with regulations or laws. These audits have penalties (fines, jail, or both) associated with them, so they are very serious. The purpose of the audit is determined by the regulatory agency and normally is specified in the regulation or law. These audits focus on detailed compliance with the regulations or laws to assure that companies are protecting the environment, the public, and their employees.

3. DETERMINATION OF AUDIT TYPE AND SCOPE

The scope of an audit is developed in conjunction with the purpose statement. The scope establishes the boundaries by identifying the exact items, groups, and activities to be examined. The auditor and the client must agree on the scope; it is documented and communicated in the audit plan to confirm a common understanding.

By looking at the specific circumstances surrounding an audit and by examining the auditee's audit history, an auditor can confirm that required corrective actions have been implemented and make judgments about which areas might require less attention. Areas that involve less risk and areas with excellent audit histories may require less sampling.

Examples of scope statements for first-, second-, and third-party audits follow.

First-party: To audit the Purchasing Manual for wireless widget production.

Second-party: To audit the heat treatment facility as it relates to contract number 95-003.

Third-party: To audit the design and manufacture of gaskets, seals, and other compounded elastomer products for commercial and automotive applications at Plant Number 1, 123 Main St., Anytown, U.S.

The scope of an audit will have a direct effect on the resources needed to achieve the audit purpose or objective. Determining the scope of an audit also keeps an auditor focused and keeps the audit from becoming a witch hunt or fishing expedition. An auditor should not seek to uncover problems in areas outside the audit's stated scope. However, if such problems emerge in the course of an audit, the auditor must be prepared to address those concerns. For example, an auditor should investigate when overdue calibration of equipment is observed even though that equipment might not pertain to the process being audited or fall within the audit scope.

The scope of an audit significantly affects resources and time requirements. If the scope is immense, a large audit team will be needed to complete the audit in a reasonable time frame. If the scope is too large for the available resources, the audit may have to be scheduled for a time when adequate resources will be available, or the scope may have to be narrowed. However, too narrow a scope wastes valuable resources too. Clarifying the scope makes audit planning and execution efficient since the availability of resources directly bears on achievement of audit objectives.

Observing Problems Outside the Stated Scope

As indicated earlier, while auditors should remain within the scope stated in the audit plan, they may discover problems beyond that scope. An auditor has an obligation not to ignore problems outside the stated scope. An auditor's reaction to such a discovery will depend on the severity of the problem, its effect on the quality system, and the type of audit being performed. Conditions outside the scope of the audit may not be included in the formal report as a finding or violation for that particular audit. Conditions should be reported directly to the client and the auditee if there is a serious condition adverse to quality or a possibility of litigation. However, minor process problems need only be reported to the auditee. For example, an unsafe practice or one with serious legal ramifications cannot be ignored, while a minor process problem may not be acknowledged in the formal audit report. A minor problem may be communicated to the auditee as feedback for quality improvement actions.

In internal audits where management's goal is to improve the quality system, problems that interfere with that goal usually are not ignored since continuous improvement of the quality system cannot be promoted if an auditor intentionally overlooks obvious problems. Therefore, the audit team may expand the stated scope and look into the problem. In an internal audit, problems within or outside the scope need to be identified so that appropriate corrective action can take place.

Sometimes an auditee will want to expand the scope of an audit. Expanding the scope is permissible before the audit begins as long as the team has time to prepare for the modified scope. If an auditee asks to have the scope expanded once the performance stage has begun, the lead auditor should suggest that the next audit encompass the additional area, since the team will not have done the necessary preparation or may not have adequate time to investigate thoroughly. There may be fewer obstacles when expanding the scope of an internal audit because the auditor's time is not constrained by a contract, nor are external management approvals required, and all parties internal to the organization should have the same organizational objectives.

In summary, auditors should stay within the scope of the audit and use their judgment when they encounter problems outside the scope.

4. DETERMINATION OF RESOURCES REQUIRED

Once an audit's purpose and scope are confirmed, an audit team must be assembled. Often, a lead auditor has already been selected and has completed some of the planning activities. The lead auditor usually participates in the selection of audit team members and may help determine the desired size and composition of the audit team. Each member of the audit team must be independent of the functions being audited. As noted in Part I, chapter B, section 3, total independence may not be possible for internal audits.

When selecting an audit team, the auditing organization must determine the number of auditors needed to complete the job. Often, the scope of an audit, the time frame in which it is to be completed, and budgetary concerns will determine whether a single auditor or an audit team is needed to complete the job. The multiple auditor, or audit team, approach allows depth of inquiry and breadth of examination. In addition, it encourages balance, since no single individual can possess all the technical knowledge and personality traits necessary in all audit situations. However, one well-trained and experienced auditor may be all that is required to conduct a meaningful and effective audit.[12]

An audit team may break down into mini-teams or subteams to perform portions of an audit. Each mini-team consists of two persons—one to interview personnel, the other to listen and take notes during the interviews. Seldom does the availability of personnel permit such luxury, except when members of an audit team are accompanied by auditors-in-training. A second way of forming mini-teams is to pair a technical specialist with a quality auditor. The quality auditor can explore the system and management controls, while the technical specialist can observe the work being done to provide a product or service.

When scheduling an audit, the lead auditor should calculate the estimated number of personnel hours needed to complete each portion of the audit, then determine the total number of team hours required for the audit. For example, if the sum of personnel hours is 10, then one auditor should be able to complete the audit in 10 hours; two auditors working as a team but in different areas should complete the same audit in five hours.

Determining the proper number of on-site audit days can be complicated when all variables are considered. However, minimum audit day guidelines have been issued for use by third-party audit organizations. Table 1 shows the minimum number of on-site days that should be spent on TL 9000/ISO 9001 quality system audits and ongoing surveillance audits. The table takes into consideration the number of employees of a company, the existing quality system, and the criteria being audited against. The table does not consider such factors as the complexity of operations or labor intensity. Audit days could be added for very complex operations, or a request to reduce the number of audit days can be submitted to the accreditation organization for simple, single-product line organizations.

Table 1. Audit day table.

Number of employees	Audit 0 > TL 9000 (On-site days)	Initial Assessment SEI to ISO 9000 & TL 9000	TickIT to TL 9000	CSOP Only to ISO 9000 TL 9000	QS 9000 Only to TL 9000	ISO 9000 Only to TL 9000	ISO 9000 & CSOP to TL 9000	On-going Maintenance Audits	Re-assessment
1–30	4	3.2	2	2	2	2	2	1	2
31–100	7	5.6	2	4	2	2	2	1.5	3
101–250	8	6.4	2	5	2	2	2	2	3
251–500	10	8	2	5	2	3	2	2	4.5
501–1000	12	9.6	3	7	3	4	2	3	5.5
1001–2000	15	12	4	9	4	4	3	4	6.5
2001–4000	18	14.4	4	11	4	5	4	5	8
4001+	21	16.8	5	13	5	6	4	5	9

Source: Table based on IAF Guidance to ISO/IEC Guide 62, Issue 1, January 1997. From the QuEst Forum Website www.questforum.org. Information subject to change. Used with permission.

The lead auditor ensures that the size of the audit team is appropriate on the basis of the amount of work to be performed, its complexity, the availability of personnel and other resources, and the desired time frame in which the audit is to be completed. Additionally, the lead auditor should consider the physical size and layout of the space in which the auditors will be working.

The following factors may be considered when determining the number of auditors needed on the audit team:

- On-site time restrictions or allocation

- Average expected interview time per interviewee

- Number of interviews (percentage of employees to be sampled)

- Time in meetings (opening, exit, auditee briefings, audit team meetings)

- Data analysis and report preparation time

- Observation of work time

- Records review time

- Meal and break times

- Lost time due to inefficiencies, such as distance from department to department

The amount of audit prework could also affect the number of auditors needed on the team. Examples include previsit communication (written and verbal), review of documents, preparing checklists, and preparing collection plans.

5. TEAM SELECTION AND IDENTIFICATION OF ROLES

An audit team is responsible to the client—the person or organization that hired or directed them to perform the audit. An audit team is accountable to the auditee because its goal is to help the auditee—that is, to assess the organization or process so that the auditee knows what is working and where opportunities for improvement exist. The members of an audit team are also accountable to the audit program manager or registrar for whom they are working. Therefore, their actions must reflect the audit organization's standards.

Lead Auditor Selection and Duties

Every audit team has a lead auditor or audit team leader. Large teams may have both. When the audit team consists of only one auditor, that auditor is the lead auditor. When more than one auditor is needed for an assignment, the lead auditor, usually an individual with supervisory experience or management capabilities, is identified prior to the other team members and participates in their selection. A lead auditor whose duties include auditing, directing, and monitoring team members usually has more auditing experience than other team members and is more familiar with the standard being audited against.

The lead auditor has ultimate responsibility for the satisfactory performance of all phases of the audit as well as for the professional conduct of the audit team members. As the representative of the entire audit team, the lead auditor is responsible for initiating and maintaining communication with the auditee. The lead auditor prepares the audit plan, conducts the opening and closing meetings, reviews the findings and observations of the auditors, prepares and submits an audit report, and evaluates corrective action. The lead auditor may also conduct daily briefings with team members throughout the audit.

Audit Team Selection and Assignments

When preparing an audit plan, the lead auditor (and/or client or audit manager) should assess the complexity of the activities to be audited and select team members who possess the qualifications or expertise needed to perform that audit. If the area to be audited is highly specialized, the auditing organization may have to outsource a specialist or consultant experienced in that area. To avoid misunderstandings, an outside specialist or subject matter expert must be briefed as to their expected role prior to an audit. Often, an audit team is a combination of quality assurance personnel, trained and experienced in auditing techniques, and technical specialists, trained and experienced in the area to be audited.[13]

Personnel are selected for specific quality auditing assignments on the basis of experience or training that indicates qualifications commensurate with the complexity of the activities to be audited.[14] Each auditor is responsible for preparing suitable working papers for the portion of the audit for which he/she is responsible. Working papers are discussed in detail later in Part II.

The responsibility of an audit team is to gather factual evidence of compliance or noncompliance of the audited area to the standard. Since the audit function intrudes on daily operations, an auditor has a duty to gather information promptly, objectively, and considerately. After comparing and analyzing observations, an audit team should be able to draw conclusions about the systems and report those findings in a timely manner.

Additionally, audit team members should be free from biases or conflicts of interest, comply with standards of ethical conduct, and exercise due care in the performance of their duties. These concepts were discussed in Part I of this handbook.

In summary, the number of personnel needed and their experience and qualifications depend on the amount of material to be covered, the availability of personnel and other audit resources, the amount of time available to perform the audit, and the subject of the audit.[15] A quality system audit of a bank will require different auditor skills than will an audit of technical areas for a chemical processing operation, or a robotics or software company.

6. REQUIREMENTS TO AUDIT AGAINST

Audits of quality programs require reference standards against which to judge the adequacy of the plans:

"The reference standards normally available include:
- Written policies and procedures of the company as they apply to quality
- Stated objectives in the budgets, programs, contracts, etc.
- Customer and company quality specifications
- Pertinent government specifications and handbooks
- Company, industry, and other pertinent quality standards on products, processes, and computer software
- Published guides for conduct of quality audits
- Pertinent quality department instructions
- General literature on auditing"[16]

Performance standards are the norms or criteria against which an activity is measured. There are four levels of performance standards:

1. **Policy Documents**—Examples include corporate policy statements, international and national quality system standards, regulatory standards, and business sector standards.

2. **Transition Documents**—Often called manuals, one should exist for each section, department, or division. Examples are corporate manual and plant manual.

3. **Procedure Documents**—These include the step-by-step requirements for doing a job.

4. **Detailed Documents**—These documents, such as drawings, purchase orders, product specifications, and inspection plans, explain specific tasks.[17]

"Standards, codes, and regulations . . . are issued by related industrial or professional associations, by national standards writing organizations concerned with the intended marketplace, by local/state/national legislative bodies and by international bodies."[18]

Why Must an Audit Basis Exist?

To perform an audit, an auditor must be aware of the audit basis, sometimes called reference standards or performance standards. The compliance or adequacy of a system cannot be measured until those requirements are defined. Regardless of the requirements, an audit must be performed against a basis for reference (e.g., organization performance standards and/or national standards such as ANSI/ISO/ASQ Q9001 or Q9004). These reference documents can include (1) quality system, product, or process standards; (2) contracts; (3) specifications; (4) policies; and (5) laws or regulations.

Standards. Certain international, national, and industry standards are mandated for many organizations. Audits verify compliance with the applicable standard, whether it be the ANSI/ISO/ASQ Q9001, AS 9001, QS–9000, or ISO 14001. At times, an organization may voluntarily adopt certain standards by incorporating them into contracts or policies even though there is no requirement to do so.

Contracts. In a second-party audit, the purchase order or other contract states the specific requirements that must be met, and an audit is performed to verify that the supplier is meeting those requirements. A contract may include references to a specific standard, such as ANSI, ASTM, FAA, or FDA standards.

Specifications. Specifications are normally used when conducting product or service audits. An auditor examines physical dimensions, placement or arrangement of items, or chemical compositions, for example, to see if they are in compliance with the specified requirements.

Policies. Internally, many companies regularly assess compliance and effectiveness with their own quality policies or policy statements. These policies are often stated in quality manuals and are the basis for the quality program.

Laws and Regulations. Many companies perform internal audits to assure that they are meeting all the requirements imposed by various laws and regulations, whether general or industry-specific. Third-party auditors within a regulatory agency use the laws and regulations, case law, and their internal requirements/guidelines as the basis for the audit.

Chapter B
Audit Design

1. STRATEGY

Regardless of whether a product, process, or system is being audited, the auditor should use a general auditing strategy, or audit path, so that data are collected in a logical and methodical manner. Effective audit planning ensures that an auditor will have the time and means to conduct a thorough investigation of the audited organization. It also enables the auditor to segment the audit by element or department, or to use the discovery method or tracing techniques to gather data. Adhering to such strategies helps an auditor gain insight into the practices actually employed throughout a company and assists in the identification of problems.

Some functions/departments lend themselves naturally to one particular auditing strategy. For example, tracing techniques may be suitable in situations where there is a natural flow of work, such as in production areas.[19]

Tracing

Tracing, or following the chronological progress of something as it is processed, is a common and effective means of collecting objective evidence during an audit. In forward tracing, an auditor starts at the beginning or middle of a manufacturing process, for example, and traces forward. In backward tracing, the auditor starts at the middle or end of a process and traces backward. Backward tracing can be more revealing than forward tracing, because the auditor examines the process from the perspective of seeing the results (product or service) of the preceding activity.

A flowchart can be used as a road map for tracing activities. When tracing, the auditor should:

- Start at the beginning, middle, or end of the process

- Choose an action, such as painting a wall, stamping, folding, or baking

- Gather information in six areas—people, equipment, method, material, environment, and measurement—for the action chosen, and record this information on a checklist (these factors are discussed in Part VII)

- Follow the path of the transaction backward or forward through the process[20]

Discovery Method

The discovery method is sometimes called random auditing. This method investigates what is currently taking place and therefore reflects prevailing work procedures. However, the discovery method offers no discernible pattern to an audit, and an auditor can become disoriented or spend too much time in the facility.[21]

In most situations, the discovery method should not have to be used if the audit has been adequately planned. However, this method could be effective if the auditor knows that a problem exists but has not yet located it. By going into the audit area and looking around, an auditor may be able to bring the problem to the surface.

Element Method

The element method is a commonly employed auditing strategy. The element method can refer to any element of any quality assurance standard or of the auditee's quality program. Examples of elements are:

- 20 elements from ANSI/ISO/ASQ Q9001-1994

- 18 elements from 10 CFR 50, Appendix B

- 15 elements from 10 CFR 830.120

- 7 categories from the Malcolm Baldrige National Quality Award

- elements from the ANSI/ISO/ASQ Q9004 *Guidance for Performance Improvement*

The auditor examines each element individually to see how it affects the entire system. This method is thorough and good to use on an annual basis. However, when an audit team is very large or is spending several weeks in a facility, the element method can become cumbersome.

Department Method

The department method is another way of dividing an auditing task and works especially well when accountability at the department level is important. The auditor focuses on the entire operation of one department rather than on segments of it by reviewing numerous quality elements within the department. This auditing strategy touches on almost everything in an audited facility. Here, the auditor's ability to identify applicable quality elements for that department is put to test. While this is an excellent strategy when the audit team wishes "to slice the apple a different way," it should not be overused. Focusing too much on one small group of people (one department) may not accurately represent what is happening throughout an organization.

2. DATA COLLECTION PLAN

An auditor must develop a plan for collecting specific evidence needed to answer checklist questions. The collection plan provides the auditor with space for recording the results of examinations and identifying people who were interviewed. The auditor should ask open-ended questions that result in verifiable data. The questions asked may deal with causal groupings such as methods, materials, machinery, people, measurement, and environment—that may affect a specific action.

Data include any observation of facts and can be qualitative or quantitative. Sources of data could include records from the auditee as well as observations that an auditor makes during audit performance, such as counting the number of press cycle openings or observing an operator during a prescribed, defined operation. Qualitative data indicate "yes, this was performed, or this step was conducted." Objective evidence must be available and reviewable for any data to be considered verifiable. Quantitative data are collected by measuring or counting, such as the number of defective pieces removed (inspected out) or the number of cycles of molding press observed during a period of time. The number of complaints that a complaint handling system received during a certain time period is another example of quantitative data.

An auditor, as part of the planning, will usually have access to work instructions or written procedures. If the quality system is mature, the written procedures will describe what records need to be maintained, who maintains the records, who collects the data, and what kinds of data are collected. As a result of this preparation, an auditor should know what data sheets or records to expect when reaching the audit site.

An auditor should have a plan in mind for what needs to be examined, and it should be described on the audit checklist. For example, an auditor will be familiar with the inspection records on a production line and may decide to examine them. Next, the auditor may decide how many inspection records need to be examined. Depending on the size of the auditee organization and objective of the audit, a sampling plan may need to be developed. See the sampling theory and procedures section of Part VII and the appendix for more information on selecting samples.

An auditor must be familiar with different data collection methods and their strengths and weaknesses. Proper training teaches auditors which methods can be used and which ones cannot be used for a specific task in particular situations. The audit program can dictate which data collection methods are for compliance and which ones can be used only for inference. Data collection plans may include interviewing, observing, reviewing records and documents, analyzing data, and statistical and nonstatistical sampling. An auditor needs to understand basic statistical methods and must be able to choose the one that gives the desired information.

3. SAMPLING PLAN

A sampling plan must be developed for each audit. The type and extent of sampling is normally the responsibility of the auditor, based on the purpose and scope of the audit. Questions regarding the adequacy of the sampling plan should be addressed by the lead auditor.

The purpose of sampling is to gain information about an entire group of units, items, things, or people based on observing and/or inspecting a segment of the group. Sampling is a technique to gain the information needed at a reduced cost (compared to 100 percent inspection). To be valid, the segment or sample selected should be representative of the entire group.

Sampling of information for an audit is not always statistically valid, however. The auditor normally does not have time to review a statistically valid sample from thousands of instruments that need calibration or thousands of engineering records. In such cases, the auditor should quantify the number of instruments or records evaluated and identify the areas where they were obtained. Items from a population could be sampled several times; each time, the auditor will identify the number (quantity) and location. This sampling technique allows the client and the auditee to appreciate the significance of the results and better focus their corrective action activities. Reviewing instruments or documents from a variety of areas, although not statistically sound, will identify if a problem is systemic or focused in certain areas.[22]

Statistically valid sampling plans are normally used for product, process, and compliance audits. It would be common for a product audit plan to require statistically valid sampling. See Part VII and the appendix for more detail on sampling plans and techniques.

4. LOGISTICS PLANNING

Audit logistical planning is necessary for both audit team coordination and establishing auditee communication links. Good planning will result in a smooth, seamless audit performance. Poor planning will make the audit team appear less professional and might jeopardize meeting audit objectives. Auditors need to arrive at the right place, with the right equipment and information, at the right time, and for a suitable duration of time to get the job done right. To help the auditor properly think through what is necessary to start the audit process, it is prudent to outline a detailed logistical plan.[23]

The logistics of an audit are a crucial part of the planning process any time the auditors must travel to the audit location. The following items should be included in the plan that is typically given to the auditee in advance of the audit:

- A timeline plan for the auditor's visit

- The opening and closing meeting location and time

- A request for an audit team meeting place, such as a conference room for team debriefings and discussions of observations, equipped with telephones, computer, or any other equipment needed to conduct audit activities

- A request for facility layout maps, office locations, confidential areas, and so on, and any special requirements such as safety, environment, or health equipment like steel-toe shoes, hard hat, lab coat, hair net, head cover, grounding devices, or safety glasses

- Travel plans, possibly identifying a rendezvous prior to the opening meeting, and possibly including an extra day to meet at a nearby hotel and get familiar with the area

Chapter C

Document Review and Preparation

1. AUDIT-RELATED DOCUMENT REVIEW

Before performing an audit, an auditor must secure documentation of the quality policies or practices and procedures of a company, so that compliance of a product, process, or system with the requirements specified in the documentation may be assessed.

Securing Quality-Related Documentation

An auditor should contact the auditee to determine the availability of quality-related documentation and to request copies. Proprietary material contained in the documents may be removed before it is sent to an auditor. Historically, paper has been the conventional form of documentation, but documentation may be in any medium that can be recorded, reviewed, and retrieved. For instance, magnetic media, computer files, voice recordings, and videotape are all acceptable forms of quality-related documentation. Many companies are now achieving a paperless office and have placed their controlled documents on an intranet for use and downloading by employees. An auditor may be asked to visit the World Wide Web site and obtain the documentation independently.

A quality auditor observes, examines, and reports compliance by assessing systems, processes, and products against quality-related documentation. Processes are compared to quality objectives and standards, while products are tested and inspected to determine conformance to

specifications or standards. Documents that specify quality requirements include:

- Quality manuals
- Procedures
- Detailed instructions
- Workmanship standards or models
- Policy manuals
- Blueprints and drawings
- Project plans
- Quality plans
- Specifications
- Strategic plans to identify quality objectives
- Certificate of compliance forms
- Industry practices/methods
- Forms used to record data
- Schedules
- Trade practices
- Service standards
- Software operating manuals
- Work instructions
- Routing cards
- Preventive maintenance plans
- Quality inspection plans
- Purchase order forms
- Flowcharts

Written procedures are reviewed before an audit starts because the
policies, specifications, and standards drive the audit preparation. In an
audit with a scope limited to training in an organization, for example, the
appropriate part of the standard that describes the training requirements

becomes part of the documentation for that audit, along with the corporate training policy, the records of training for the individuals involved, and the quality plan for training.

Using Quality-Related Documentation

Reasonable documentation is secured before an audit so that the auditor can determine if the system is properly designed. An on-site audit will then determine if the system is functioning satisfactorily. Information contained in documents must be appropriate, adequate, and current if the documentation is to be used in decision making. The quality manual, a master list of documents, or other similar documentation should instruct the auditor where to locate and how to obtain applicable documents. Reviewing these documents before the audit helps an auditor prepare working papers and determine where to concentrate effort during the performance stage.

Documentation should meet minimum expectations in identifying the organization's requirements and what the policy of the organization is relative to meeting those requirements. The audit team should review the documentation to assure that it meets and complies with the requirements of the applicable standards and laws/regulations. A matrix or table relating each requirement to the location in the company's documentation where it is addressed will greatly help the audit team make this determination as well as help the company ensure that all requirements have been adequately addressed.

2. AUDITEE'S PERFORMANCE HISTORY REVIEW

An auditee organization will have a performance history unless the audit is an initial audit or qualification survey. Knowledge of the performance history will help ensure that positive practices continue and problems are corrected.

When prior audit information exists, it should be reviewed as part of an auditor's checklist to ensure that corrective action has been implemented effectively. Sometimes a prior observation was reported that was not a violation, but an emerging trend. During audit preparation, an auditor may examine data to see if this trend has continued or if some action has been taken to reverse it.

Another reason to review past audit records is to identify specific areas likely to have continuing or repeat problems and to determine the status of actions taken earlier to resolve any noncompliance. The audit team should verify that the corrective actions implemented following previous audits have remained in effect and that they have prevented the problem or noncompliance from recurring.[24]

For internal audits, performance data may already be available to the auditor. For second- and third-party audits, the performance data may need to be requested before or during the audit. Performance data may relate to the product, process, or system.

One of the most common performance records reviewed by auditors is the prior audit report. The review may be for the auditor's professional benefit, or the client may request that the auditor verify corrective actions from prior audits as part of the audit purpose. If the client has a concern about the objectivity of the prior audit, the client may instruct the current audit team not to review the prior audit.

Performance records to be reviewed may include:

- Prior audit reports

- Customer feedback

- Corrective and preventive action records

- Product returns

- Product warranty claims

- Product quality levels

- Process and unit performance compared to goals

- Organization and business performance

- Customer surveys

- Field reports

3. PREPARATION OF AUDIT CHECKLISTS, GUIDELINES, LOG SHEETS

An audit checklist is the primary tool for bringing order to quality audits. With a well-planned and well-defined checklist, success is achievable. Without a checklist, an auditor has a disjointed, disorganized activity and no place to record failed efforts. Before developing the checklists, an auditor must know what the governing requirement's documents say.

A completed checklist provides:

- Objective evidence that an audit was performed

- Order and organization

- A record that all applicable aspects of the quality program were examined

- Historical information on program, systems, or supplier problems

- The essence for the closing meeting and audit report

- An information base for planning future audits

- A vehicle for time management

The purpose of a checklist is to gather information during the course of an audit that the auditor will need to justify the audit findings and conclusion. The checklist guides each member of the audit team to ensure that the full scope of the audit is adequately covered. The checklist provides space for recording facts gathered during fieldwork, with places to answer questions and numerous areas for taking notes.

A checklist is a set of notes and instructions about specific things and specific areas, with specific questions to ask and specific techniques to use during an audit. Checklists or written procedures are used to assure continuity and comprehensive coverage of the area of interest and to provide evidence of the questions that were reviewed and a record of the review.[25]

A checklist may contain a standard set of information that every auditor looks for, such as the following:

- Does the person being audited have access to written procedures and applicable work instructions?

- Is the procedure up-to-date?

- Does the scope of this employee's training cover the observed activities?

- Is the organizational structure proper for what the employee is expected to do in the observed procedure?

- Are appropriate records being maintained?

The specific format and construction of a checklist may vary from auditor to auditor depending on what works best for the auditor. Some checklists are yes/no questions that reference a specified requirement; others are open-ended interview questions that test the limits of a procedure; and yet others are statements providing additional instructions for the auditor. Variations of checklist question/statement may be: "Does the person being audited always have access to the latest version of the procedure?" "Verify, through observations, discussions, and review of documents, that individuals have access to written procedures and applicable work instructions that cover their activities."

In addition, many checklists contain a set of questions for each section of the requirement standard that is being audited against. This part of the checklist includes questions about management responsibilities, training, quality planning, and so on. These "canned" or generic checklist items should be supplemented with time-specific and circumstance-specific questions and observations that the auditor wants to make during that audit. Checklists should always be reviewed to make sure they are still current, since standards change.

Deviations from the checklist may result from a change in the audit schedule or an observation that indicates a possible problem. A checklist can be expanded as is necessary, while staying within the scope of the audit.[26]

An audit checklist is flexible; audit observations need not be restricted to what the auditor has planned. Also, it is permissible to abandon or make adjustments to the checklist items during daily meetings. A checklist is nonlimiting—it does not restrict what an auditor needs to do provided the auditor stays within the scope of the audit; it is simply a way to plan so that the auditor knows what to look for and observe in the given area.

The audit checklist may be forwarded to the auditee prior to the audit. This is a choice of the auditing organization. Normally, for first- and second-party audits, if the auditee requests a copy of the audit checklist, it is provided in the spirit of cooperation. Some audit organizations issue disclaimers when checklists are shared to remind the auditee that the checklist is not the standard and that areas not on the checklist may be examined as long as they are within the purpose and scope of the audit.

It may benefit the auditor to review previous audits after the checklist is completed to see if anything should be added that was a concern in the past. The reason for waiting to review previous audits is to avoid bias in audit preparation due to some historical event. If a previous audit had a corrective action that requires follow-up, this is the time to add it to the checklist. There may even have been some customer complaints that were not completely answered. These are important issues that cannot be ignored.

Guidelines are additional documented instructions considered good audit practice that may provide additional information for conducting the audit. Guidelines are not mandatory and are normally prepared in a statement format.

Log sheets are another kind of working paper prepared in advance of an audit. A log sheet contains auditor notes and becomes a record of activities performed during an audit, what the auditor observed, and who the auditor talked to.

Example log sheet

One example of a log sheet is a white ruled pad that chronologically details where the auditor went and who was interviewed.

Example Area Guidelines for an auditor

- Make sure posted instructions are signed and that any changes are also signed.
- If cyclical reports are kept, be sure older ones are marked as historical or reference. The same thing applies to drawings or specifications.
- Everyone should be able to use the intranet to view practices and specifications. Make sure all stations are capable.
- Changes to WNs, routings, and OISs must be initialed.
- All product should be identifiable (e.g., routing, tag) and nonconforming material segregated in the MRB area or clearly marked.
- Housekeeping need not be what we do for CAT VIPs, but there should be some orderliness, and debris should be removed.
- Anything that needs to be calibrated should have a current label. Also check for dates that may expire next week.
- Personal training records must be current and available.

Audit Checklist Form

Enterprise: _____   Audit Team: _____
Location: _____   Team Member: _____
Date Audited: _____   Area Audited: _____   Team Member: _____

Check 1 or Both		Document	Element	Contact		Checklist Item	Findings/Comments
ISO	QS			Who	Where		

Form 1. Audit checklist form.

Chapter D
Communication and Distribution of Audit Plan

An audit plan is a written description of the various elements of an upcoming audit. An audit plan is not the same as an audit schedule. The audit plan describes what will be covered in a particular audit or sequence of audits. The audit schedule states what audits will be performed within a certain block of time.[27] Figure 8 shows a sample audit plan.

Communication of an Audit Plan

Before issuing an audit plan, the lead auditor should contact the auditee by telephone to verify the proposed date of the audit. After an audit plan has been finalized, the date and logistics of the impending audit should be confirmed in writing. For an internal audit, notification is done by memo or published schedule. For a second- or third-party audit, it is done by letter. The notification letter or memo should be addressed to the senior person in charge of the area to be audited. For internal audits, this person is probably the department manager or area superintendent. For second- and third-party audits, this person is usually the plant manager or president.[28] Figure 9 shows a sample audit notification letter.

Even if the lead auditor prepares the letter or memo, the client should sign it. This formal notice should be delivered before the field visit. The timing of the notice should be consistent with organizational procedures and common courtesy, varying from one week to several months. Advance notice of 30 days is common but not required.

Audit Plan—2/22/XX

Audited Organization: ABC Industries, ABC Fla.

Purpose:

To assess conformance (compliance) and effectiveness of the quality management system against internal and external performance standards and to report findings.

Scope of the Audit:

The ABC production facility and support activities will be included in the audit. The audit includes all departments that support the production of gizmos that are responsible for meeting ISO 9001 requirements. The areas of interest include the Purchasing, Quality Assurance, Laboratory, Distribution, Order Entry, Scheduling, Production, and Training departments.

Requirements:

As specified in ANSI/ISO/ASQ Q9001 and existing ABC company policies and procedures.

Applicable Documents:

The Quality (policy) Manual(s)—QM9001

Unit procedures that cover the ANSI/ISO/ASQ Q9001 requirements

Other regulatory requirements and industry standards

Overall Schedule (detailed interview schedule to follow):

March 23, 20XX

8:00 A.M.	Orientation for auditors (safety and environment)
9:00 A.M.	Opening meeting (for auditees)
9:30 A.M.	Tour/review documents
10:30 A.M.–4:00 P.M.	Interviews and observations
4:00 P.M.–5:00 P.M.	Audit team meeting

Figure 8. Audit plan.

March 24, 20XX

      8:00 A.M.–8:30 A.M.   Daily briefing with ABC coordinator

      8:30 A.M.–1:00 P.M.   Interviews and observations continued

      1:00 P.M.–3:00 P.M.   Audit team meeting, preparation of report

      3:00 P.M.–4:00 P.M.   Closing meeting

Team Members:

    John Smith, Lead Auditor, ASQ CQA

    Jane Doe, ASQ CQA

Approved: _____   Approved: _____
        Audit Organization   ABC Industries

Figure 8. *Continued.*

Distribution of an Audit Plan

Members of an audit team receive copies of the audit plan, as does the auditee. The auditee is responsible for distributing the audit plan within the organization.

Several parallel activities are involved in the preparation of an audit plan: scheduling the audit, notifying the auditee, and lining up audit resources. Once the audit plan is prepared, it is formally communicated to the auditee. The lead auditor should publish the audit plan, notify the client and the auditee of the impending audit, and confirm that any special needs or plans, such as travel requirements and security clearances, have been arranged. Once these steps have been completed, the performance stage of the audit is ready to begin.

Mr. Dale Smith   February 23, 20XX
ABC Industries
1 ABC Blvd.
ABC, FL XXXXX

Dear Dale,

The audit team will perform a quality system audit of the ABC facility to assess conformance to ANSI/ISO/ASQ Q9001 standard requirements. The scope of the audit will be limited to the requirements stated in ISO 9001 (ANSI/ISO/ASQ Q9001) and existing internal quality system policies and procedures. The audit process will be conducted according to recognized auditing conventions as defined for ASQ Certified Quality Auditors.

You should plan for the audit to require two days of on-site interviewing and verifying of requirements. A draft report will be left after the audit, and the final report will be forwarded within two business days. The auditors will be Jane Red and myself .

The on-site audit is scheduled for March 23rd through March 24th. The audit team will need a room with a table, telephone, and electrical outlets for computers and printers. The audit plan is enclosed. As agreed, please forward the quality manual to my attention to arrive no later than two weeks before the scheduled audit.

Thank you for your cooperation in making the necessary arrangements to the planned quality audit. If you have any questions I can be reached at the (XXX)-XXX-XXXX.

                                        Sincerely,

                                        John Doe

                                        John Doe, ASQ CQA

                                        Chip Jones

                                        Chip Jones, Client

Copy: Jane Red
Enclosures: 1

Figure 9. Notification letter.

SIDEBAR

Problems Commonly Encountered During the Audit Planning Stage

Problems likely to be encountered during the planning stage of an audit include difficulties related to the availability of personnel and other audit resources and scheduling the audit.

Availability of Audit Team Personnel. A common detriment or hindrance to effective planning for an internal audit is the reluctance of some organizations to release their people to do effective audit planning. Most audit team members are not full-time members of a quality assurance staff or of an auditing organization. They are either volunteers or people drafted from other areas of the company, such as production, accounting, sales, and personnel. It is often difficult for them to find the time that is needed to effectively plan an audit—generally four to six hours per person.

Availability of Other Resources. One problem is the lack of availability of other resources, such as funding, that can have an effect on audit planning. Another problem is that the auditee may fail to forward the necessary documents to the auditor in time to allow adequate preparation.

Scheduling Difficulties. Often other events take priority and make the audit difficult to schedule. Such events could include a major reorganization or merger. Perhaps the auditee has just received a major contract, or the audit is scheduled at the same time a regulatory agency plans a visit. The audit is an important event, but sometimes other events take higher priority.

Auditee Availability. At times, in spite of all good intentions, some auditees can not be available due to prior business commitments or personal emergencies.

Part III

Audit Performance

[32 of the CQA exam questions or 21%]

The performance phase of an audit is the actual fieldwork. It is the data-gathering portion of the audit that covers the time from the auditor's arrival at the audit location through the exit meeting.[29]

Chapter A
Audit Management

The lead auditor is responsible for managing the audit. Prior to arriving at the audit location, the lead auditor should confirm that all other auditors were properly prepared and that they are aware of the place and starting time. The lead auditor is determined by the client or audit program manager and should not be confused with national certification programs that classify auditors as an *auditor* or *lead auditor*.

1. AUDIT TEAM MANAGEMENT

The lead auditor should convene the audit team in a quiet portion of the facility or in a conference room at least once a day throughout an audit. Some teams prefer to hold daily meetings in the morning, while others prefer to hold them before lunch or at the end of the day. The timing of the meeting is less important than the topics discussed.

First, audit team members share the information they have gathered so far. Then team members propose conclusions or identify potential problem areas on the basis of the information gathered. If contradictory information has been gathered or if team members disagree about what has been observed, the team must gather additional information. Finally, in an effort to keep the audit on schedule, the audit team discusses what areas may need more or less attention than originally thought. This discussion redirects or modifies the remaining audit schedule, which helps keep the audit on track and prevents the audit team from becoming distracted by minor issues.

Between meetings, the audit team members are "on their own." If a team member runs into a problem during the audit and is uncertain about how to handle a situation, the member should contact the lead auditor immediately.

In summary, daily meetings help an audit team (1) discuss and confirm observations and potential findings, (2) determine how they might relate to other areas, (3) plan for the next day, and (4) prepare for the daily meeting with the auditee.

2. COMMUNICATION OF AUDIT STATUS TO AUDITEE

At the beginning or end of each day, an audit team should meet with the auditee to discuss what will be or has been done that day. This meeting gives the lead auditor an opportunity to explain what has been looked at, what will be observed next, and where problems may exist.

Communicating potential findings every day serves two purposes. First, the auditee can communicate potential findings up the command chain so that auditee management is aware of problems before the exit meeting. Second, the auditee can either confirm or deny that a problem exists. An auditee who insists that a problem does not exist can offer more data in an attempt to convince the auditor that there is no problem.

A daily meeting of the audit team and auditee can help prevent difficult situations, such as auditee management's refusing to accept the audit team's findings at the exit meeting. If an auditee will not agree to a daily meeting, the lead auditor must take responsibility for informing the escort and area supervisors of potential findings in an area. For internal audits, formal meetings may not be needed or desirable. However, the auditee should still be informed daily of progress, whether by voice mail, e-mail, on-the-spot conversations, or other means.

3. AUDIT PLAN CHANGES

The lead auditor ensures that any change in the audit plan or schedule is proactively discussed during the opening meeting and obtains consensus for changes. The lead auditor needs to be flexible enough to make audit plan and schedule changes at the auditee's request. This is critically important to ensure that the audit gets off to a good start. At the same time, the lead auditor must be understanding if the auditee refuses to make schedule changes at the request of the audit team.

The lead auditor ensures that all discussed and agreed-upon schedule changes are fully documented in a revised schedule, and communicated to all involved parties or departments prior to the interview process. The auditors are responsible for ensuring that audit plan changes do not result in sacrificing the original time allocations established to effectively evaluate conformance to requirements.

Chapter B
Opening Meeting

Soon after the arrival of the audit team at the audit site, the audit team and auditee gather for an opening meeting, sometimes called a preaudit conference or entrance meeting. This meeting starts the data-gathering phase of the audit.

1. PRESENTATION AND REVIEW OF THE AUDIT PLAN

The principal objectives of the opening meeting are to:

- Introduce audit team members to auditee management
- Establish communication links and role of the escort
- Communicate the audit plan by 1) reviewing the scope and purpose of the audit, 2) reaffirming the reference standards being used, and 3) describing the methods and procedures to be used during the audit
- Inform the auditee how the results will be reported (nonconformances, findings, or other) and the methods used to classify and prioritize results
- Inform the auditee of the possible outcomes of the audit
- Confirm logistics, such as hours, escorts, tentative schedules, needed facilities, and availability of resources
- Confirm time and date for exit meeting as well as interim auditee daily briefings

Additionally, if applicable, the opening meeting may:

- Include a review of previous audits

- Help ensure that the audit team understands the confidentiality agreement

- Verify required safety and security clearances

- Identify local language issues and concerns (different languages used in the work place, slang, word usage level)

- Identify work agreement requirements between management and labor that may affect the performance of the audit

The opening meeting establishes the best climate for developing rapport and sets the ground rules for conducting an audit. Before an audit starts, individuals should know the daily audit schedule and what to expect in the exit meeting, written report, corrective action requests, and possible follow-up. The structure of the opening meeting should be flexible and the level of formality will depend on several factors, including the audit scope, the purpose, the size of the audit team, and whether the audit is internal or external.[30]

While an opening meeting should always take place, in the case of an internal audit, it is frequently a short, informal meeting. Often there is more interaction between the audit team and management in the preparation stage of internal audits. Since internal audits usually occur on a fairly regular basis, all parties normally understand what will be examined before the audit takes place.

Roles and Responsibilities of an Auditor

The entire audit team should attend the opening meeting, which is conducted by the lead auditor. The lead auditor prepares the meeting agenda and often hands out copies in advance. At the opening meeting the lead auditor:

- Introduces audit team members and presents their credentials

- Restates the purpose and scope of the audit in a clear and diplomatic fashion

- May refer to previous audits of the facility and previously required corrective action

- May ask specific questions as a result of the document review or other information provided to the audit team

- Solicits areas of interest from the auditee or mentions areas of specific concern

DAY ONE: March 23, 20XX

Item/Element	Area/Function	Contact	Auditor	Time
Opening meeting	Conference room	All	All	9–9:30 A.M.
Document Control	Quality assurance	Ms. Apostrophe	Mr. Brackets	10–11 A.M.
Customer Requirements	Marketing	Mr. Colon	Ms. Dash	10–11 A.M.
Design and Development Control	R&D	Ms. Parentheses	Mr. Brackets	11 A.M. – 12 P.M.

Figure 10. Detailed audit schedule.

- May present the audit checklist to the auditee
- Sets the detailed audit schedule (see Figure 10 for an example)
- Describes the quality-related documentation used to develop the audit plan
- Ensures meeting minutes and attendance are recorded. These duties may be completed by the lead auditor, or the lead auditor may assign the duties to an audit team member
- Verifies that auditee's management has communicated to employees and other interested parties, such as a union, that the audit is being conducted

The lead auditor should also describe the audit process and the anticipated benefits. The lead auditor should allow time in the schedule to answer any questions from auditee personnel.

Roles and Responsibilities of an Auditee

Auditors expect at least one representative of management to attend the opening meeting. The management team member may be the person who coordinated the audit on behalf of the auditee organization or someone else. Other responsible and interested parties, such as the supervisors or managers of the areas to be audited, may attend. In some cases, the lead auditor may specifically request certain representatives or may suggest minimum attendance based on the auditor's judgment (for example, if the room is too small to hold many people, if the wrong people want to attend,

or if there are culture issues). The auditee's senior management representative should be invited to introduce his/her attendees.

The auditee should be expected to achieve consensus with the auditor
on the following:

- The individual who will represent the auditee on all matters
  during the audit

- Auditor access to areas, and activities to be audited

- Facilities for the audit team's use

- Support personnel to be provided: escorts, specialists, line
  personnel, etc.

- Safety and regulatory requirements

- Protection of proprietary rights[31]

If members of an auditee's staff disagree with or need clarification on
any of the lead auditor's statements, they should express an opinion or ask
for clarification at this time. For example, if the stated scope of the audit
does not match the auditee's expectations, the auditee must point out this
fact at the opening meeting, rather than during or on completion of the audit.

Sometimes an auditee may wish to make a presentation to acquaint
the auditor with the firm or give a plant tour to familiarize the auditor with
the facility. Brief presentations or tours are permissible and at times highly
desirable; but if the time spent on these activities becomes excessive, it is
the lead auditor's responsibility to politely call a halt to the proceedings
so that the audit schedule remains intact.

SIDEBAR

When an audit is not moving along as planned, the auditor can say:

"I'm really enjoying this conversation, but all of us have a lot to do; so
what do you say we get started."

"This tour has been very helpful, but I think it has accomplished what I
needed; so let's start the audit interviews."

"Since we have so many areas to cover today, can we speed things up so
we don't have to stay after working hours to complete the audit?"

"What's next on the schedule?" (The auditee notes the next step from the
provided copy of the audit agenda.) "OK, let's move on so we don't
affect the operation."

2. CONFIRMATION OF AUDIT LOGISTICS

A number of logistical issues need to be settled at the opening meeting. The number of issues will depend on whether the audit is internal or external, the size of the organization, the size of the audit team, and the complexity of the area to be audited. Issues include but are not necessarily limited to:

- Meeting rooms for audit team use and for daily auditee briefings
- Office space for auditors
- Access to necessary facilities and equipment required for verification activities
- Documents and records needed
- Special safety, environmental, or security issues
- Facilities for the safe storage of confidential records
- Access to telephones
- The distances between areas to be visited
- Housekeeping items (rest rooms, lunchroom, break area)
- An escort
- Tours[32]

An auditee should provide an escort for each subgroup of the audit team. (An exception can be made for internal audits if the auditor is already familiar with the organization and activities being audited.) The escort accompanies the auditor on the entire data-gathering portion of the audit and serves as a liaison between the auditing organization and auditee management. The escort performs personnel introductions and provides clarifying information as needed. For example, an escort can suggest a way of rephrasing a question, perhaps by substituting terminology more familiar to the person being interviewed. However, the escort should refrain from answering questions for the auditee unless asked to do so by the auditor.

Other duties of the escort include:

- Providing or requesting supplies and records required by the auditor
- Acting as an observer for management, and providing an overview of the auditor's observations, findings, and conclusions to auditee management

- Acting as a guide for the auditor

- Confirming or denying that a discrepancy or nonconformity has been found before moving on to the next area to be audited

- Ensuring that auditors comply with company rules, including safety rules

3. DISCUSSION OF AUDITEE CONCERNS

It is not unusual for an auditee to have concerns about an audit. Auditees may be unfamiliar with the auditor's mode of operation. Or an overly conscientious auditee may be obsessively concerned about potential deficiencies. The opening meeting can serve to allay these and other auditee concerns.[33]

For third-party audits, the lead auditor addresses and obtains consensus to the following potential concerns of the auditee during the opening meeting:

- Audit plan or schedule changes

- Nonconformance or nonconformity reporting

- Process for providing additional evidence to address a potential nonconformance or nonconformity

For second-party audits, the lead auditor addresses all clarifications related to the criteria or guidelines against which the audit will be performed and the usage of the audit results.

For first-party audits, the lead auditor addresses concerns related to reflection of auditee job performance based on the audit results. Auditee difficulties with the implementation of procedure or work instruction is the greatest concern during first-party audits. It may be helpful if the auditor emphasizes that the systems and processes are being audited and not the individual employees.

Chapter C
Data Collection

An audit team should employ one or a combination of several, auditing strategies during the data-gathering phase of an audit. As data are gathered, the audit team should reassemble periodically to sort it and to form tentative conclusions. If the data that have been gathered are unclear or contradictory, the audit team should determine the need for additional data that can be used to confirm or deny tentative conclusions. The audit team is also responsible for ensuring that an auditee representative is made aware of potential problems as they surface.

The data-gathering process normally takes most of the time and effort in the performance phase of an audit. The job of an auditor is to collect factual information, analyze and evaluate it in terms of the specified requirements, draw conclusions from this comparison, and report the results to management.[34]

When using a particular audit strategy (department or element), the auditor must be aware of the interconnectedness of the departments and quality-system elements. If an auditor's focus is too narrow, the results of the investigation will not be comprehensive or reflect the actual situation. For example, an auditor conducting an audit of the sales department should recognize the interconnection between the process of identifying customer requirements, activities related to design requirements, customer feedback activities described in control of nonconforming product and corrective action, credit approval guidelines, and so on.

In auditing, information or objective evidence can be gathered in several different ways. The auditor may examine documents and records, interview employees, physically examine samples of product, and observe work in progress. The auditor must sort and summarize the objective evidence gathered (observations) into a format that will be useful to the client and/or auditee.

1. DOCUMENT/RECORD EXAMINATION

An auditor must be well-trained in methods for examining documents and records. A document specifies what *should* be done; a record specifies what *has* been done. *Documents* are written instructions or procedures that establish a practice or tell a person how to do a job. Examples of documents include written work instructions, purchase orders, procedures, diagrams, drawings, and blank forms. In contrast, *records* result when a particular step or process is performed as directed in the documents.

Records are evidence that practices outlined in documents have been performed. Thus, records verify that the actions specified in documents have indeed taken place as required.

Reasons for Examining Documents and Records
Documents and records must be examined for the following reasons:

- To ensure that documents adequately meet higher tier requirements, such as policies, codes, and standards

- To ensure that records provide the objective evidence to demonstrate product acceptability and the appropriate implementation of system/process controls

- To provide the auditor with an understanding of the system/process under investigation

Document and record examination may reveal incomplete, conflicting, or incorrect information that must be addressed by the audit team. The implementation (deployment) of documents (policy, procedure, plan, etc.) are normally verified through examination of records, interviewing, physical examination and observing work.

Document and Record Considerations
To ensure that documents and records reflect actual practice, the auditor should verify that they are secure, permanent, current, and accurate.

Records should not be accessible to unauthorized personnel. They should be backed up or stored in more than one location. Written records should be permanent—written in ink, unless environmental circumstances do not allow recording data in ink. For example, some chemicals used in laboratories may cause reactions when they come in contact with ink, so an alternate means of recording data would be permissible. If records must be changed, the changes should be dated and signed or initialed. The original information should be kept intact so that the new information and the reason for the change can be assessed. Erasures and use of correction fluid are strictly forbidden on records.

Documents should be current and available to the people who need them. Sometimes, what an auditor sees on the production floor does not match the documentation because the documentation has not been updated as procedures have changed.

Some documents and records reside in computer programs. Access and changes to documents, as well as changes to computer code, must be controlled. For records, controls should be in place to limit who can access records, enter data as a record, control record changes, and control code changes to the software.

Tracing is a common means of collecting objective evidence (facts) during an audit. An auditor may read a procedure or become familiar with a method and then observe others attempting to accomplish the procedure. If it cannot be done, the auditor needs to determine whether the procedure is inaccurate, which could indicate that the person who wrote the procedure did not understand the process or that the process was changed and the document was not updated. The alternative is that the process is being improperly performed, which could indicate that employees have not been adequately trained.

An auditor may examine items to verify information. For example, if a record says "this cabinet was painted blue," the auditor examines the item to see if it is indeed blue. If the records states "there are 10 nonconforming items awaiting disposition," the auditor should go to the nonconforming hold area to count the number of items awaiting disposition.

Documents and records can be sampled to verify that they are accurate. Sampling is employed when 100 percent inspection is not practical. To test the accuracy of a document, an auditor reads it and then goes to where the work is being performed to observe and/or interview operators about the process. In the case of records, an auditor can sample portions of a record by verifying that the recorded result occurred. This verification can be done by talking to the person who recorded the information or by alternate means, such as cross-checking a log calculation.

2. INTERVIEWS

Interviewing, the process of obtaining information from another person in response to questions, is an important and widely used form of data collection in auditing. However, verbal statements are hearsay unless corroborated. Auditors must realize that the interviewee may have a hidden agenda or certain biases when responding to questions.

Interviews are normally conducted one-on-one; but an audit team may occasionally find it necessary to interview groups of individuals or to conduct interviews by telephone or videoconferencing. While one-on-one, face-to-face interviews are preferable for obtaining information, other methods can conserve resources.

Interviews are used in audits to gain insights, clarify information, confirm or deny suspicions, and elicit details that may not be brought out by other audit activities. Arter has suggested using a six-step interview process developed by Frank X. Brown.[36]

1. Put the interviewee at ease.

2. Explain your purpose.

3. Find out what they are doing.

4. Analyze what they are doing.

5. Make a tentative conclusion.

6. Explain your next step.

When conducting an interview, the auditor should begin by introducing himself or herself and putting the interviewee at ease. The purpose of the interview should be explained, followed by general, open-ended questions that get an interviewee talking about the job. An auditor may simply say, "What are you doing?" or "What tells you to do that?" If the interviewee's answers confirm the documentation, the information has been corroborated. If not, the auditor needs to probe by asking more specific questions to ascertain if a work problem does indeed exist, or whether the interview is being hampered by miscommunication. An auditor may not understand the process the interviewee describes, or the interviewee may misinterpret or fail to understand a question. An escort can often help clarify communication problems resulting from unfamiliar terminology by rephrasing a question. An escort should not be permitted to answer for an interviewee, however.

When auditors make a conclusion about whether necessary controls are in place, they must communicate the preliminary conclusions to the interviewee and/or escort. For example, an auditor could say, "That's good. It looks to me as though you have a thorough understanding of the requirements of your job and are doing good work." An auditor who suspects a potential finding could say, "It looks like we might have a problem in this area. I can't see where those controls are placed." Such comments give the interviewee an opportunity to offer more information. If the interviewee is able to allay the auditor's concerns, no problem exists.

The auditor usually takes notes throughout an interview and should take a few minutes at the end of each interview to ensure that the notes will be complete and meaningful when reviewed later in the day. If extensive note-taking is necessary, it may be best for the auditor to step out of the room or into a secluded location to record observations so that the interviewee will not become unnerved by the auditor's recording large amounts of information.

In all communications with the auditee, the auditor must focus on the situation, issues, documentation, activities, and/or behavior—not on the person. When communicating with auditee management, the auditor should avoid naming individuals whenever possible.

People respond readily to inquiries and offer helpful suggestions for improvements if they feel that the audit team is sincere, appreciates their views, and has their needs and interests at heart. Each person involved with an organization has a unique perspective, as does each member of the audit team. One person can filter information differently from another, miss an angle, or stop short of getting the full story. For these reasons, facts stated and other data collected during an audit interview must be corroborated to ensure accuracy. The information can be corroborated in one of three ways:

1. Another person, preferably from another group or management level, says the same thing.

2. Another member of the audit team hears the same thing from the same or a different source.

3. An item, document, or record verifies the action.[37]

Steering the Auditor Toward Specific Interviewees

Several types of problems may occur during interviews, and auditors should be trained in techniques that minimize such interference. One such problem occurs when an auditee attempts to steer the auditor toward specific interviewees. Auditees often prefer that auditors interview certain personnel and avoid certain others. However, this person's knowledge may not be typical of others in the organization. Therefore, the auditor should take charge of the selection process.

An auditor should approach an area and look around to see who is doing what jobs. Candidates for interviews can be randomly chosen as long as it is safe to interrupt them in their jobs. The auditor should follow the interview protocol described on the preceding pages.

If an auditee insists that a specific person is unavailable for interviewing, the auditor should be considerate but persistent if the interview is vital to the success of the audit. Without being threatening, the auditor can suggest that the person's unavailability may prolong the audit. A statement such as "I may have to stay over for another shift" may gain the auditor the desired cooperation.

Answering for the Interviewee

Another common problem occurs when an escort or area supervisor answers for the interviewee or intimidates her/him. An escort generally stays within listening distance and takes notes, but should step back slightly. An ideal arrangement is for an auditor to sit or stand between the interviewee and the escort, facing the interviewee.

An escort is to be an observer only and should not be involved in the interview unless there are communication problems. An auditor can minimize an escort's participation in the interview by directing questions to and maintaining eye contact with the interviewee. For example, questions about machine setups and the measuring of parameters are normally beyond the knowledge of an escort. If an escort starts to answer for an auditee, the auditor needs to redirect the question to the interviewee, avoiding eye contact with the escort. If an escort continues to interfere, an auditor should say, "I prefer to get the information from the staff member."

Asking Leading Questions

A different kind of problem occurs if an auditor asks leading questions, expecting to hear certain answers. An auditor should not lead an interviewee

The auditor should say	Not
How (where, when, who, what, why) do you record the test results?	Do you record the test results in the lab log book?
How do you know this value is right?	This instrument is calibrated, isn't it?
What is the first thing you do?	First you set up the equipment, right?
How do you know this is the current (correct) version of the drawing?	Is this drawing current (correct)?
How were you trained to perform this procedure?	Did you read the standard operating procedure during training?
What are the reporting requirements for nonconformances?	Don't you have to notify your supervisor whenever a nonconformance occurs?
What is the standard procedure for responding to customer complaints?	When a customer calls, don't you have to record the details on Form XX?
Is this equipment calibrated? How do you know?	Does this sticker indicate that the equipment is calibrated?
How do you know how to do this operation?	Do you follow the procedure for this operation?
What do you do with the finished product?	Do you place the finished product on the rack?

Figure 11. Open-ended questions contrasted with closed-ended questions.

with the questioning. Leading questions can be avoided if the auditor asks open-ended questions, such as those in Figure 11. Additionally, if an auditor goes into an interview expecting to hear certain answers, the audit results likely will be biased.

Communication Problems

Communication problems or other conflicts may occur between auditor and interviewee. Communication problems are probably the principal difficulty that must be overcome during an audit. An auditor can minimize the effects of miscommunication by relying on the escort to correct misunderstandings and by corroborating all information through one of the methods already mentioned.

An auditor who does not have a good grasp of the process being audited may not ask the right questions and may realize only after completing the interview that important issues were not addressed. To recover from such an oversight, the auditor may revisit the area or raise the issue at the daily meeting for necessary action.

Other types of conflicts may include employees who are hostile to anyone in authority. Sometimes interviewees are unable to concentrate because they are distracted by the fact that their jobs are not getting done. People are afraid to say, "I am very busy. I need to complete this test. Can you come back in 10 minutes?" A good auditor will sense when an interviewee is preoccupied, move off, and find other ways to keep the audit moving. Additionally, the auditor should guard against reacting improperly to employees who have "hidden agendas" or "axes to grind."

3. PHYSICAL EXAMINATION

The types of physical examination tools used by auditors can vary widely depending on the industry. An auditor needs to be familiar with the tools and techniques applicable to the industry or company being audited. In addition to knowing which tool to use in what situation, the auditor should be aware of the problems that can arise if tools are used incorrectly or inconsistently. If the auditor has no experience with the necessary tools, a technical expert should be included as part of the audit team.

Physical examination tools are normally associated with product audits. In a heavy manufacturing environment, an auditor may use calipers, steel rules, or micrometers, for example, to take measurements. An auditor may also observe others using these tools in order to verify that a product meets certain characteristics. In most circumstances, it is essential for tools to have been properly calibrated; however, exceptions do exist (e.g., a volt meter may be used to determine if power is turned on or off, not to measure voltage). If the auditor uses measuring devices that require periodic calibrating, the auditing organization should follow an accepted calibration program.

Beyond examination of finished product, all tangibles can be physically examined and characterized in some way. Tangible items that have physical properties may include markings on tags, types of packaging materials, condition of work area, and (housekeeping), condition of equipment. Physical examination is one of the most reliable sources of objective evidence.

Before taking an inspection tool in hand, the auditor should be aware of work rule restrictions that may exist in union shops.

4. OBSERVATION OF WORK ACTIVITIES

An auditor observes "work in progress" to see if it meets requirements. An auditor gains this knowledge by monitoring a process being performed to see how the work is being done.

Observation means "to watch attentively" or "to watch or be present without participating actively." Hence, auditors must be well-trained in observation techniques so that they learn how to observe closely but not obtrusively. Because an auditor's presence may be distracting to people at work, the auditor needs to minimize any interference resulting from it. An auditor also should realize that disrupting a worker may be unsafe.

An auditor needs to know when to observe work. For example, if auditors desire to observe work being done by different shifts, they should be aware of when shift changes will be taking place. Auditors should avoid retaining people through shift changes or during their breaks.

Most importantly, auditors need to understand what to observe and what they have seen. For example:

- The auditor should establish if the *product* is made according to the documented procedures by the individuals responsible for using the specified equipment. The auditor records the results of observations.

- When looking at *equipment,* the auditor should note the type, condition, use, and any identification tags or numbers. The auditor should also establish that the equipment has been properly maintained and calibrated, if applicable.

- The auditor should verify that *employees* are familiar with policies and procedures, that they know their responsibilities and roles, and that they have the necessary training, skills, experience, and authority to perform their jobs.

• When reviewing *documents* an auditor should verify contents, type, scope, format, readability, and date. How the document has been filed and distributed and the method by which modifications have been made are also important.

By listening and watching, an auditor should be able to ascertain if what the worker is doing supports the procedures outlined in quality-related documentation. It is usually best if an auditor observes people doing their actual work rather than creating work for them.

Chapter D
Audit Working Papers

Working papers are the documents required to facilitate the auditor's investigation and to record and report results. Working papers are an aid to the auditor and should not restrict the scope of the audit activities or hinder the effectiveness of the investigation or report.

1. DOCUMENTATION OF AUDIT TRAIL

Auditors require papers to record audit results during fact-finding interviews. The following working papers may be used during audits:

- Related audit procedures/instructions/guidelines
- Sampling plans
- Pertinent audit standards (if any)
- Questionnaire (questions requiring evidence)
- Audit checklists (yes/no, sufficient/deficient, acceptable/not acceptable)
- Memory jogger's
- Auditee feedback/evaluation forms
- Log sheets/forms
- Forms to record negative results that require corrective or preventive action
- Attendance record form

The audit checklists and questionnaire provide objective evidence of conformance and provide consistency between auditors. Forms and other papers are used to record objective evidence.

The lead auditor should approve all working papers used during the audit. Working papers should provide a place to record observations and provide the history of the audit.

2. RECORD OF OBSERVATIONS

Recorded observations provide the objective evidence for reporting the results of the investigation. It is imperative for observations to be recorded rather than rely on the auditor's memory. Observations must be traceable back to where they were made to ensure creditability.

Auditors should obtain the auditee's acknowledgment of observations identified as a nonconformance or finding. Auditee acknowledgment provides a support for the auditor's work during the exit meeting. This acknowledgment also confirms the auditee's review and acknowledgement that nonconformities were noted. Obtaining the auditee's acknowledgment of nonconformities prior to the exit meeting ensures a more productive exit meeting.

Observations can be positive or negative. Positive observations may be reported as a positive practice, noteworthy achievement, or a positive finding. Negative observations may be reported as part of a nonconformity or finding.

Chapter E
Audit Analysis

Throughout the course of an audit, team members continually attempt to analyze data as it is gathered. In their daily meetings, team members attempt to examine, sort, and verify evidence. If information appears to be contradictory, the audit team seeks more data to confirm or deny a position.

Once the data-gathering phase is closed, audit team members meet a final time to analyze and classify the evidence collected before presenting audit results to the auditee at the exit meeting. The team sorts and discusses all facts uncovered during the audit. Each finding must be a clear and concise statement of a general problem—for example, "work instruction documents are not controlled, which could cause cost overruns and schedule delays." Each finding statement should be followed by a brief restatement of the particular control element that is in need of attention—for example, the quality program requirement for controlling documents. Then the facts that show the basis for the statement should be listed and numbered.[38] All findings should be supported by linkage to a requirement (standard, internal policy, procedure, or organization objectives).

Auditors gather data as objective evidence to determine the degree of conformance to quality objectives and/or standards and to identify areas for continuous improvement. The main uses of gathered data are for analysis, summary, verification, and presentation.

Analysis is the evaluation of information and data gathered during the audit for the purpose of determining conformance to quality objectives and/or standards. The analysis will be the basis for reporting nonconformities and audit findings. This evaluation may be the result of the auditor's professional judgment, or the auditor may use statistical techniques. The auditor needs to be able to apply good judgment as well as have a working knowledge of statistical analysis techniques. Whatever the method of evaluation or analysis used, the auditor must ensure that decisions made from data and information gathered during the course of the audit stand up to scrutiny by others.

An auditor must be able to summarize the results of data analysis into a unified statement about the adequacy and effectiveness of the process represented by the analyzed data. The auditor should examine patterns or trends and consolidate similar observations into a single finding.

Prior to the final presentation to the auditee, the audit team members should review the final results, judgments, and analyzed data to confirm the accuracy of the data and the decisions derived from that data. In the event of a conflict between members of the audit team as to the acceptability of the audit results, the lead auditor is responsible for resolving all issues and determining what should be reported. The other members of the audit team must support the decision of the lead auditor. Verification is done primarily to prevent errors in the reporting of audit results.

Facts of the audit are presented at the exit meeting and in the final audit report. The method of presentation depends on the type of data analysis used. The reporting method should enable the auditee to understand the finding to facilitate investigation and to take proper corrective action.

1. CORROBORATION AND OBJECTIVITY OF EVIDENCE

An auditor measures compliance with and conformance to specified requirements by gathering and analyzing objective evidence, "information which can be proved true, based on facts obtained through observation, measurement, test, or other means."[39] Objective evidence is uninfluenced by prejudice, emotion, or bias. It is anything that can be proved or disproved when required activities are taking place. Records, witnessing an event, and discussions with personnel could all be sources of objective evidence. Sampling different sources is a means to verify the observation as objective evidence. Two auditors examining the same objective evidence should be able to reach the same conclusion.

An auditee presents evidence to an auditor to prove that the audited system works as the auditee has explained it and that written documentation exists to support the system. If something cannot be observed, then it must be verified with a record. A check sheet that confirms a particular activity, or minutes from a meeting can be objective evidence. If an auditor talks to a supervisor and gets one story, and then talks to several operators independently and hears the same explanations, that auditor has corroboration of the evidence for the investigation. Techniques to corroborate information from interviews were presented in chapter C, "Data Collection."

Corroboration methods are used by the auditor to make more certain about or to validate data that could be considered unreliable or questionable. Information from interviews must be corroborated by asking another person or checking records and documents. Another corroboration method may be to check different shifts or departments to establish consistency or inconsistency.

Evidence should be collected on all matters related to audit objectives and scope. Evidence can include procedures or work instructions and proof of their implementation, examination of personnel training and qualification records, examination of process controls and records, and reexamination of selected work. Evidence needed to support the auditor's findings may be physical, testimonial, documentary, or analytical. Objective evidence may be obtained internally from the organization under audit, externally from third parties, or by comparing evidence obtained from two or more sources. Evidence obtained from independent, external sources is generally more reliable than information obtained from internal sources. Knowledge obtained through physical examination, observation, computation, and inspection is more reliable than interview comments. Evidence derived from records is likewise more reliable than oral evidence. Any evidence should be sufficient, complete, and relevant, to be useful as a sound basis for audit findings and recommendations. A rational relationship should exist between the cost of obtaining evidence and the usefulness of the evidence.[40] For example, the costs involved in shutting down a manufacturing plant to obtain data or in traveling to 100 service centers to verify that employees know the quality policy may not be justifiable.

2. DATA PATTERNS AND TRENDS

At its final gathering before the exit meeting, audit team members evaluate the accumulated data; they sort it, see what supports it and what it supports, and look at it away from the situation to see what it means. Any finding should be clear to a reasonable person. The auditor has to look at the evidence found, its relation to the purpose of the audit, and its importance to the entire scheme that has been audited.

The lead auditor must make every effort to resolve contradictory evidence or open issues prior to reporting the results of the audit. However, if contradictory evidence has been gathered and the audit team cannot obtain additional data, the contradiction should be included in the audit report as a finding or observation, and clarification should be requested. A supplemental report can be generated if needed to clarify the original audit report.

Through analysis of audit data, the audit team can distinguish between systemic and isolated incidents. An auditor who detects a possible problem looks for a recurrence. If subsequent data show recurrence of the incident in several places, it is a systemic incident. Data that reveal a trend and pattern may also support a conclusion that an incident is systemic rather than isolated. For example, if one piece of equipment is overdue for calibration by about a month, but all other equipment is in calibration, the auditee may have a good calibration program and the one piece of equipment is an isolated case. However, if a high percentage of equipment has not been calibrated on schedule, the problem is systemic.

Thus, an auditor needs to look at things from a system standpoint and try to assess how the overall system is working. If, after preliminary evaluation of data, a problem appears to be systemic, the auditor may need to draw another sample. Once it has been determined whether a problem is a systemic or isolated event, it can be classified for reporting purposes.

3. CLASSIFICATION OF OBSERVATIONS

An auditor uses several techniques to classify and prioritize observations before the exit meeting. In any audit, risk is associated with reporting a finding on the basis of available data. An auditor may fail to identify a significant problem or may identify a problem that is not significant. Evaluation is often based on a relatively small sample and, therefore, involves a large sampling risk. A problem or noncompliance may be classified as a nonconformity, noncompliance, or finding. The auditor should also group "like" observations under similar findings or nonconformances.

The risk-benefit ratio is a method of analyzing the risk of reporting (based on the sample) or not reporting compared to the benefit to be gained by reporting or not reporting an area of concern. Criticality refers to the importance of an observation. If there is significant opportunity for project failure or a safety concern, a critical activity or item should be reported after one occurrence as opposed to multiple occurrences for an item of lesser importance.

Additionally, observations may be classified as improvement points or positive practices (not a violation of a requirement). An observation of a process or system that is very effective may warrant reporting the observation as a positive practice.

Depending on the client, the industry, and audit procedure requirements, auditors may define and report other classifications for observations. The other classifications include concern, observation, issue, and continuous improvement point. They are not violations of a requirement; but based on the auditor's experience, they are noteworthy and in some cases they could develop into a problem if not corrected. All classifications of observations should be identified along with expected follow-up actions.

4. CLASSIFICATION OF NONCONFORMANCES

An auditor must sort and classify facts based on the severity of the problem, the frequency of occurrence, and the risks associated with the problem. The terms *noncompliance* and *nonconformance* are frequently used to report the results of the audit. In common practice, these terms are used interchangeably. The most critical problems are often called major nonconformances. Reporting problems found during the audit as nonconformances is one of the most popular reporting techniques. A nonconformity is nonfulfillment of a specified requirement (ANSI/ISO/ASQ A8402-1994, 2.21) or alternatively a failure to meet a requirement. Most quality system registrar auditors are taught to report nonconformances, and consequently many auditors of registered organizations adopt the same method of reporting. A nonconformance may be systemic or isolated and major or minor, depending on its effect on the product, service, or system.

Some audit organizations report problems found during the audit as findings. In general, the reporting of findings is a technique in which only systemic issues or conclusions regarding individual processes or systems are reported. Some findings are more important than other findings—all findings don't have the same importance to the organization being audited.

The methods used to classify audit results vary from organization to organization. Some organizations classify findings as major or as category 1 findings, while observations are classified as minor or category 2 findings. Others simply report the findings in the order of their importance. Sorting and classifying nonconformities and findings is a method to assess their significance.

Minor nonconformities usually do not denote a system breakdown, but they could result in one in the future if not properly corrected or contained. Whatever terms are used to report the results of the audit, they should be clearly defined by the audit organization.

5. CONCLUSIONS

For audits that are measuring compliance, or fulfillment of requirements, the lead auditor should report the overall degree to which those requirements are being met. The audit conclusion should match the audit purpose. For example, if the purpose of the audit is to determine if the existing controls comply with international standards and are being maintained, then the audit conclusion should state the degree to which this has been accomplished.

Some audits measure not only compliance, but also the efficiency and effectiveness of the controls that are in place. If a control is attempting to achieve a certain result, an auditor can determine if the desired outcome is being achieved by analyzing observations such as: "the presence of damaged material in a warehouse indicates that material handling procedures may be ineffective"; "the use of nonconforming material in finished product indicates poor control of nonconforming material"; and "obsolete drawings and procedures in a manufacturing area indicate that the document control system is ineffective."

The lead auditor's overall assessment of results plays a critical role in meaningful audits for improvement. The following items should be considered in the lead auditor's assessment:

- Quality management system maturity

- Overall system effectiveness, rather than segmental ineffectiveness

- Implementation of corrective and preventive actions and their effectiveness

- Internal quality audits and their effectiveness related to continuous improvement mechanisms in place

- Employee awareness, and dissemination of established quality policy
- Teamwork and employee involvement with management participation, and demonstrated resource commitment
- Auditee organization's business and strategic plans, culture, and values
- Critical system issues, rather than nitpicking trivialities
- Opportunities for improvements, without acting as a consultant
- Positives

An auditor can get an indication of the effectiveness of controls by the nature and number of nonconformances observed.

The final audit team meeting is held after improvement areas have been identified and just prior to the exit meeting. The team collects all information and identifies significant areas to be mentioned at the exit meeting. The team:

- Decides on the content and emphasis of the report
- Summarizes all nonconformities and/or findings
- Finalizes a list of opportunities for improvement
- Decides on a list of positive practices or noteworthy achievements

Based on the conclusions formed at this meeting, the lead auditor prepares a preliminary draft of the audit report. The draft report can be handwritten or typed on a computer. Part IV of the handbook presents additional information about audit conclusions and reporting the results of the investigation.

Chapter F
Exit Meeting

The exit meeting, sometimes called a post-audit conference or closure meeting, ends the performance stage of an audit. At the exit meeting, the lead auditor presents a draft or preliminary audit report to the auditee.

1. PRESENTATION OF AUDIT RESULTS

The exit meeting is a presentation of the audit results to the auditee organization and, in some cases, the client. The client may choose not to attend the exit meeting, in which case the auditor is giving the auditee a preliminary view of the information that will be provided to the client. The purpose of the exit meeting is to present audit observations to senior management to ensure that audit results are clearly understood. The exit meeting normally takes place following the conclusion of the interviews and the final team meeting.

The lead auditor should circulate an attendance roster for the exit meeting. Attendees should include the audit team, at least one auditee management representative, and other personnel deemed appropriate by auditee management. For example, the escort may be present to help explain details of findings. Usually, the same people attend the exit meeting as attended the opening meeting. Sometimes higher levels of management attend, since they want to be informed of the audit results. The lead auditor should do most of the talking, and a member of the audit team should keep minutes of the meeting. The minutes should include any agreed-on changes to the audit report.

Individual auditors may present their own findings, or the lead auditor may present all findings and rely on the appropriate auditor to clarify and answer questions. Discussions should be kept brief and pertinent and should clarify the audit findings, not justify the audit method.[41] Finally, the lead auditor should present the audit team's conclusions about the quality system's overall adherence to requirements and its effectiveness.

The primary duty of the lead auditor at the exit meeting is to be a clear communicator. To avoid misunderstandings, the lead auditor should provide written findings or nonconformances to the auditee organization at the exit meeting. Findings, nonconformances, and audit reports should be marked "draft" or "preliminary," since they have not been approved by the client and also may need to be edited for language and grammar. The audit team's written findings or nonconformances and the team's ability to explain the results in person are important factors for ensuring that the auditee understands the results and will be able to identify necessary corrective actions.

Presentation techniques employed by the auditor will vary depending on whether it is a first-, second-, or third-party audit and on what methods are considered most suitable for the situation (Pass or Fail). First-party audit exit meetings tend to be less formal than second- or third-party audit exit meetings. One of the toughest challenges for the lead auditor is the delivery of bad news. The actual methods and equipment (flip chart, data projector, or overhead projector) used will also depend on the availability of resources and what best fits the situation (mature system, awarding a contract, small organization). Different presentation techniques are covered in Part VII, Chapter B.

2. DISCUSSION OF FOLLOW-UP ACTIONS

The lead auditor is expected to clarify all follow-up actions to the auditee and client and to arrive at a consensus. The lead auditor will have an open discussion with the auditee organization at the exit meeting to determine adequate time for corrective action plans and/or corrective action implementation. The following are some guidelines for discussion with the auditee:

- Clearly defined nonconformance/finding
- Process for effective corrective action determination/implementation

- Emphasis on timely corrective actions with accurate root cause determination

- Follow-up audit dates or follow-up corrective action review

- Areas and departments to be audited in follow-up audit

The most serious problems need the auditee's urgent attention, while the less important ones are treated with the time frame and priority they deserve. If the auditee needs additional time to analyze the root cause of a serious problem, the auditor should allow it. The timing of corrective action is dependent on its importance and complexity and the availability of the resources needed for corrective action.

3. EXPECTATIONS OF AUDITORS, AUDITEES, AND CLIENT

Role of an Auditor
The exit meeting is conducted by the lead auditor, who should:

- Present the summary

- Read the results of the audit without interruption from the auditee

- Discuss audit details

- Allow individual auditors to clarify statements or respond to specific questions about the areas they audited

- Indicate how audit results are categorized and prioritized

- Explain the required follow-up and expected corrective action response[42]

- Obtain and verify acknowledgment from the auditee representative

- Ensure that minutes and an attendance record are kept

- Affirm confidentially of the report

A big problem at exit meetings occurs when communication between an auditor and auditee was not reported to the top of the command chain before the meeting. The auditee, caught off guard, may become defensive. Daily meetings help prevent this problem. If an auditee does not want daily meetings, the auditor can prevent problems by promoting communication during the audit. An auditor who suspects that information is not getting to the top should casually, but deliberately, inform management of audit findings.

The formal, official audit report should be issued to the auditee by the client (or lead auditor, if authorized to do so by the client) within the time period previously agreed to or specified by organizational procedure.

Role of an Auditee

The exit meeting should be attended by senior managers of the areas that were audited. Attendance by several layers of management should be discouraged; it often leads to arguing and unproductive time since employees often feel obligated to defend their positions to their supervisors.[43]

At the exit meeting, auditee representatives have the responsibility to listen attentively. There should be no extensive discussions unless the auditee needs clarification of items in the audit report. If the auditee and auditor disagree as to whether a finding exists, or have different opinions on the degree of criticality of a finding, the auditee can present its view of the situation as part of its response to the requests for corrective action.

Role of a Client

The auditor should invite the client to attend the exit meeting. If this proves impractical, the auditor should arrange to debrief the client. The auditor expects the client's support in resolving any findings or issues. In some cases, the client and the auditee are the same and must undertake both roles.

SIDEBAR

Problems Commonly Encountered During the Audit Performance Stage

The following are examples of the types of problems commonly encountered during the performance stage of an audit.

Losing Track of Time or Scope. Problems regarding a lack of time or loss of focus or scope are frequently encountered during audits. Daily meetings that assess the audit's progress should help prevent such problems. Also, properly prepared working papers can help eliminate problems related to time management or the focus of the audit.

Unreasonable Absence or Unavailability of Key Personnel. An auditor needs to be able to work around the absence of key personnel. However, if this situation is happening regularly during an external audit, the auditor may need to call a meeting with management or stop the audit. If an obstruction exists and no mutual agreement can be reached at the meeting, the auditor should report to the client for advice on how or whether to continue the audit. Of course, unreasonable absence assumes reasonable notification by the auditor or audit organization of the impending audit. In an internal audit, people often take the availability of the audit team for granted. They may feel free to handle their own crises as they arise because they believe it should be easy for the audit team to reschedule.

Interference from Internal Problems. Employees sometimes wish to involve the audit team in internal problems. For example, if employees believe that their performance would improve with the addition of a certain piece of equipment, they may attempt to enlist the auditor in lobbying management for the purchase of such equipment. It may be necessary to state that auditors do not get involved in advising the auditee how to run their business.

Extensive Discussions or Arguments. The auditee may attempt to prolong the exit meeting with extensive discussion or arguments. The exit meeting is not a time for negotiation; the lead auditor should present the information contained in the draft audit report, make sure that the auditee understands the results and what is expected in the way of a corrective action plan, and end the meeting.

Lack of Effective Communication. Communication barriers pose a threat to the successful completion of an audit. This is why training in interviewing techniques is so important. Unless the auditors can word questions in an unbiased and concise manner, they may not receive accurate responses.

Part IV

Audit Reporting

[10 of the CQA exam questions or 7%]

The purpose of the quality audit report is to communicate the results of the investigation. The report should provide correct and clear data that will be effective as a management aid in addressing important organizational issues.[44] The audit ends when the report is issued by the lead auditor. However, follow-up and closure actions may be necessary, as will be discussed in Part V.

Chapter A
Review and Finalize Audit Results

After audit results have been reported at the exit meeting, the lead auditor formally communicates the audit results in a written audit report. While the audit team may have prepared a handwritten or typed report to present to the auditee at the exit meeting, that report should have been clearly marked "draft" or "preliminary." The exit meeting should include discussion of all significant findings so that the auditee is not surprised by information in the final audit report. The final audit report formally communicates the audit results to the client and the auditee. The audit report is prepared, signed, and dated by the lead auditor. It should be reviewed and approved by the management of the auditing organization as well as by the client before it is sent to the auditee.

The audit report should be sent to the auditee in accordance with a mutually understood time frame. Short timelines between performing and reporting about the audit are highly desirable. When a significant amount of time passes between the end of an audit and the issuance of the audit report, the urgency of the corrective action is diminished, misunderstandings or miscommunications are more likely to occur, the auditee may be less motivated to resolve problems, and the audit program may be viewed as inefficient.

An audit report serves the following functions:

- It supplies information that verifies adherence to requirements or that initiates corrective action and system improvement.

- It guides management and their consultants in subsequent decisions and activities.

- It establishes a record of the investigation and conclusions.

A report should be sent even if there are no deficiencies. Organizations may compare the results year to year to identify positive and negative trends. This same type of analysis is valuable to the auditor, auditing organization, and auditee (internal department, supplier, or customer).[45]

Chapter B
Written Report Format and Content

1. AUDIT DETAILS

While the format of the written audit report can vary widely from company to company or industry to industry, certain information always should be included. Most audit reports contain an introduction, a summary, a listing of the findings/nonconformities, and requests for corrective action.

An audit report should not normally name individual employees of the auditee in connection with specific findings, observations, or nonconformances; a report should refer to positions, titles, or systems when identifying deficiencies. However, an auditor may encounter a situation where naming an individual is appropriate and essential for effective corrective action—if the individual has special or unique knowledge of a situation, product or process.

There is no standard length for audit reports. However, reports should be concise and should contain prescribed information. The content may depend on the size and complexity of the auditee organization and the number of findings/nonconformances identified, as well as client or audit organization report procedures and guidelines.

Reports may or may not contain attachments. Attachments (or exhibits or examples) may include minutes from the exit/opening meeting, attendance roster of exit/opening meeting, requests for corrective action issued at the exit meeting, nonconformance forms issued at the exit meeting, and charts, calculations, documents, records, or other material required by audit procedure or that add value to the report.

The audit report starts off with an introduction or background. Much of the introductory material included in an audit report can be completed from the audit plan before the audit is performed. The audit report introduction:

- States the purpose and scope of the audit
- Identifies the auditee, client, and auditing organization
- Identifies the audit team members and the lead auditor, and presents their qualifications
- Specifies the audit dates and locations
- Specifies the standards (manuals, procedures, international standards, etc.) used for the audit
- Addresses confidentiality issues
- May list auditee personnel involved in or contacted during the audit
- Lists report distribution

Normally, an audit report identifies an area of nonconformance in the auditee's system and does not contain detailed technical information about a proprietary process or material. Any confidential information that may appear in an auditor's notes or in the completed checklist must either be protected to prevent disclosing a confidence or destroyed. The official records contain a copy of a blank checklist, which does not contain proprietary information.

Additionally, the introduction may mention the auditee's audit history, discuss the methods used during the audit, and mention the records or documents that were examined as part of the audit. Each report should be uniquely identified by title, number, letters, or a combination so that the report can be properly referenced and retrieved.

2. COMPLIANCE

The results of the audit may be indicated as findings, nonconformities, deficiencies, adverse conclusions, or significant observations and conclusions. The most common terminology used to report the results of an audit are *nonconformity* and *finding.* The terminology used should be defined to ensure the auditee's understanding. Observations made during the audit that violate a requirement should be reported and their importance should be taken into account. Within each category, further classifications of critical, major, and minor may exist.

Each problem area should be listed in one or two sentences. The report should include facts or examples that support or explain each finding or positive practice. The results of the audit may be listed in order of importance, in sequence of the procedure or performance standard clauses, or in no particular order. Noteworthy accomplishments, positive practices, or processes that work exceptionally well may be included and can be listed at the front or back of the report, depending on the auditor's preference. The auditor should note that the findings are symptoms, the causes of which remain to be identified.

The results section of a formal report should include the following information:

- Audit findings/nonconformities and number

- Specific requirement

- Details or specifications of the nonconformity or finding

- Provisions for auditee's response

- Provisions for recording corrective action and follow-up activities

- Recommendations (if required by client) for correcting deficiencies, or suggestions for improving the quality program

When the client requests recommendations from the auditor, the recommendations should be clearly marked or placed in an appendix or separate report. In most cases, the auditee is under no obligation to implement auditor recommendations. Some auditors use the term *suggestion for improvement* as a less formal term with a lesser chance of being misinterpreted as directive in nature.

The audit report should explain how the results of the audit are classified and prioritized. For an example of an audit report format, see Figure 12.

To: Auditee responsible for reply

From: Lead auditor

Subject: Audit of (procedure, title, and number or subject)

Reference: List of procedures audited and to which reference is made in the list of findings, i.e., quality manual dated XX-XX-XX, MIL-STD-XXXX, etc.

I. Present audit

A. General
State the purpose and objectives of the audit, where and when it was performed, and what was included or excluded; be specific on quantities audited.

B. Summary
Provide a synopsis of the most significant audit findings.

C. Findings
For each discrepancy state the requirement, document the observations, show the effect, and identify the responsible supervisor contacted relative to each finding.

II. History

A. Audit history
State previous audit results and corrective actions taken.

B. Analysis and evaluation
Provide auditor's analysis and conclusion, including an evaluation of corrective actions taken.

III. Required action

A. Response
The persons listed below are requested to review and respond to this audit within 15 working days from the date of this report. The response should include the following:

1. Corrective action taken and reason finding existed.
2. Action taken to correct the cause.
3. Date by which the corrective action will be complete.

(continued)

Figure 12. Typical audit report format.

Source: From *How to Plan an Audit,* ASQC Quality Audit Technical Committee, Charles B. Robinson, Editor. ASQC Quality Press, 1987, pp. 38–39.

Example

    Action addressee: Finding #

Director of engineering   I.C.1
Director of operations   I.C.2, 3, & 7
Director of quality assurance   I.C.4, 5, & 6

B. Follow-up
Reference material pertaining to this audit is available from (the auditor) at extension XXXX/XXXX. Replies will be followed up and corrective action will be confirmed.

                                       —————————
                                       Lead auditor

Figure 12. *Continued.*

3. SYSTEM EFFECTIVENESS

A *system* is a collection of processes supported by an infrastructure to manage and coordinate its function.[46] Typical systems are document control systems and training systems. In a system, processes interact and work together to achieve a common goal or objective.

It has become increasing popular to identify an audit as either a compliance audit or management audit. *Compliance audits* determine if there are rules and if they are being followed, not the effectiveness or suitability of the rules. *Management audits* seek to determine both compliance and effectiveness of controls. Management audits are also called "performance improvement audits" and "value-added audits." A product, process, or system audit can be either a management audit or a compliance audit, depending on the wishes of the client.

Effectiveness of a process or system is determined by its ability to achieve its objectives or intended purpose. Assessment of effectiveness goes beyond determining the degree of conformance to requirements and maintenance of procedures. When discussing effectiveness of corrective action, Russell and Regel state that system effectiveness has two components: whether it is achieving the desired result and whether the process is capable, efficient, and consistent with objectives.[47] One measurement of *effectiveness* is the degree to which objectives are achieved in an efficient and economical manner.

Other auditors in the field use the words *effectiveness and suitability,* or *effectiveness and efficiency* to describe the same type of assessment. A suitability audit might say that the sum of the processes is achieving the desired results. Or it may say that even though the process is performing according to requirements, those requirements are deficient. For example, "because there is no requirement to review the software load specifications on a monthly basis, incorrect loads are occurring because the platform is changing so rapidly" or "the document control system is unsuitable to meet business needs, even though it is fully compliant with ISO 9001 and implemented throughout the facility." Or the opposite may occur: "the audit may conclude that ISO 9001 is too cumbersome for the backyard swing-set assembly business; it is not suitable for my business needs." This type of quality audit comes quite close to that being performed by Institute of Internal Auditors operational audits. Process audits can also examine suitability.

Whether the words *effectiveness* or *suitability* are used, what is important is that quality audits may be performed to assess processes and systems in order to verify that organizational objectives are being met. An internal audit, as defined by the Institute of Internal Auditors, that does not report the extent to which objectives and goals have been met is not an effective management-oriented audit.[48] An audit that examines effectiveness does not substitute for management's responsibility to monitor performance. Rather, audits provide an additional source of information to assist management in their evaluation.[49]

<table>
<tr><td>SIDEBAR</td></tr>
</table>

As part of a training class on how to audit for effectiveness, the actual production area was audited. The receiving area had procedures for nonconforming product control. They were maintained; there was nonconforming material; and the nonconforming components were properly marked and stored. Everything was excellent. Then the students were asked to find out how long the nonconforming items had been in the hold area. Most of the items had been in the hold area for over 30 days, with one for nine months. An objective of the organization was to reduce working capital cost, yet expensive components were being held without disposition for up to nine months. Everyone agreed that this was not meeting organizational goals and was an area for improvement.

4. CONCLUSIONS TO BE REPORTED

In many cases, the overall conclusions are reported in the summary section of the audit report. The summary or abstract is a synopsis of the audit results. It should include the following information:

- Statements pertaining to the observations of nonconformities and findings

- The audit team's judgment of the extent of the auditee's compliance with the applicable standard

- The system's ability to achieve defined quality objectives

The team will be recognized as competent and unbiased if the summary presents a professional, honest, and straightforward picture.[50]

The conclusions reached based on the objective evidence can be positive and/or negative. There may be strengths as well as weakness to report.

- For a third-party registrar audit, the conclusion may be to recommend registration or not recommend registration of the organization's quality system.

- For a second-party audit, the conclusion may be to continue doing business or not to continue doing business with a supplier.

- For a second-party audit, the conclusion may be to withhold payment on future invoices until specified findings are corrected and verified by the client.

- For a first party audit, the conclusion may be that the department functions well but is falling short of organizational objectives.

- For a first-party audit, the conclusion may be that, pending resolution of the audit findings, the department may continue to function provided that specified compensatory actions are immediately implemented.

- For a first-party audit, the conclusion may be that, due to the conditions observed, the interval for periodic audits of the area will be extended (or shortened).

5. REQUEST FOR CORRECTIVE ACTIONS

Management of an audited organization should be asked to review and investigate the audit findings to determine the root cause and take appropriate corrective action. They should be asked to respond to the report in writing. The response should clearly state the root cause, corrective action planned or taken to prevent recurrence and the scheduled completion date for the corrective action. If corrective action is not appropriate, the response should specify the reason for no action.[51]

All requests for corrective action should ask the auditee to determine:

- Short-term (remedial/containment) action planned, if appropriate

- The root cause of the problem

- Long-term corrective action planned for the cause

- Schedules and responsibilities for these actions[52]

To prevent a nonconformity or problem from recurring, an auditor will ask the auditee to give attention to and take action on certain items. Depending on the audit's purpose and scope and the delegated responsibility of the auditing organization, the client may assume this function. In some cases, the auditor may not have any responsibility for the corrective action phases of the audit process. Especially in many third-party audits, the auditor may collect and interpret information and provide this information to the client, who in turn manages the corrective action phase. Therefore, it may be appropriate to substitute "client" for "auditor" here and in other follow-up activities.

Adverse findings may be recorded on a separate sheet called a "corrective action request" or "discrepancy notice." A corrective action request is a statement of what the condition should be and what it is, and it includes several examples of what occurred. Serious problems are normally supported by many incidences, but an auditor can also record single instances of major problems, such as the lack of or total breakdown of a system. An auditor issues reports or corrective action requests for areas in which the auditee needs to take action. The auditee needs to identify and correct the root cause of the problem.

On receipt of the formal audit report, an auditee may employ the same or similar techniques to determine which problems the organization should concentrate on correcting first, based on the significance or cost of the inefficiency. After making this determination, an auditee can focus on preparing a corrective action plan that addresses the remedial action or other action to eliminate the problem.

Chapter C
Issue Written Report

1. OBTAIN APPROVALS

The audit report should be reviewed and approved in accordance with the audit organization's procedures and guidelines. Normally, the lead auditor prepares and signs approval of the audit report. The lead auditor approves any inputs to the audit report by audit team members. In many organizations the client and/or audit program manager review and approve the audit report before final release. Procedures may require other approvers due to risk or communication issues within the organization.

There is no limit to the number of people who can review the audit report. The lead auditor may ask audit team members to review the report. Auditee management could review the report to identify factual errors and misunderstanding. Allowing auditee management to review a draft audit report has inherent risks; review may be construed as negotiation unless very clear instructions have been provided to auditee management. Additionally, too many reviewers and approvers could create lengthy delays in issuing the final report.

2. DISTRIBUTE REPORT

The distribution list for an audit report should be noted on the report. Distribution is at the discretion of the client unless this task has been delegated to the lead auditor or auditing organization. An internal audit report is normally distributed to the supervisor of the audited area as well as to someone in higher management. An external audit report typically goes to a division manager or CEO. In addition, the auditing organization maintains a copy of the report in its official files, and each member of the audit team also retains a copy.

The lead auditor should not automatically send a report directly to the auditee unless approved to do so by the client. The client is given the option of receiving the audit report first and of attaching a cover letter before the report is distributed to the auditee. This procedure promotes accountability of the auditing function.

Responses by the auditee to requests for corrective action should be sent to the same distribution.

Chapter D
Audit Records Retention

The lead auditor and audit team members must follow organizational procedures concerning the retention of audit records. Audit records should be reasonably secure to prevent inadvertent access by outside parties. All audit records should be considered confidential. For high-risk areas, there may be elaborate procedures for securing or destroying audit records.

Under normal circumstances, auditors keep records until the next scheduled audit. If an auditor is certified, the auditor may need to keep records for three years or the specified renewal period.

Audit records may include:

- Notice of the audit

- Opening and exit meeting attendance and minutes

- Completed working papers

- Draft and final copy of audit report

- Corrective action responses and relevant feedback

- Final close-out note to the auditee

Part VI, chapter B discusses audit retention practices.

Part V

Corrective Action Follow-Up and Closure

[12 of the CQA exam questions or 8%]

"The audit is completed upon submission of the audit report to the client" (ANSI/ISO/ASQ Q10011-1-1994, clause 6.0). Some audit organizations interpret the guidance of the international audit standard to mean that the auditor should not be involved in audit follow-up activities. However, many organizations involve the auditor or lead auditor in follow-up audits and some aspects of the corrective action/improvement process. Someone—whether the client, lead auditor, auditor, audit program manager, management sponsor, or corrective action team leader—must be assigned the nonauditee duties discussed in this section.

Chapter A

Corrective Action Follow-Up

The auditee is responsible for taking corrective action and keeping the client informed of its progress. Sometimes, an auditee will look to the auditor for a solution or recommendation, but the auditor should proceed with caution. While not precluded from providing a solution, the auditor may not have the technical knowledge to address and solve the problem. In addition, an auditor who advances a solution takes ownership of the problem. An auditor who has studied a process may have an excellent understanding of it and may be able to offer assistance to an auditee who seems genuinely confused about what is expected in the way of corrective action. It is important, however, that the auditee take responsibility for the solution. An auditor who participates in implementing or modifying a quality system compromises objectivity in regard to later audits of that area. For these reasons, many company auditors and most third-party auditors are prohibited from recommending corrective action.

Both internal and external audit results can be input to the corrective action process. The corrective action process can result in significant benefits to an organization. The purpose of this part of the handbook is to make suggestions on how auditors can most effectively carry out their responsibilities relative to correcting the deficiencies found during the audit. It is not a discussion about the organization's corrective action process.

1. CRITERIA FOR ACCEPTABLE CORRECTIVE ACTION PLANS

The auditee's management is responsible for setting priorities on corrective action requests as a result of a quality audit. An auditee should draw conclusions in order to focus on those problems that provide the greatest benefit for the least effort and expense. As the group responsible for developing the corrective action plan, auditee managers have to know what their resources are and what to fix first.

An auditee sets priorities by looking at the range of problems in relation to the entire system and noting where problems are clustering. Additionally, the auditee is responsible for recognizing the potential for similar conditions elsewhere in the organization or system and taking the necessary steps to rectify those problems. The quality system audit is not intended to identify each and every instance of a problem—it is not a 100 percent inspection activity. Rather an audit looks for trends that might suggest a systemic problem.

After receiving the formal audit report, the auditee should prepare a corrective action plan and issue it to the auditor within a specified time. The first step in the development of a corrective action plan is the identification of the problem and the determination of the root cause. After a problem has been identified, the auditee may sometimes take immediate or short-term corrective action. Such action, usually considered remedial or temporary, is a quick containment action and is not necessarily the action needed to solve the problem permanently. On the other hand, long-term corrective action is permanent and addresses the underlying cause. An auditee needs to implement a solution to ensure that the problem will not recur.

Once a deficiency and its root cause have been identified, the corrective action plan can be developed. The plan should cite action already taken to correct the deficiency and to preclude a similar occurrence. The plan should identify not only the action to be taken but also who is responsible for that action and by what date preventive action will be in effect.[53]

Overall, fundamental corrective action and preventive action components in a corrective action plan should accomplish the following objectives:

- Identify the problem and isolate the important triggering event
- Identify the underlying cause of the problem
- Identify the potential that the problem will occur in other areas

- Find a solution for the causes and develop a plan for solving the problem
- Identify the manager's responsibility for the corrective action plan
- Document the corrective action plan
- Establish timelines and provide a schedule of the dates when action is to be initiated and completed[54]

The audited organization may maintain that the audit team has made an error and provide information as to why no corrective action is needed. The auditee may also attest that, in the organization's view, corrective action has already been implemented and is effective. Or, the auditee may acknowledge that the corrective action request has been received and that it is understood, but that more time is needed to work on it and a plan to address the problem will be prepared at a specified future date. The auditor must assess the situation to either approve or not approve requested extensions.

2. ACCEPTABILITY OF PROPOSED CORRECTIVE ACTION

The client (or lead auditor, if assigned to do so) coordinates the review of the auditee's response to the corrective action request. The lead auditor may, likewise, assign review responsibilities to the individual auditor who found the problem. The lead auditor should approve the acceptance of corrective action plans reviewed by individual audit team members.

Corrective action must be timely, effective, and prevent recurrence of the same problem or the occurrence of a new one. It is sometimes necessary to implement immediate remedial or containment actions. Such actions may not prevent recurrence but may enable a process to continue, pending the implementation of a long-term solution. For example, when an automatic measuring device on a production line is found to be out of calibration, immediate action is taken to check the measured parameter with a hand-held calibrated instrument before releasing components for use and revising the procedure. A technical specialist may have to assess the proposed corrective action plan if the auditor or client does not have the expertise to do so.

If the proposed corrective action plan seems feasible and reasonable, the auditor should accept it. Either the auditor or a designee may verify that the auditee is doing what has been promised and is meeting the requirements of the corrective action. The auditor often follows up with a visit to the work area to check that corrective action has been implemented, to assess its effectiveness, and to confirm that it prevents recurrence of the problem.

When attempting to evaluate a proposed corrective action plan, an auditor should make sure that the auditee is treating the problem and not a symptom of the problem. The proposed solution might address the issue on the surface but may not prevent the problems from recurring, so the auditor should ask whether the corrective action plan is specific enough to ensure that changes will be permanent. Another question is whether the proposed solution will cause another problem.

Corrective action must be timely. It is permissible for an auditee to request reasonable extensions, since some problems take longer to solve. However, the auditee may be asked to provide periodic status reports with supporting evidence on the corrective action.

Corrective action must prevent reoccurrence. It must identify and address a root cause in order to prevent the same problem in the future.

The principle of corrective action is that conditions adverse to quality must be identified and corrected. The root cause must be determined. Steps must be taken to preclude repetition, including the reporting of these actions to management. True corrective action is difficult to implement, since the real causes of problems are seldom easy to identify.[55]

A five-step process is recommended for corrective action:

1. Document what the problem is, and "stop the bleeding" (that is, implement immediate remedial or containment action).

2. Conduct an investigation to identify root causes.

3. Design and implement the corrective action, and verify its effectiveness.

4. Ensure that the noncompliance is managed and controlled to avoid the potential of recurrence.

5. Analyze the effects of the findings on the product being manufactured. For example, what, if anything, does the organization need to do (remedial/containment action) about products shipped or active systems while it was in noncompliance?

Follow-up action may be accomplished through written communication, review of revised documents, reaudit after the reported implementation date, or other appropriate means.[56] The auditee's plan should be accepted if there is a reasonable chance that it will correct the problem and preclude a recurrence.[57]

3. NEGOTIATION OF CORRECTIVE ACTION PLANS

Findings should be clearly stated by the auditor, and the auditee should indicate that they are understood. However, the auditor and the auditee may not agree on the proposed action plan or the timing of the corrective action. In most cases, additional explanation of the requirements and/or the conditions that led to the identification of the finding may be sufficient for the auditee to develop an effective corrective action plan. Some situations are complex and require serious evaluation by both the auditor and the auditee.

The auditor should not assume that the auditee is automatically wrong because there is a difference of opinion. Forcing one's will on the auditee is unacceptable and may lead to disastrous results for the audit function. Instead, the auditor might attempt to understand the auditee's interpretation of the requirement and the underlying reasoning for the proposed corrective action. The auditor may learn that the auditee's proposed action plan addresses system issues that were not identified during the course of the audit. If the auditee's reasoning is valid, the auditor should accept the proposed action plan. On the other hand, if the auditor has identified specific weaknesses in the action plan, these should be presented to the auditee so that they may be understood and addressed. Because of the difficulties of being involved in a team approach to corrective action but not recommending solutions, many audit organizations have chosen not to participate in any follow-up activities.

The review of the corrective action plan may indicate that the auditee is not responsive or is evasive or that the proposed action is inadequate. When a response is questionable or unacceptable, the auditor should immediately contact the auditee to resolve the auditor's perception. A simple telephone call could alleviate the auditor's concern by clarifying the corrective action plan.

4. METHODS FOR VERIFYING CORRECTIVE ACTION

A review of the corrective action response and its timeliness is, in some instances, all the follow-up action that is required by the client or the organizational procedures. One method of verification is for the auditor to return to the work area, observe the new process, ensure that the paper-work has been done, and ensure that employees have been trained in the new method. Performance records may also be used by auditors to verify corrective action.

The auditor's evaluation should be documented to ensure that all findings on the corrective action request have been addressed. The auditor records actions taken to verify the corrective action and the results of that verification. The auditor may record the verification on a corrective action form, an audit report, or both. The auditee's action must be traceable to facilitate verification.

All the audit findings in one report do not have to be closed at the same time, but may instead be closed out individually. Verification for such corrective actions does not have to be done immediately. Verification may be combined with another visit, if possible, or another auditor may be asked to verify the corrective action and bring supporting information to the lead auditor. A finding may be closed pending final verification.

5. FOLLOW-UP AUDIT SCHEDULE, AS REQUIRED

Follow-up audits may be required in some situations, but many organizations do not require them due to cost considerations. Instead, follow-up activities are included with the next regularly scheduled audit. When follow-up audits are performed as a separate activity, the audit schedule is determined by the findings from the original audit. These audits can also provide independent verification of corrective action effectiveness.

Follow-up activities may be accomplished in another way. The auditee may provide the auditor with periodic reports containing evidence that the corrective action plan has been implemented and is effective. In this way, the auditor may be able to verify that the action plan is effective without the added expense of an additional on-site visit. The auditor still has the option of verifying the effectiveness of these activities in a subsequent visit.[58]

6. VERIFICATION OF CORRECTIVE ACTION COMPLETION

For effective implementation, the auditor should verify that people did what they said they were going to do and that everyone involved in the change is informed (see Form 2). People can be informed by means of a discussion, a training session, a memorandum, or by another method. This is important for a new process, process changes, or personnel changes.[59]

Request for Corrective Action		
CA REQUEST NO: ☐ INTERNAL ☐ EXTERNAL		AUDIT/WN/PO:
ISSUED TO:		
REQUESTED BY:		PART NO.:
DATE:		
C/A REQUESTED FOR:		
C/A REQUIRED DATE: RETURN TO ATTN: John Doe		

Corrective Action Response
PROBABLE CAUSE:
C/A TAKEN:
EFFECTIVITY DATE: SUBMITTED BY: DATE:

REVIEW OF C/A:
☐ SATISFACTORY   ☐ UNSATISFACTORY   ☐ CA IMPLEMENTED & EFFECTIVE:
COMMENTS:
REVIEWED BY: DATE:

Form 2. Sample request for corrective action form for first-party audits.

Source: Provided by Solar Turbines, 1998 Malcolm Baldrige National Award Winner. Used with permission.

7. EFFECTIVENESS OF CORRECTIVE ACTION

Auditors must review the results of the corrective action plan to determine that the actions were implemented and that they achieved the desired result. The auditee should determine the appropriate measures to be monitored to demonstrate effectiveness. The auditor will then be able to verify the corrective action by comparing the end result to the original conditions.[60]

Effective implementation of a corrective action plan is not the same as effective corrective action. The first is an indication that the actions were implemented, while the second is an indication that the actions worked. There are two elements involved in effective implementation:

1. Achieving the desired result is proof that the process improved and the actions implemented are consistent with business goals.

2. The fact that the process is capable, efficient, and meets stated objectives requires evidence that it consistently achieves the desired results in a cost-effective manner.

The auditor does not determine effectiveness by verifying that a change occurred. Effectiveness is verified when the auditor has determined that a change has occurred and that the product and process achieved the desired result.[61]

8. STRATEGIES WHEN CORRECTIVE ACTION IS NOT IMPLEMENTED OR IS NOT EFFECTIVE

Auditors and/or clients must be objective when determining what strategy to employ when corrective action is not implemented or is not effective. Change may be required in both the audit function and the auditee's organization. Auditors will need to draw on their communication and negotiation skills to ensure that the appropriate actions are initiated. The auditor must evaluate each occurrence of lack of implementation or ineffective corrective action based on its own merits.

Rather than assume that the auditee is at fault, the auditor should reevaluate the corrective action and follow-up process with an open mind. Perhaps an incorrect conclusion was reached due to a lack of time to verify evidence. Available evidence may indicate an error in judgment on the part of the corrective action team, or there may be inadequate resources. The lack of resources may be due to a change in business conditions beyond the auditee's control. Lack of success when attempting to implement corrective action does not always indicate a lack of management commitment.

When the corrective action is not implemented, the auditor should take time to evaluate the situation thoroughly before making any attempt at escalation (i.e. getting higher-ups involved). Jumping into the role of enforcer prematurely puts the auditor in a negative position. It is in the auditor's best interest to be viewed as one who is interested is assisting the auditee to achieve the desired results. As a last resort, the auditor may need to go up the chain of command to the next level of management.[62]

When the corrective action is not effective the auditor/client should either recycle the finding or issue a new finding (referencing the original) to start the corrective action process again. Failure of the corrective action to be effective is serious and should be considered for a form of rework. If this is a frequent recurrence, the corrective action process may be suspect.

For a third-party and some second-party audits, failure to implement a corrective action could result in suspension, being taken off the approved list, or loss of registration.

Chapter B
Closure

After verification of corrective action implementation, the auditing organization may prepare a follow-up report and distribute it in a manner similar to the original audit report.[63] Closure requires verification that corrective actions have been implemented as planned. The auditor notifies the auditee by letter that the audit is closed. The auditor may then discard certain papers accumulated during the audit, but is generally required to retain other records for specific time periods.

Advice on Retaining Records

One auditor divides records into two categories. The first are defined as quality records and are retained for evidential purposes. The second type of retained paper is personal auditor records that may be needed as objective evidence for auditor certification purposes, or information that may help in future audit preparation. Examples may be handwritten notes and completed checklists. All other records and papers can be destroyed.

For internal audits, one organization issues a blank tailored worksheet (similar to a checklist) to the auditor. The auditor fills in the blanks, retitles the worksheet as a report, and deletes the worksheet from the database.

Another auditor reports: "Several years ago, the company I worked for conducted a study to determine the cost of retaining QA records. The study concluded that each sheet of paper in the record cost about $12, and the company was retaining millions of sheets of paper. Because of the cost implications, I encouraged a legal and pragmatic approach to determine what data must be kept and the earliest destruction date. Care should be taken not to retain data solely to satisfy an auditor; there must be another benefit."

According to another auditor, records to maintain are a copy of the original checklist, the audit report, and auditee-auditor correspondence related to the findings and response.

1. CRITERIA FOR CLOSURE

A letter of closure assessing the auditee's corrective action plan implementation and effectiveness may be submitted to the client and/or auditee as applicable. The audit is formally closed when the auditor issues the letter.[64]

When the client is not the auditee, communication between an auditor and auditee will usually go through the client, since the client is the primary link with the audited organization. For an external audit, the contract may specify a contact person. Internally, close-out reports go to the original distribution of the audit report, such as the audit manager and the audited organization. A summary report of all audits performed and their closure status goes to upper-level managers.

Sometimes each corrective action request is individually tracked. Tracking each individual corrective action and closing out a portion of an audit is acceptable. On resolution of each finding, written notification should be sent to those who received a copy of the initial report. This written notification not only satisfies the auditing department's records; it also lets the auditee know that the corrective actions have been accepted. If a satisfactory resolution cannot be reached with the auditee, the finding should be forwarded to upper management for resolution and then closed out if so directed.

2. TIMELINESS

The primary concern with timeliness is the completion and verification of the effectiveness of the corrective action. An administrative concern may be the timely closure of a request for corrective action or the audit report once the corrective actions have been verified. The audit should be closed out as soon as the corrective action is verified and not carried as open item or as a backlog activity.

Timeliness of corrective action does not mean that all corrective actions will be closed in 30 days. Timeliness with regard to corrective action is not compared against a fixed time period but rather an agreed upon specified time period. The specified time should be based on the importance and the availability of resources. Some corrective actions may be completed in a few minutes, while others may take weeks or months. The auditor is limited to reaching agreement with the auditee on the date for completion for each corrective action plan. If these are completed on schedule, then corrective action is timely. There are times, however, when delays occur that are beyond the control of the auditee. The auditor should accept these when there is sufficient evidence that the auditee has initiated actions and recorded the reasons for the delay in completing the action plan.

Problems Commonly Encountered During the Audit Reporting and Closure Stage

The following are examples of the types of problems commonly encountered during the audit reporting and closure stage.

Lack of Response or Inadequate Response. Sometimes an auditee will fail to take the action specified on the corrective action plan. The auditee may fail to notify the auditing organization when action is taken, or the action taken may not be sufficient to warrant closing out the finding. The auditee may lose sight of the original intent of the corrective action request and address a different issue. At times, an auditee may not understand what a standard says or means and may argue the issue's importance or relevance. As a result, an auditee may try to fix a problem haphazardly without understanding the need for action or training. Sometimes the person involved in fixing a problem was not involved in the audit and may not have all the needed information. An auditee may try to pit one audit team against another and argue that the other audit team had no findings in a certain area.

On-the-Spot Corrective Actions.   Some organizations may ask for a list of findings prior to the exit meeting so that corrective action can be implemented before the auditors leave the building. The immediate management response should be recognized by the audit team, but in most cases the underlying cause of the problem is not eliminated.

Continual Requests for Extensions. Sometimes an auditor and auditee may not agree on the significance of a problem. When vested interest is not the same, agreement on the importance or priority of solving a problem may be difficult to achieve. An auditee may request continual extensions for fixing the problem. Excuses can range from "We're working on a big order and don't have time to fix it right now," to "We forgot."

Part VI

Audit Program Management

[10 of the CQA exam questions or 7%]

The purpose of this part of the body of knowledge is to understand the management controls needed for an effective quality audit program. Auditors conduct audits under a prescribed set of rules that are controlled by management. Recognition of audit program management responsibilities will result in an effective auditor program that meets customer needs and requirements.

Chapter A
Administration

An audit program is the organizational structure, commitment, and documented methods used to plan and perform audits. Operational effectiveness of the audit program depends on clearly defined objectives.

A well-managed audit program:

- Plans and performs the audit
- Strives to standardize and improve its performance
- Produces audit results that are meaningful
- Verifies compliance
- Promotes continual improvement within the organization

Some audit organizations may chose to limit the objective of their audit program to verification of compliance to standards while others also evaluate management controls.

All management systems, including quality auditing, consist of four fundamental activities: planning, performance, measurement, and improvement. Often referred to as the PDCA cycle (Plan-Do-Check-Act), these activities are basic to any total quality management approach.[65]

PDCA is commonly known as the Shewhart Cycle, named after Walter A. Shewhart, a pioneer in statistical quality control, who created it. The Japanese call it the Deming Cycle, after W. Edwards Deming, who first described the cycle to them.[66]

The plan stage, or preparation phase, starts with the decision to conduct an audit. It includes all activities from audit team selection to the on-site gathering of information. Part II of this handbook discusses the audit preparation phase.

The do stage is the performance phase. It begins with the on-site opening meeting, continues with the gathering and analysis of data, and concludes with the exit meeting. Part III of this handbook discusses the performance phase of auditing.

The check stage, or reporting phase, of the PDCA cycle covers the translation of the audit team's conclusions into a tangible product. It includes publication of the formal audit report.

The act stage, or closure phase, of the PDCA cycle consists of reactions to the report and the recording of the entire effort. For audits resulting in the identification of weakness, the closure phase includes tracking and evaluating the follow-up action taken by others to fix the problem and prevent recurrence. Corrective action flows from this part of the closure phase.[67] Parts IV and V of this handbook discuss the reporting and closure phases of auditing.

1. AUDIT PROGRAM OBJECTIVES

The first step in successfully implementing an audit program is to define its objectives. While objectives vary from one organization to another, they often include the following statements:

- Perform and present audits meaningfully (in terms that appeal to the customers of the audit process)

- Ensure regular performance of required audits, and ensure frequent audits of critical functions

- Ensure that audits are performed only by trained, qualified, and independent auditors

- Promote a strong alliance between the audit function and the auditee

- Standardize the auditing process, and form a basis against which to measure continuous improvement of the audit program

- Support the objectives/strategies/goals of the organization

Audits are valuable tools for evaluating a company's ongoing compliance and performance when they meet management's needs. Benefits realized from the performance of an audit are weighed against the cost of performing the audit. "Such costs include:

- The auditor's time spent preparing, performing, following up and completing an audit.
- The auditee's time spent participating in and following up the audit results.
- Overhead costs associated with an audit."[68]

Audit program objectives should address the reporter's questions: who, what, where, when, why, and how. Rudyard Kipling provided the following rhyme that sums up the reporter's role. "I keep six honest serving men. (They taught me all I knew.) Their names were What, and Why, and When, and How, and Where and Who."[69]

- Who performs and who participates in the audits?
- What activity or system is being audited?
- Where are the audits performed?
- When are the audits performed?
- Why are the audits performed? What is the driving force behind the audit?
- How is the audit performed?

SIDEBAR

I received lots of complimentary feedback from an auditee who was very close to the process he managed. The staff auditor coached the new internal auditor to ask the reporter's questions. I had coached the new internal auditor that the *why* question was not philosophical. The answer to *why* gives the reason or driver for an activity. After the audit, the manager said that he had learned more from attempting to answer and document the driver for the activity than from any previous audit experience. It reinforced the actions needed for an activity. It also identified actions he did not have to take.

2. IDENTIFICATION AND JUSTIFICATION OF RESOURCE REQUIREMENTS

A group responsible for performing audits should have a documented, formalized program. The program that includes selecting and training auditors and monitoring their performance is robust.[70]

Some companies have a separate audit group to perform internal audits. This group may consist of a few professionals. It reports to either an audit manager or the quality manager. Other companies use part-time or subcontract auditors. Sometimes an audit program coordinator or quality manger recruits and trains individuals to perform audits part-time, in addition to their regular assignments. Either arrangement or a combination of both is acceptable as long as the auditors are well-qualified, technically competent people who know the audit system and can perform internal audits.

SIDEBAR

An external auditor relayed the experience of one company that designated the tool-room attendant to be the internal auditor. This person reported directly to the president of the company. The person was knowledgeable about the processes but had no direct influence on the quality of the process. All the plant personnel knew the tool-room attendant. The company president asked the tool room attendant to observe operations, interview operations and support personnel, and write up findings based on the observations. These observations went directly to the president of the company. Personnel responded well to the situation.

SIDEBAR

I manage our internal audit program in addition to other related duties. My arrangement is to have 80 to 100 engineers, operators, buyers, material planners, and so on perform one audit per year in addition to their other duties. This leaves a great deal of planning, evaluating, and so forth in my hands, but it provides a wide range of perspectives from the auditors.

The justification for resources is based on the audit program schedule. The audit program schedule should be based on internal organizational needs and external requirements, such as regulatory and ISO requirements. The audit program manager should ensure there will be sufficient resources to conduct the quantity and type of quality audits required. If there are objections to the amount of resources needed, then management should reassess organizational needs and external requirements.

3. MANAGEMENT'S RELATIONSHIP TO THE AUDIT FUNCTION

An audit program is an extension of the management function. An audit should identify with systems, not with people. Support by senior management helps the rest of the organization keep a positive attitude about the audit. When management emphasizes the importance of the audit function and its usefulness to the organization, that attitude permeates the entire organization. If management fears or resents the intrusion of the auditing function, this attitude will likewise infiltrate the organization. An audit program set up to collect worthwhile information provides management with two primary benefits:

1. Verification of on-going system compliance to requirements

2. Identification of improvement opportunities within the organization

Management's responses to audit results are also important. If obtained data improves the management system, the employees will see the benefits. This is especially true in an internal audit program, which helps a company identify its own weaknesses before customers or others do.

On the other hand, if an auditor or management focuses on the people being audited rather than on the processes or systems, the value of the audit program can rapidly decline. Rarely is it one individual's fault when there are many audit findings or when system implementation is poor. System structure is often the cause of such problems.

SIDEBAR

While auditing a company that I had visited many times in the past, I noticed coldness and unwillingness to cooperate on the part of many of the employees. I had found these same employees to be very friendly and cooperative during prior audits. Finally, someone confided to me that results from the previous audit I had performed provided a basis for employees' performance appraisals. Although I tried to discuss the situation with the manager of that area, he insisted that performance appraisal was a proper use of audit results.

One auditor's reaction to this dilemma was to state in the audit report that this was an inappropriate use of the audit results and that corrective action eliminating the practice of using audit results in employee performance appraisals was required. In another case, the auditor declined future audit assignments in that particular department.

4. CREDIBILITY OF AUDIT FUNCTION

A credible audit is a meaningful audit. Competent individuals who gather and handle all information pertaining to the audit in an unbiased and ethical manner provide a credible audit. An audit group should be structured so that it does not report directly to the manager of the function being audited. Management must use the audit results appropriately to establish and maintain the credibility of the program. The misuse of audit results or failure to initiate corrective actions will erode the credibility of the audit program regardless of the performance of the auditors.

Using a knowledgeable, experienced, skilled, capable, and well-trained auditor is the most effective way to enhance the credibility of the audit function. Becoming an ASQ Certified Quality Auditor is one way for an auditor to demonstrate competence. The use of unqualified auditors who possess little knowledge or who do not have the ability to assist management in making good decisions or improving a process can discredit the entire audit process.

SIDEBAR

I am familiar with the attitude of one company in choosing members for its internal audit group. Rather than selecting its best employees and training them as auditors, this company uses the audit group as a means of relieving its worst employees. These people are exactly the wrong ones to be in that position.

A good auditor does not have to be an expert in the area being audited. The auditor does need to be knowledgeable in the discipline of quality auditing. The auditor needs to have an understanding of what is being observed. At times, an auditor must be able to grasp that understanding in minutes. If the auditor needs help, he/she should ask another member of the audit team to verify an observation or to assist in other ways.

Auditors need to be able to communicate effectively, both orally and in writing. A large part of the job consists of interviewing. A good auditor must ask intelligent, proper questions and listen attentively. Part III of this handbook discusses interviewing techniques.

An auditor needs to be tactful and offer feedback in a positive, nonintimidating manner. An auditor needs to be especially considerate of an auditee's employees. The audit process is disruptive to daily operations and can cause inconvenience for employees. The auditor shows sensitivity to those being audited by sticking to the proposed audit schedule and not retaining employees through their coffee or lunch breaks. If people see the audit process as a nuisance, they are less likely to cooperate, and the auditor runs the risk of being unable to complete the assignment well or on time.

SIDEBAR

As an auditee, I had received an audit agenda for a third-party audit. The first item on the agenda was a quick plant tour. However, as we started the tour, the auditor requested to see a certain area of the plant not scheduled for that audit. As we were about to leave the area he said, "I know it's not on the agenda, but I would like to ask a couple of questions here. It won't take long; I don't want to get off schedule, but I'd like to start here." A day and a half later, the auditor was still in that area asking questions. He never audited another department in the entire facility.

An auditor aims to keep the credibility of the audit function on a high plane. The auditor does this by looking at information objectively and avoiding ethical conflicts. An auditee must trust that an auditor will not divulge proprietary information to competitors or other outsiders who can use it to their benefit. Even internally, auditors must be careful to maintain confidences. This is especially true when the locations or departments report to different management.

The credibility of the audit function is enhanced if the role of the audit function is communicated and understood by all stakeholders. Fear of the audit function will reduce its credibility. The credibility of the audit function is enhanced if the auditors act professionally and the program is professionally managed. The audit function should be managed and made accountable the same as other functions within the organization.

5. LINKAGE TO BUSINESS PERFORMANCE

Just as an audit program's mission should be linked to the organization's mission, the audit program's results should be linked to the organization's needs. Linking results to needs demonstrates that the audit program recognizes and is committed to the organization's success. It aligns itself with the business purposes. One method of linking audit results to issues that affect the organization is to group benefits in terms of cost savings, risk reduction, and increased opportunity.[71]

Cost Savings

Audit-related corrective action may produce savings by:

- Lowering cost per unit, per service, or per entry

- Lowering daily expenses

- Reducing working capital requirements

- Lowering capital expenditure

Such organizational savings offset some of the cost of supporting the audit program. The total saving, then, is the net of the savings produced less the cost of the audit program.

Figure 13 illustrates the program cost and savings accrued from audit activities. This is an illustrative sample only. Details regarding particular savings vary from company to company and industry to industry. The sample shows that the audit program saved the organization $236,000 over the cost of the audit program's expenses. Distilling the savings further, some internal audit programs may subtract costs incurred by the auditee, such as preparation time, lost productivity, and corrective action initiation. It all depends on what numbers best measure audit program progress or contribution.

Audit Program Expense	Yearly Cost*	Audit-Related Cost Savings*				
		1st Qtr	2nd Qtr	3rd Qtr	4th Qtr	Net
Salaries	$57		($60)			($3)
Indirect	96		(233)	($56)	($24)	(217)
Overtime	25			(20)		5
Fringes	61		(102)	(26)	(8)	(75)
Subtotal	$239		($395)	($102)	($32)	($290)
Outside Services	$50		($23)			$27
Maintenance Supplies	7					7
General Supplies	13					13
Travel	2					2
Office Supplies	3					3
Subtotal	$75		($23)			$52
Depreciation	$4		($7)			($3)
Rent	5					5
Subtotal	$9		($7)			$2
Gross Operating Expenses	$323		($425)	($102)	($32)	($236)

* In thousands of dollars

Figure 13. Sample auto program contributions.

Risk Reduction

Audit programs should avoid equating their value with only the costs saved. In some cases, cost saving is irrelevant because the organization seeks to reduce risk, such as the risk of noncompliance to a law, regulation, or standard. For instance, organizations required by government regulation to have an ISO 9001 registered quality system to remain in business cannot refuse an audit of a third-party registrar simply to save money.

Risk reduction in terms of safety, health, and environment concerns is another way that audit programs contribute to business performance. Audit results may reveal risks to the organization's wealth or well-being. Auditing may reveal situations that could result in fines, legal violations, negative publicity, or customer loss. In some cases, auditing is needed to provide positive demonstration of due diligence within the framework of legal relations.

Increased Opportunity

Identification of opportunities is of significant interest to management and a potential audit-related contribution. The results of the audit and subsequent follow-up actions may increase the organization's opportunity to develop new products, open new markets, add new services, or increase services or production capacity.

6. LINKAGE TO CONTINUOUS IMPROVEMENT

In the 1970s, the principal focus of audits was to attain compliance. Today, companies are shifting their focus from compliance to customer satisfaction. Many firms see this as an operational imperative. Fewer and fewer organizations feel completely at ease with their current customer relationship. Listening to the voice of the customer and acting on that intelligence to develop new products becomes a necessary marketing strategy.[72]

Definition of Continuous Improvement

Continuous improvement is a quality philosophy that assumes that organizations can always make improvements. In *The Change Agents' Handbook,* Hutton explains, "No matter how much improvement has been accomplished, there are always practical ways of doing even more with less—providing an even better product or service at the same or lower cost."[73] The marketplace is constantly shifting. Continuous improvement allows organizations to meet customer needs and remain competitive.

Continuous Improvement in the Audit Program

When management looks at the data collected in audits, they can begin to analyze the data and act on the conclusions. This analysis of causes, corrective actions, and preventive actions provides direction for audit program improvements. In *After the Quality Audit,* Russell and Regel provide some concrete techniques to integrate continuous improvement into the audit process, including:

- Establishing teams to implement opportunities for improved audit service performance

- Providing training and resources to assist introduction and implement indicated changes

- Developing an audit program structure that supports future anticipated demands from the customer, market, regulatory agency, and other external and internal requirements[74]

Continuous improvement is an ongoing process. The audit program never finishes making improvements. The successful implementation of one improvement simply flows into the next investigation.

Within the audit organization, the audit program provides the seeds for change and the continuous improvement process. The audit program serves as a primary source of corrective action input. When the audit program becomes trusted and credible, employees may share information with auditors that they would not typically share with management. Employees' candid suggestions, ideas, complaints, and observations are invaluable to continuous improvement.

SIDEBAR

In a small manufacturing firm, the general manager coached the truck drivers on observation techniques. The transportation supervisor debriefed the drivers after every delivery. He asked for observations that supported other marketing information and potential opportunities for improvement. The delivery routine was one more source being cultivated for information on competitive advances. This same company actively encouraged all employees to forward observations on improvement opportunities and listened to and acknowledged each observation. Management exhibited a uniform posture about external and internal observations made by its employees.

The audit also provides an improvement support network. An organization may welcome corrective action and fully intend to complete it, but it may fail to implement the action. By providing support throughout the corrective action process, the audit program can promote process completion while gaining insight into how corrective action helps or hinders the organization.

SIDEBAR

In a service organization, day to day fire-fighting left little time for focusing on corrective action. After experiencing significant numbers of nonconformances, management started to see a pattern of common cause. Then management directed that a root cause analysis be used. The actions determined and implemented significantly reduced customer complaints. The comment by several managers after the actions were complete was: "We should have done this years ago."

7. EVALUATION OF AUDIT PROGRAM EFFECTIVENESS

Periodic evaluations of all audit programs and audit teams causes improvement opportunities to surface. Audit programs are evaluated through periodic management reviews. Management can review records, analyze performance, or appoint an independent audit team to review audit results. In the case of a multisite company, auditors from another location can come in annually to audit the audit team. This evaluation could include:

- Observing audit teams perform an audit

- Examining auditor training records and audit schedules

- Looking at sample audit results, corrective actions, and follow-up activities to see if the program is working as intended

Additional data can be collected by asking an auditee to rate audit team members in the areas of:

- Interviewing skills

- Interaction with personnel

- Reporting results

Critical reviews by peers, subordinates, and superiors provide exceptional opportunity for growth and maturity. While it may be slightly unpleasant to those being reviewed, it also helps keep things in perspective.

SIDEBAR

One auditor I know very well said that after a particularly successful series of audits, his ego was starting to inflate just a little. He was helping to identify and solve the problems of the corporate world. Key people were getting excited about quality. Action that would change the way the corporation was thinking were becoming common. His ego quickly deflated, however, when he bragged of his accomplishments to his wife, who said, "Well, that's nice dear. Do you suppose you could do something about the leak in the toilet?"

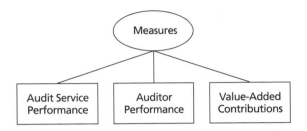

Figure 14. Audit program measures.

Source: Adapted from *After the Quality Audit,* by J. P. Russell and Terry Regel (Milwaukee, WI: ASQC Quality Press, 1996).

Management should treat the audit function the same as other organizational functions and departments.[75] There are three measures for monitoring program effectiveness, as shown in Figure 14. Effective measures of an audit program include audit service performance, auditor performance, and value-added contributions.

Measures are effective only to the extent that they meet the audit program's needs. An audit program must select its measures based on documented standards and objectives. In addition, it must use data collected over time to accurately reflect ongoing program performance.

Audit Service Performance

This measure determines if the audit program meets customer expectations. Sources of input data for managing the audit program may include:

- Performance evaluations from audit customers

- Focus groups to gather direct customer feedback

- Audit-related loss of customer time, resources, or both

- Contract term fulfillment

- Quality of audit deliverables, including audit reports

- An independent auditor to audit the audit program

- The number and severity of external audits performed on the audit organization[76]

Auditor Performance

This measure assesses the competency of individual auditors as well as consistency among team members. To apply the measurement, management could:

- Observe auditor performance during an audit
- Review customer performance evaluations
- Review audit deliverables
- Employ an independent auditor to evaluate auditor techniques
- Appraise general auditor credentials

Value-added Contributions

This measure looks at how the audit program improves the organization's business performance. To apply the measurement, management could:

- Compare planned completion of corrective action to actual completion
- Track the number and severity of noncompliances issued by external audits
- Plot the corrective action from the initial performance level through the stated performance goal
- Determine the degree to which planned corrective action is effective the first time
- Identify the number of "recycled" corrective actions that failed to address root causes the first time
- Identify the number of repeat problems due to the same cause
- Determine the benefit of corrective action
- Benchmark audit performance against other companies in the same industry
- Plot measures, such as types of customer complaints, warranty costs, and scrap and rework costs, and compare trends to audit results

8. SUMMARY OF AUDIT PROGRAM RESULTS FOR REVIEW

In many organizations, the audit program is a key preventive element in the overall cost of quality. In these organizations, management has a vested interest in the audit program's annual results.

According to ANSI/ISO/ASQ Q9004-1-1994: 6.3 Reporting:

> "The financial reporting of quality activities should be regularly provided to and monitored by management in order to provide for an:
>
> - Evaluation of the adequacy and effectiveness of the quality system
> - Identification of additional areas requiring attention and improvement
> - Establishment of quality and cost objectives for the following period."[77]

Audit program management should address three main questions in its annual summary.[78] The first question is: *How did the audit department contribute to the organization last year?* Management wants to know what the audit program contributed to the organization's business performance during the previous period.

The audit program should not attempt to address this question directly before the review. It must compile and define program contributions throughout the review period as discussed in sections 1, 5 and 7 of this chapter. Figure 15 summarizes the actions described in each section. These

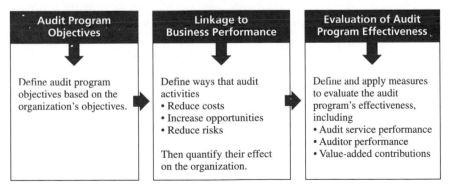

Figure 15. Audit result linkages.

activities secure meaningful data. The data drive the management summary. The audit program direction comes from the analyses of the consolidated data. The significance of the audit program and trends are derived from the analyses. Typically, the significance and trends reflect areas of strength as well as points of vulnerability in the program. Therefore, the audit program annual contribution to the organization is the result.

The second question is: *What will the audit program contribute to the organization next year?* Based on historical trends, the audit program can recommend future audit activity and define its intended benefit to the organization.

The third question is: *Is there anything management should know to avoid future risks to the organization's wealth?* The audit program should identify potentially critical information, such as regulatory changes or defunct programs, and include them in the summary report.

Typically, the audit program's summary report is one of many that competes for management attention. It must be concise, accurate, and eye-catching. Accompanying graphs, matrixes, and data summaries must capture and focus attention on the issues. Figure 16 provides two samples that can enhance the summary report. Graphs such as these allow management to appreciate the value of the audit program at a glance. "Expectations are what people buy, not things."[79]

9. LONG-TERM AUDIT PLANNING

Long-term audit planning completes the loop in audit administration. The process begins with defining a mission statement and establishing objectives. From the mission and objectives flow the audit program and its boundaries (scope), policies, and high-level procedures. These documents guide daily activity. The process ends with long-term planning. The program patrols the boundaries and ensures that the policies and procedures still make sense before the process proceeds.

The *Malcolm Baldrige National Quality Award 1998 Criteria for Performance Excellence* states that the role of long-term or strategic planning is "to align the work processes with the company's strategic directions, thereby ensuring that improvement and learning reinforce company priorities."[80] The criteria outline the steps involved in strategic planning, with three steps especially important for the audit program.

Step 1: *Identify information that might affect the program's future opportunities and directions. Attempt to take as long a view as is practicable.* This

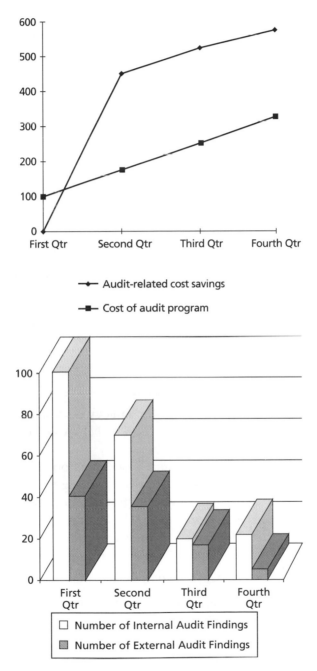

Figure 16. Charting results.

Customer-Related

- Who are our customers?
- What do they need and want?
- How are we doing in their eyes?

Auditor-Related

- What are the auditors' needs and concerns?
- What do they need to do a great job?
- How are we doing in their eyes?
- Who is making a real effort?
- How do we say thank you?

Organization-Related

- How does the organization's structure support what we are trying to do?
- What organizational issues will ultimately affect us (e.g., new product lines, new business risks, new management structure)?
- How can we make better use of management experience and support?
- How can we help management improve?

Figure 17. Open-ended questions.

first step provides the realistic content for strategy development. Figure 17 provides a focus list of open-ended questions to help with the identification process.

Step 2: *Define a strategic direction.* Based on information gathered in step 1, the audit program devises a long-term strategy to guide ongoing decision making, resource allocation, and program management.

Step 3: *Put the strategy in operation.* The audit program develops and deploys an action plan to make the strategy operational. This process includes:

- Defining new processes to accommodate strategic change

- Defining key measures, indicators, or both to track progress

- Communicating new strategic direction and new processes to the audit team and the organization

- Providing resources to support the new strategic direction, including procedures, training, and incentives.

Chapter B
Process

Auditing often is a function of an organization's quality department, although it may also reside in the manufacturing, operations, compliance, or technology department. Regardless of where the auditing function resides, it must be (1) independent of the audited areas, (2) supported by management, and (3) deployed positively.

Management of the audit function includes the following activities:

- Establishing a reporting relationship for the audit function
- Establishing audit authority, operational freedom, constraints, and boundaries
- Ensuring the availability of adequate resources for all audits
- Determining whether to use a single auditor or an audit team
- Staffing and training auditors
- Establishing procedures, processes, and criteria for an effective and efficient audit program
- Establishing methods for evaluating an audit program
- Establishing audit schedules
- Confirming audit dates and any requested changes of audit dates
- Setting priorities for audit subjects
- Reviewing audit performance
- Providing periodic reports to management on the status of the quality audit program

An audit manager or audit coordinator is responsible for:

- Preparing an overall audit schedule

- Budgeting resources

- Assisting with or overseeing other administrative duties related to the auditing function

Additionally, the audit manager staffs and trains the audit department and monitors and evaluates auditors in the performance of their duties.

1. DEVELOPMENT AND IMPLEMENTATION OF AUDIT PROGRAM PROCEDURES

Documented procedures are critical to the success of an auditee's quality system. A procedure answers the reporter's questions: who, what, where, when, why, and how. "Documentation of procedures is objective evidence that:

- A process is defined

- The procedures are approved

- The procedures are under change control."[81]

Procedures also allow for distribution control, ensuring that those who need information have access to it.

The same ideas apply to the audit program. Procedures are critical to the program's success. They promote constancy within the audit execution. Procedures also provide a means to define and enforce intangible standards and expectations, such as ethical behavior.

Procedure Development

Three areas typically require procedures, as shown in Figure 18.

Procedures for audit scheduling should include:

- Guiding principles for developing audit schedules

- Focus areas for auditing

- Process for creating an overall periodic audit schedule

Procedures for auditor maintenance should include:

- General auditor qualifications

- Standards for ethical conduct

- Process for selecting and approving new auditors

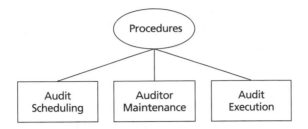

Figure 18. Areas requiring procedures.

- Process for training new and existing auditors
- Process for assessing auditor performance

Procedures for audit execution should include:

- Process for planning audits
- Process for conducting audits, to include
  — Recording and reporting audit results
  — Providing corrective action follow-up
- Process for retaining and handling audit records
- Process for billing audit customers, such as
  — Invoicing and collecting payment from third-party audit customers
  — Conducting internal money transfers for first- and second-party audit customers

Overall, audit procedure development is a collaborative effort. Individual auditors should take advantage of practical knowledge and experience to develop functional, streamlined procedures. Audit program managers should use their strategic perspective to direct the audit program and ensure that appropriate procedures are established and maintained.

Procedure Implementation

For successful procedure implementation, the audit program must communicate with the auditors and the organization. Each auditor must understand the importance and proper use of procedures. Members of the organization should also have a general understanding of audit procedures to avoid confusion.

To complete a procedure's implementation, audit program management should schedule a follow-up audit to verify the procedure's effectiveness. If a procedure fails to facilitate an audit process, modify or replace it.

2. DEVELOPMENT AND IMPLEMENTATION OF AUDIT PROGRAM SCHEDULE

When scheduling an audit, an audit program manager typically identifies the client and the client's requirements and obtains initial information about the auditee. The audit program manager may also select the audit team (often with recommendations from the lead auditor) and identifies other resources needed, such as a technical specialist or consultant. Audit program management should issue an audit program schedule and update the schedule as changes occur. Many audit organizations issue schedules annually, semi-annually, or quarterly. The auditee facility should have a copy of the plan in advance, showing the time period (week or month) that an audit will occur at the site.

Some audit program managers develop schedules using a horizontal and vertical audit strategy. A *horizontal audit* is an audit of one system, such as training, across several departments. A *vertical audit* is an audit of several systems, such as testing, test equipment, test status, and nonconformances, within one department.

To develop a schedule, the audit program uses three process steps. The first step is to identify auditees. With limited resources, the audit program must determine which areas warrant scheduled audits. Some areas may need an audit each year. Others may require an audit to maintain registration or satisfy a regulatory requirement. Still others may need an audit to monitor new products or processes. There should be some type of defined rationale for developing audit schedules or audit program plans.[82] The rationale may include factors such as routine check, regulatory or registrar requirements, changes to processes, new product or service introductions, previous audit results, or reported problem areas.

The second step is to assign available resources. The audit program must assign available resources, particularly a team of auditors, to execute required audits.

The third step is to schedule individual audits. The audit program has to organize the required information to schedule activity for the upcoming year. Figure 19 shows a partial example of an audit schedule of a services organization.

PRI	ANNEX	JAN.	FEB.	MAR.	APR.	MAY.	JUN.	JUN.*	JUL.	AUG.
1	3a-HWCATS	5-Jan					3-Jun	ABC		
1	3b-ES&H						3-Jun	ABC	6-Jul	
1	3c-HazMAT						3-Jun	ABC	13-Jul	
1	8b-Elect Power			30-Mar			3-Jun	ABC		
1	8d-Elect Distribution		2-Feb				3-Jun	ABC		
1	8f-Pot and NonPot Water	12-Jan					3-Jun	ABC		
1	9-Transpo Veh&Equipt						3-Jun	ABC		2-Aug
1	11-Medical Services						3-Jun			
1	15-POL Systems	26-Jan					3-Jun	ABC		
1	20-Bldg/Struct Maint						3-Jun	ABC	27-Jul	
2	2a-Tech Library						3-Jun	ABC		
2	2b-Human Resources						3-Jun	ABC		
2	2c-Finance/Accnt						3-Jun	ABC		
2	2d-MIS						3-Jun			9-Aug
2	2e-QP&S						3-Jun	ABC		
2	2f-Program Director						3-Jun	ABC		
2	2g-Hono Office						10-Jun			
2	2h-Health&Safety						3-Jun			16-Aug
2	2i-Contract Administration						3-Jun	ABC		

*External audit by ABC Registrar.

Figure 19. Sample audit schedule.

To implement an audit schedule, the audit program should notify auditees and auditors of the upcoming schedule and update and redistribute the schedule as changes occur.

3. AUDIT RECORD-KEEPING REQUIREMENTS

The auditing organization retains all audit documents and records by agreement between the client, the auditing organization, and the auditee, or in accordance with any regulatory requirements. Auditors should adopt reasonable procedures to ensure the safe custody and retention of working papers for a period of time sufficient to satisfy pertinent legal and administrative requirements.[83]

Properly retained working papers, reports, and other documents from an audit facilitate future audit planning, review of audit work, preparation of reports on the work of audit departments or groups, and proof of compliance with audit standards. Retain complete reports, including supplemental documents, at least until the next formal audit is complete. When a period of certification is involved (typically three years), it may be advisable to retain audit records until the next certification period. This provides evidence that the findings of an earlier audit have been identified, corrected, and maintained.[84]

Audit records are maintained primarily as evidence that the quality program has been evaluated and, secondarily, to show that the audits were planned, conducted, and reported according to established procedures. Included in the category of quality records of the audit system are audit schedules, audit plans, audit reports, completed audit checklists, auditor qualification records, and audit follow-up records.[85]

Long-term Records

Audit records are classified as either long-term or short-term records, depending upon their use and the length of time they are kept.[86] Long-term record retention practices, vary, depending on organizational needs and product or operation risk. It is a good practice to ask the general counsel of an organization what the required length of time for record retention should be. Auditors in regulated industries, such as pharmaceuticals or nuclear power, should check with their legal staffs or contract administrators.[87] Often, these records are lifetime records that need to be retained for the life of the program, product, device, or facility.

Examples of long-term records include:

- Audit notification letter and audit plan
- Blank checklists
- Audit report and cover letter
- Response from the auditee
- Follow-up audit or verification results
- Closing letter

Short-term Records

The length of time to keep short-term records varies from organization to organization. Some may keep short-term records until the next audit, automatically destroy records after a specified time period, or keep them for three years due to the recertification cycle and other rationales. Short-term records include:

- Copies of auditor qualification records
- Completed checklists (working papers)
- Documents and records obtained from the auditee
- Additional correspondence

The organization responsible for conducting and reporting audits should maintain the original supporting records generated during the audit and used to prepare the final report. In all cases, label official audit records and documents to be retained. The retention time for the audit files should be consistent with organization policy and legal requirements.

Chapter C
Audit Personnel

1. QUALIFICATIONS

While a formal post-secondary education and previous work experience are helpful for those desiring to work as quality auditors, auditing is a learned discipline. An auditor's qualifications result from a combination of formal education, training, orientation, experience, continued professional study and work, passing examinations, a good performance record, and acceptance by peers, subordinates, clients, auditees, and employers.[88]

Education and Experience
Quality auditors should have a combination of work experience and education. Authorities such as the American Society for Quality (ASQ), the Registrar Accreditation Board (RAB), or their own organization qualify auditors. One method of proving qualification is to become an ASQ Certified Quality Auditor (CQA). To become a CQA, an auditor must have experience in one or more of the areas identified in the quality audit Body of Knowledge, at least a high school education, and a commitment to the ASQ's Code of Ethics. In the past, auditors usually had a general background in the quality field. Today, many quality auditors have diverse backgrounds and advanced technical degrees or have service industry degrees in areas such as hotel management.

Interpersonal and Other Skills
Regardless of education or training, an auditor who lacks certain interpersonal skills will not be able to conduct an effective audit. Good communication skills, both oral and written, are essential, as are excellent listening skills.

Auditing methods include listening, questioning, evaluating, judging, recording, planning and controlling an audit, administering, leading, supervising, and decision making. Interpersonal communication skills such as tact, adaptability, and the ability to analyze evidence and draw conclusions from it are especially important in auditing.[89] An auditor often must criticize other people's work or at least question the validity of someone else's actions. Tact helps. Furthermore, an auditor must be able to handle situations where conflict is imminent. These skills, taught to people, need considerable exercise.

An auditor must be able to understand the technical materials presented during an audit. Depending on the complexity of an audit, the auditor must be able to ask probing questions and get to the heart of the problem.

Analytical skills are essential to gathering and synthesizing audit information. According to ANSI/ISO/ASQC Q10011-2-1994: 7.0 Personal Attributes, good analytical skills include:

- Perceiving situations realistically

- Understanding complex operations from a broad perspective

- Understanding the role of individual units within an organization[90]

Personal Traits

Auditors require certain personal traits to complement a strong skill base. Specifically, an auditor should be:

- Independent
- Systematic
- Trustworthy
- Persistent
- Positive
- Curious
- Open-minded
- Mature
- Tenacious
- Patient

An auditor must be able to present a case clearly and concisely. Auditors do not make assumptions; they verify evidence. An auditor should be unbiased, never going into an audit looking for something specific (hidden agenda) and trying to prove it. An auditor also needs to realize how far a team's authority extends and should not exceed that authority. Auditors develop most of the necessary interpersonal and other skills through experience and training.

2. SELECTION

Based on clearly defined qualifications, the audit program manager must select competent auditors. Russell and Regel's *After the Quality Audit* stresses that the people selected to perform quality audits should be the organization's best people.[91] Who the "best" people are, however, may differ from one audit work assignment to another depending on their backgrounds.

> **SIDEBAR**
>
> In a Department of Energy nuclear facility, the contracting operations company used senior managers from other nuclear facilities as management self-assessment auditors. These senior operations managers were extremely skilled at identifying the significant safety issues facing the operation managers of the facilities. The self-assessments identified significant issues, and company management addressed them in a very timely manner. The operations managers performing the management self-assessment were on temporary assignment from their normal operational duties.

Audit management must consider a variety of factors for a particular audit assignment to secure an auditor with the most appropriate skills. Figure 20 summarizes some of the key factors.

Even with well-defined auditor criteria and a well-defined work assignment, selection of individuals to be auditors may become arbitrary without additional structure. Figure 21 outlines features within sample procedures that may be used to evaluate particular auditor qualifications.

The results of the evaluation & selection should be recorded and communicated to auditor candidates as quickly as possible.

Work Assignment-Related

- Conducting audits against quality system standards, for hardware, software, process or service industries.
- Service or product type and its associated regulatory requirements (e.g., health care, food, or nuclear devices)

Audit Team-Related

- Audit team size
- Audit team skill composition
- Audit team leadership requirements

Auditor-Related

- Professional qualifications or technical expertise required in a particular discipline
- Personal skills required to deal with a specific auditee
- Language skills required
- Real or perceived conflict of interest

Figure 20. Assignment considerations.

To evaluate education

- Review the candidate's written work.
- Obtain evidence (such as an exam administered by a national certification body) that the candidate has the required knowledge and skills.
- Administer a separate competency exam using a company scenario.

To evaluate experience

- Seek outside confirmation of the candidate's experience level.
- Interview the candidate to assess experience in detail.

To evaluate personal skills and traits

- If available, consider information from previous employers and colleagues.
- Interview the candidate to assess work style and personal style.
- Perform role plays.
- Observe the candidate working under actual audit conditions.
- Administer a personality test.

Figure 21. Evaluation considerations.

3. TRAINING AND RECERTIFICATION

An auditor must have training to ensure competence in auditing skills, related standards and regulations, general structure of quality assurance programs, auditing techniques, and other work specific skills. Competence can be developed through the following methods:

- Orientation on related standards

- Implementation procedures

- Training programs on subjects related to auditing

- On-the-job training[92]

Auditors should maintain their technical competence through continuing education and current relevant auditing experience. ANSI/ISO/ASQC Q10011-2-1994 suggests training with subsequent examination in standards used within the audits and auditing techniques. In addition, auditors and lead auditors need management skills.[93]

Companies can offer an organization-wide certification program for all auditors that includes training. Recognition and certificates to identify auditors approved according to the company's standards provides positive feedback to the auditors. An auditor needs training in:

- The standard to be applied

- Objective evidence-gathering

- Interpersonal relations

- Auditing methodology

Auditors should be trained to write audit observations on the checklists and notes used by audit teams as well as to gather evidence. At least one team member should be familiar with the department operation or the scope of audited activities.

A lead auditor usually has more experience, may be more highly trained in the applicable audit standards, and may have more training in conducting audits. Policies and procedures defining the qualifications for lead auditors often require a certain number of years of experience or performance of a specific number of audits before promotion to this level.

Auditors should be recertified. Continuing their training helps auditors maintain skills and knowledge. Training may include a refresher course periodically. The refresher course, coupled with experience in performing audits, is a reasonable expectation. Such requirements help an auditor keep up with changes in standards.

Training ensures that auditors keep current on the organization's policy and procedures in auditing techniques. Audits provide a learning opportunity to help an organization improve its operations continuously. Auditors should likewise strive to improve their performance continuously.

Continuing Education Resources for Auditors

The field of quality auditing changes. Auditors must strive to keep abreast of changes and trends. Quality auditors must embrace current technology to avoid becoming liabilities rather than assets. Committed quality professionals increase their knowledge and improve their skills through continuing education. The following are continuing education resources:

- Reading technical literature (auditing-related books, newsletters, and periodicals)

- Reading case studies

- Reading research papers

- Attending seminars and classes

- Participating in professional organizations

- Consulting with peers[94]

- Attending the ASQ Quality Audit Division annual conference

More colleges and universities are providing network courses over the Internet. This technology provides easy access to courses in remote locations. Near-realtime communications can be arranged.[95]

Many continuing education opportunities are available through the ASQ. The Quality Audit Division offers annual tutorials to reflect current events and trends in auditing and holds a quality audit conference to expand auditors' knowledge in quality and related fields. Many other organizations offer correspondence courses in standards and quality management. Continuing education requires attending conferences or taking formal courses. Books and magazines are also available to expand an auditor's knowledge.

The ASQ requires an auditor who has passed the CQA examination and has been certified by the ASQ to recertify within three years. This can be accomplished by earning recertification units (points) and retaking and passing an examination. An auditor must collect a specified number of points in a three-year period to remain certified. Points accumulate by attending regular ASQ section meetings. Points are also awarded for:

- Completing additional course work
- Being employed in the field
- Writing about topics included in the Body of Knowledge
- Attending or leading seminars or training sessions

Recertification encourages auditors to remain in touch with the audit curriculum and maintain a professional level of expertise. Some companies have additional training and qualification requirements for members of their internal audit functions.

Many opportunities exist for auditors to learn about the technical aspects of quality. Private consultants teach auditing courses and do on-site auditor training. More colleges are teaching statistical process control courses, and courses related to auditing are part of the curriculum at some technical schools.

Auditors may benefit from staying abreast of technology outside the field of auditing, as specified in the Certified Quality Auditor's Body of Knowledge. For example, auditors may take courses in leadership or computer training classes. They may brush up on their facilitation and presentation skills, public speaking techniques, and time management techniques. All enhance auditors' performance and professionalism.

Auditors are better qualified and better trained than ever before. Continuing education opportunities for auditors, once scarce or unheard of, are abundant and diverse. In the twenty-first century, management can expect to reap the benefits of properly performed audits by exceptionally well-trained personnel.

An informal type of internal continuing education is networking with other auditors. Team interactions can play a vital role in ensuring that auditors follow unified policies and perform similarly. Auditor discussion groups can review unusual situations, findings, or problems encountered during an audit. The entire team can benefit from the experience and gain new skills and insights. Such discussion promotes:

- Team spirit within a department
- Open communication
- Uniformity of auditing practices

Some auditing departments plan weekly meetings to accomplish this growth. They may even keep minutes of the meetings for future reference. All such discussions must remain within the department. Outside discussion is unethical and compromises a department's integrity.

Auditing is not a stagnant process; it is a continuous learning experience. The aim of the auditor should be to:

- Stay current with product processes

- Conform to changes in general auditing standards

- Meet the ever-changing needs of management.

Internationalization of Businesses

As auditing has become increasingly global, many auditors are finding the ability to speak a second language to be essential. The auditor should be able to use tactics that ease cultural differences, such as:

- Employing an interpreter to facilitate an audit

- Familiarizing him/herself with cultural differences that could affect relations with the auditee

- Preventing serious misunderstandings by becoming acquainted with local customs

These tactics avoid cultural differences that interfere with the audit process.

SIDEBAR

While performing an audit of a supplier in Japan, I worked late one evening, as was often my custom at home. When I opened the door to exit the office provided for my use, I noticed that all employees of the company were still at their workstations. The Japanese culture apparently dictated that every employee remain until I had left for the night. I became embarrassed that my conduct had detained so many people unnecessarily. Of course, I left promptly at 5:00 the following evening.

4. PERFORMANCE EVALUATION

According to ANSI/ISO/ASQ Q10011-3-1994: 4.5.1 Performance Evaluations, "Audit program management should continually evaluate the performance of its auditors . . . to improve auditor selection and performance and to identify unsuitable performance."[96] Three steps are required for an effective performance evaluation.

Step 1: *Communicate expectations.* A meaningful performance evaluation is one that measures performance against clearly defined standards. Audit management must provide consistent explanation of these standards during the initial training session. Proper training provides auditors with day-to-day performance expectations as well as insight into the basis for performance evaluation.

Step 2: *Evaluate the auditor's performance.* Performance evaluation should assess the competency of individual auditors, as well as the consistency between them, against established standards. As mentioned earlier, audit management measures performance by:

- Observing auditor performance during an audit
- Reviewing customer performance evaluations
- Reviewing audit deliverables
- Employing an independent auditor to evaluate auditor techniques
- Appraising general auditor credentials

Step 3. *Communicate the auditor's performance.* Audit management should report performance evaluation results to the auditor. To improve performance, an auditor must understand his or her strengths and weaknesses. Audit management should review evaluation results with the auditor and they can work together on a training plan to improve performance.

This completes the evaluation loop. The performance evaluation provides a monitoring function for competency. The evaluation feeds back ways to improve the auditor selection process.

Part VII

General Knowledge and Skills

[49 of the CQA exam questions or 33%]

The purpose of this part is to present fundamental terminology and auditor communication skills, and to introduce quality tools that auditors need to understand and apply. The topics in this part are core knowledge for quality auditors.

Chapter A
Auditing Basics

1. QUALITY CONCEPTS, TERMS, AND DEFINITIONS

Quality has been defined as fitness for use, conformance to requirements, and the pursuit of excellence. Even though the concept of quality has existed from early times, the study and definition of quality has been given prominence only in the last century. Following the industrial revolution and the rise of mass production, it became important in the 1920s to better define and control the quality of products. Originally, the goal of quality was to ensure that engineering requirements were met in final products. Later, as manufacturing processes became more complex, quality developed into a discipline for controlling process variation as a means of producing quality products.

In the 1950s, the quality profession expanded to include quality assurance and quality auditing functions. The drivers of independent verification of quality were primarily industries in which public health and safety were paramount. In the 1980s, businesses realized that quality wasn't just the domain of products and manufacturing processes. Total quality management principles were developed to include all processes in a company, including management functions and service sectors.

Over the past several years, there have been many interpretations of what *quality* is beyond the dictionary definition of "general goodness." *Quality* has been defined as fitness for use, reduction of variation, value-added, conformance to requirements or specifications, and so on. ANSI/ISO/ASQC A8402-1994 calls *quality* the totality of features and characteristics of a product or service that bear on its ability to satisfy given needs. Simply, *quality* can be thought of as "meeting customer requirements" or "achieving customer satisfaction." Another description of quality that takes into account the customer and the provider of the product or service is "Quality for the customer is getting what you were expecting and quality for the provider (supplier) is getting it right the first time."[97]

A system of *quality management* includes all activities of the overall management function that determine the quality policy, objectives, and responsibilities and their implementation.[98] The quality management system is the means of establishing a quality policy and objectives and of achieving those objectives.

Quality assurance and quality control are two aspects of quality management. *Quality assurance* consists of "all the planned and systematic activities implemented within the quality system, and demonstrated as needed, to provide adequate *confidence* that an entity (item) will fulfill requirements for quality."[99] The confidence provided by quality assurance is twofold—internally to management and externally to customers, government agencies, regulators, certifiers, and third parties. While some quality assurance and quality control activities are interrelated, *quality control* is defined as "operational techniques and activities that are used to *fulfill requirements* for quality."[100] While quality assurance relates to how a process is performed or how a product is made, quality control, is more the inspection aspect of quality management. *Inspection* is the process of measuring, examining, and testing to gauge one or more characteristics of a product or service and the comparison of these with specified requirements to determine conformity. Products, processes, and various other results can be inspected to make sure that the object coming off a production line, or the service being provided, is correct and meets specifications.

Quality auditing is part of the quality assurance function. It is important to ensuring quality because it is used to compare actual conditions with requirements and to report those results to management. "A quality audit is not an alternative to an inspection operation. . . . The quality auditor may use inspection techniques as an evaluation tool . . . but the quality audit should not be involved in carrying out any verification activities leading to the actual acceptance or rejection of a product or service. A quality audit should be involved with the evaluation of the process and controls covering the production and verification activities."[101] Auditors make observations and report their findings. An *observation* is an item of objective evidence found during an audit. A *finding* is a conclusion of importance based on observation(s). (Refer to the ANSI/ISO/ASQC A8402-1994 glossary for additional terms and definitions.)

2. THEORIES AND PRACTICES IN QUALITY AUDITING

Audits are independent, unbiased fact-finding exercises that provide information to management. This information identifies opportunities and reduces the risk of decisions made by management. It is management's responsibility to take appropriate actions based on the audit information provided.

> "The audit is a long-established and well-respected activity in the accounting profession. . . . Because of many similarities in the activities of the accounting and quality fields, quality professionals have adopted the same word 'audit,' complete with some of the same modifiers."[102]

Quality audits emerged shortly after World War II and gained momentum when the military began issuing standards and specifications for products. Quality auditing originally resembled an inspection activity and was developed primarily in large manufacturing industries, such as electronics, and in high-risk fields, such as the nuclear and aerospace industries.

Audits are planned, objective, and independent investigations of products, processes, or systems. By examining documentation, implementation, and effectiveness, quality auditing is used to evaluate, confirm, or verify activities related to quality. "The quality audit may be a single occurrence or a repetitive activity, depending on the purpose and the results of both the audit and the product/service, process, or quality system concerned."[103] A properly conducted quality audit is a positive and constructive process. It helps prevent problems through the identification of activities likely to create problems. Problems generally arise from the inefficiency or inadequacy of the concerned activity.

> "All companies and enterprises, regardless of size, can benefit by examining their activities and management systems. This applies to local government, civil service, commerce and the service industries as well as manufacturing industries."[104]

The principles of quality auditing apply to any type of management assessment. No valid reason exists for separating management auditing into subcomponents. Management controls the resources. The goals of quality, safety, environmental stewardship, and efficiency are all driven by the same set of rules: define requirements, produce to requirements, monitor achievement of requirements, and continuously improve on requirements.[105]

What Do Audits Measure?

Quality audits examine products, processes, & systems with respect to predetermined standards. Within this context, quality audits evaluate one or more of the following: the adequacy of the documentation, compliance to the documented procedures, implementation and maintenance of the procedures, and the effectiveness of the procedures to accomplish intended objectives. Audit methods and techniques used to verify these measures are discussed in Part III of this handbook.

Adequacy is defined as "the state of being sufficient for a specified requirement." Quality audit evaluation for adequacy usually consists of reviews to verify the sufficiency of documentation for defining work and of records as evidence of satisfactory work completion. This typically includes such items as legibility, understandability, and implementability. Adequacy alone, however, does not verify whether work was performed correctly unless it is evaluated in conjunction with compliance, or the implementation and maintenance of the documented system.

Compliance refers to the affirmative indication or judgment that the auditee has met the requirements of the relevant specifications, contract, or regulation. In auditing, the terms *conformance* and *compliance* are used interchangeably to report the results. However, many regulated industries tend to favor the use of the terms *compliance* and *noncompliance.* In the ISO quality management system assessment process, the terms *conformance* and *nonconformance* are normally used. The term *compliance audit* is also used to indicate that the purpose of a quality audit is to determine the degree of compliance to rules.

Compliance looks for strict adherence to a set of rules, which may include requirements and standards. The compliance audit is not the arena for questioning these rules; they are set and identified for the audit. Examples of audits involving compliance include regulatory and high-risk.

Regulatory audits are used in cases where activities are regulated by government. Among these regulated activities are production of energy, stewardship of the environment, production of food, protection of workers, and use of medical products. Auditors verify that the applicable laws and regulations in these areas are being implemented to ensure the health and safety of consumers.

High-risk audits are used when the consequences of failure are unacceptable, such as in the launching of airplanes, submarines, and rockets. A complete and thorough audit of the finished product is necessary before it is activated or placed into service. The audit checks inspection records, craft qualification records, design review records, and other forms of proof.[106]

A *management audit* assesses compliance and whether procedures and instructions—and the implementation of those procedures and instructions—meet pre-established goals and objectives. Compliance verifies the accomplishment of a set of rules, and adequacy verifies the proper translation of those rules into procedures, whereas effectiveness measures the achievement of those rules and procedures. The goals verified as part of effectiveness are usually related to overall quality objectives or continuous improvement of the organization.

How Do Audits Measure Results?

Quality auditing is an information-intensive activity. Therefore, auditors need clear, useful information to make effective auditing judgments and decisions. Information must be based on data, but merely obtaining data does not guarantee that the information will be useful. To collect data successfully, an auditor must know what questions to ask and collect, process, analyze, and present the specific data needed to answer that question. In addition, an auditor must ensure that the data they collect represent objective evidence, "information which can be proved true, based on facts obtained through observation, measurement, test, or other means."[107]

Data must be precise and accurate so that an auditor can form reliable conclusions. When using measurement and test devices, the auditor needs to verify that data-generating equipment has been properly maintained and calibrated. If an auditor is relying on auditee's data, the auditor needs to ensure that the audited company has an effective calibration system for measuring and testing equipment. The objective of the system is to ensure that inspection and test equipment is adjusted, replaced, or repaired before it becomes inaccurate. The system should consist of:

- Labels, tags, color codes, or other means of tracing the measurement device to the individual calibration record

- A requirement for calibration practices

- Certified primary company or reference standards traceable to industry or to national, or international standards, such as the National Institute of Standards and Technology (NIST)

- Listings by department of calibration status and delinquents (instruments that are out of calibration cannot be used to certify product and must be removed from service until calibrated)

- All personally owned tools that are used, which should be in the system and calibrated

- Inspection check of calibration by an inspection department before signing off on items.[108]

In addition to defining accuracy of inspection equipment, an auditee's calibration procedures must address the issue of remedial action if equipment is found to be out of calibration. In other words, how did the out-of-calibration equipment affect the products that were manufactured or tested with that piece of equipment? If necessary, production should be halted or a product recall issued.

3. BENEFITS AND CONSEQUENCES OF AUDITS

The performance of a quality audit provides management with unbiased facts that can be used to:

- Provide input for management decisions, so that quality problems and costs can be prevented or rectified

- Inform management of actual or potential risks

- Identify areas of opportunity for continuous improvement

- Assess personnel training effectiveness and equipment capability

- Provide visible management support of the quality program

- Verify compliance to regulations

"The tasks of management include: (1) identifying possible sources of problems, (2) planning preventive action to forestall problems, and (3) solving problems, should they arise. . . . Most problems are quality problems related to the quality of work being performed, the quality of items being received, the quality of information being communicated, the quality of available equipment, the quality of decisions made. . . . Since all quality problems have a cost associated with them, avoiding, preventing, and solving these problems prevents and reduces unnecessary costs."[109]

The benefits that a quality audit provides vary depending on whether the audit is a first-, second-, or third-party audit. For example, possible benefits of a first-party audit include the assurance that procedures are adequate and utilized and the early detection of a problem, which gives management the opportunity to investigate and identify root causes, take immediate corrective actions, and ultimately prevent problems from happening again.

Second-party audits benefit the supplier as well as the customer because they help eliminate the shipping of nonconforming products and reduce costs and waste. This in turn builds confidence between the supplier and customer, promotes a better understanding of customer expectations, and provides an avenue for quality technology transfer between the customer and supplier. Second-party audits also help ensure a better final product by verifying that there are appropriate controls for inputs into the system.

Third-party audits typically verify compliance to specified regulations or standards. The regulations and standards may be required by law, such as FAA or FDA regulations, or may be voluntary, such as ISO 9001. The benefits of passing a third-party audit may be permission to continue to operate, recognition in the form of a certificate or registration, or an award.

"The usual purposes of quality audits are to provide independent assurance of the following conditions:

- Plans for attaining quality are such that, if followed, the intended quality will, in fact, be attained
- Products are fit for use and safe for the user
- Laws and regulations are being adhered to
- There is conformance to specifications
- Procedures are adequate and are being followed
- The data system provides accurate and adequate information on quality to all concerned
- Deficiencies are identified and corrective action is taken
- Opportunities for improvement are identified and the appropriate personnel alerted."[110]

4. ROLES AND RESPONSIBILITIES OF CLIENT, AUDITOR, AND AUDITEE

A quality audit involves three key participants who may interrelate in a number of ways. Described by function, these participants are the client, the auditor, and the auditee.

The *client* is the person or organization who has requested or commissioned an audit. The client usually is senior management, and the audit is typically of an organizational unit under the client's jurisdiction, of independent suppliers, or an application for third-party registration.[111]

The *auditor* is the person who plans and carries out an audit. An auditing organization employs auditors to carry out audits. The auditing organization may be internal to a company or an independent organization, such as the auditing group of a quality program registrar or consulting organization.

The *auditee* is the organization to be audited. The auditee may be a division of the client's organization or an entirely separate entity, such as a supplier. At times, and often in internal audits, the client and auditee are the same person or department.

Following are examples of external audits:[112]

Situation: Organization desiring recognition or approval of its capability to meet a particular standard such as ISO 9001
Client: The organization desiring registration or certification/registration
Auditee: The organization desiring certification/registration
Auditing organization: The organization granting the certification/registration using an auditor employed by the auditing organization or hired to conduct the audit.

Situation: Customer organization desires to evaluate a supplier
Client: The interested purchasing agent
Auditee: The potential or existing supplier
Auditing organization: Member(s) of the customer organization staff or auditors under contract to the customer organization

Situation: Regulatory organization verifies that supplier or operator is in compliance with requirements
Client: The regulatory agency
Auditee: The potential supplier or operator
Auditing organization: Employee(s) of the regulatory agency or auditors under contract to the agency

An example of an internal audit is:[113]

Situation: Organization desires to determine the degree of conformity of its own organization elements to a predefined quality program
Client: Upper management team desiring to use the technique
Auditee: The element(s) of the organization to be evaluated
Auditor: Employee(s) of the organization

5. CHARACTERISTICS OF SYSTEM, PROCESS, AND PRODUCT AUDITS

A *quality audit* is "a systematic and independent examination and evaluation to determine whether quality activities and related results comply with planned arrangements and whether these arrangements are implemented effectively and are suitable to achieving objectives."[114] There are three distinct types of quality audits: product (which includes services), process, and quality system.

Product Quality Audit

A *product quality audit* is an examination of a particular product (hardware, processed material, software or service) to evaluate whether it conforms to requirements (i.e. specifications, performance standards, and customer requirements). If an audit is being performed on a service instead of a product, then it is called a *service quality audit.* Elements examined may include packaging, shipment preparation and protection, user instructions, product characteristics, product performance, and other customer requirements.

Product audits are conducted when a product is in a completed stage of production and has passed the final inspection. The product auditor uses inspection techniques to evaluate the entire product and all aspects of the product characteristics. A product quality audit is the examination or test of a product that has been previously accepted or rejected for the characteristics being audited. Such an audit is a reinspection or retest of the product to measure the effectiveness of the system for product acceptance. It includes performing operational tests to the same requirements used by manufacturing, using the same production test procedure, methods, and equipment. The product quality audit verifies conformance to specified standards of workmanship and performance. This audit can also provide a measure of the quality of the product going to the customer. The product quality audit frequently includes an evaluation of packaging, examination for cosmetics, and a check for proper documentation and accessories, such as proper tags, stamps, shipment preparation, and protection.

Process Quality Audit

The process quality audit is performed to verify that processes are working within established limits. *A process quality audit* examines an activity to verify that the inputs, actions, and outputs are in accordance with defined requirements. A process quality audit covers only a portion of the total system and usually takes much less time than a system audit. The boundary of a process audit should be a single process, such as marking, stamping, cooking, cutting, coating, setting up, starting up, or installing. A process audit is very focused and usually involves only one auditor or work crew.[115]

A process audit is a verification by evaluation of an operation or method against documented instructions and standards, to measure conformance to these standards and the effectiveness of the instructions. Such an audit is a check of conformance of process, personnel, and equipment to defined requirements such as time, temperature, pressure, composition, amperage, and component mixture. It may involve special processes, such as heat treating, soldering, plating, encapsulation, welding, and nondestructive examination. A process audit checks the adequacy and effectiveness of the process controls over the equipment and operators as established by procedures, work instructions, and process specifications.[116]

Quality System Audit

A quality audit conducted on a quality management system would be called a *quality system audit*. It can be described as a documented activity performed to verify, by examination and evaluation of objective evidence, that applicable elements of the quality system are appropriate and effective and have been developed, documented, and implemented in accordance and in conjunction with specified requirements.

A quality system audit evaluates an existing quality program to determine its conformance to company policies, contract commitments, and regulatory requirements. It includes the preparation of formal plans and checklists on the basis of established requirements, the evaluation of implementation of detailed activities within the quality program, and the issuance of formal requests for corrective action where necessary.[117]

Criteria contained in the American Society of Mechanical Engineers (ASME) codes, nuclear regulations, good manufacturing practices, or ISO standards, for example, may describe a quality system. Normally these descriptions state what must be done but do not specify how it must be done. The "how" is left up to the organization being audited. An auditor looks at the management systems that control all activities from the time an order comes into a company (i.e. how that order is handled, processed, passed on to operations, what operations does in response to that order) through delivery of the goods, sometimes including transportation to the site.

A system audit looks at everything within the quality system: the processes, products, services, and supporting groups, such as purchasing, customer service, design engineering, order entry, and training. It encompasses all the systems of the facility that assist in providing an acceptable product or service.

6. CHARACTERISTICS OF INTERNAL AND EXTERNAL AUDITS

An audit may be classified as internal or external depending on the inter-relationships that exist among the participants. *Internal audits* are first-party audits, while *external audits* can be either second- or third-party audits. Figure 22 illustrates the classifications commonly used to differentiate between types of internal and external quality audits. The figure is provided as a guide to classifications, but there is no absolute rule because there are exceptions.

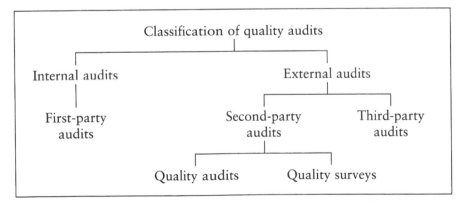

Figure 22. Classifications of quality audits.

7. CHARACTERISTICS OF FIRST-, SECOND-, AND THIRD-PARTY AUDITS

First-party Audit

A first-party audit is performed within an organization to measure its strengths and weaknesses against its own procedures or methods and/or against external standards adopted by (voluntary) or imposed on (mandatory) the organization. A first-party audit is an internal audit conducted by auditors who are employed by the organization being audited, but who have no vested interest in the audit results of the area being audited. Companies may have a separate audit group consisting of full-time auditors, or the auditors may be trained employees from other areas of the company who perform audits as needed on a part-time basis in addition to their other duties.

A multisite company's audit of another of its divisions or subsidiaries, whether locally, nationally, or internationally, is often considered an internal audit. If, however, the other locations function primarily as suppliers to the main operation or location, audits of those sites would be considered second-party audits.

Second-party Audit

A second-party audit is an external audit performed on a supplier by a customer or by a contracted organization on behalf of a customer. A contract is in place, and the goods or service are being, or will be, delivered.[118]

A *quality survey,* sometimes called a *quality assessment* or *quality examination,* is a comprehensive evaluation that analyzes such things as facilities, resources, economic stability, technical capability, personnel, production capabilities, and past performance, as well as the entire quality system. In general, a survey is performed prior to the award of a contract to a prospective supplier to ensure that the proper capabilities and quality systems are in place.[119]

SIDEBAR

An auditor told of one case in which an organization actually went out to give a supplier an award for the perfect product they had been receiving. However, during the award process it was discovered that the supplier had absolutely no quality system in place! The supplier was able to ship acceptable product simply because its employees were good sorters.

Third-party Audit

A third-party audit is performed by an audit organization independent of the customer-supplier relationship and is free of any conflict of interest. Independence of the audit organization is a key component of a third-party audit. Third-party audits may result in certification, registration, recognition, an award, license approval, a citation, a fine, or a penalty issued by the third-party organization or an interested party. Third-party audits may be performed on behalf of an auditee's potential customers, who either cannot afford to survey or audit external organizations themselves or who consider a third-party audit to be a more cost-effective alternative. For example, government representatives perform mandatory audits on regulated industries, such as nuclear power stations, airlines, and medical device manufacturers, to provide assurances of safety to the public.

Recognition Purposes. Companies applying for the Malcolm Baldrige National Quality Award, which recognizes world-class companies and establishes the criteria necessary to compete internationally, must submit to an examination. More than thirty-five states have programs modeled after the Malcolm Baldrige National Quality Award program, and some municipalities present similar awards. Japan's Deming prize is another example of such an award. The United States and Japan are not unique; many countries have established similar criteria.

Registration Purposes. Companies in certain high-risk categories—such as toys, pressure vessels, elevators, gas appliances, and electrical and medical devices—wanting to do business in Europe must have their management system registered by audit to either ANSI/ISO/ASQC Q9001-1994 or ANSI/ISO/ASQC Q9002-1994 requirement criteria. Contractors to federal agencies are recognized as registered suppliers by auditing against standards.

Customers suggest or demand that their suppliers conform to ANSI/ISO/ASQC Q9001-1994 or ANSI/ISO/ASQC Q9002-1994 criteria. The U.S. Federal Acquisition Regulations (FARs) currently state that government contractors who comply with the ISO 9000 requirement standards are not required to comply with other quality standards. Many national standards have been canceled, and users have been referred to the U.S.-adopted ANSI/ISO/ASQC Q9001-1994 or ANSI/ISO/ASQC Q9002-1994 requirement standards. A third-party audit normally results in the issuance of a certificate stating that the auditee complies with the requirements of a pertinent standard or regulation.

Third-party audits for quality system registration should be performed by organizations that have been evaluated and accredited by an established accreditation board, such as the Registrar Accreditation Board in the U. S., as being competent to perform audits of companies desiring to achieve quality system registration.

8. CHARACTERISTICS OF QUALITATIVE AND QUANTITATIVE ANALYSIS

During an audit, an auditor must analyze many different types of information to determine its acceptability with the overall audit scope and the characteristics, goals, and objectives of the product, process, or system being evaluated. This information may be documented or undocumented and includes procedures, drawings, work instructions, manuals, training records, electronic data on a computer disk, observation, and interview results. The auditor must determine if the information is relevant to the audit purpose and scope.

Quantitative data means either that measurements were taken or that a count was made, such as counting the number of defective pieces removed (inspected out), the number of customer complaints, or number of cycles of a molding press observed during a time period. In short the data is expressed as a measurement or amount. IIA's *Internal Auditing: Principles and Techniques,* suggests that there are many sources of quantitative data, such as:

- Test reports
- Product scrap rates
- Trend analyses
- Histograms
- Regression analyses
- Ratio analyses
- Lost-time accidents
- Frequency distributions

- Chi square tests
- Risk analyses
- Variance analyses
- Budget comparisons
- Mean, mode, median
- Profitability
- Cost/benefit studies[120]

In contrast, *qualitative* data relates to the nature, kind, or attribute of an observation. Qualitative data may include single observations or data points. Examples are: last month's withholding tax deposit was three days late; the paycheck was wrong; the injection needle was contaminated; the wrong reference standard was used; the purchase order specification gave the wrong activity level; computer equipment was missing from the clerk's office; regulatory violation. Whether the evidence is qualitative or quantitative, it should be objective, unbiased and proven true.

The auditor must analyze data to determine relevancy. Some data are important and should be reported due to frequency or level. Other data are important due to the nature or kind of the information even though an event occurred only once.

With quantitative information, the determination of acceptability is fairly straightforward for two reasons. First, a direct comparison can be made between the information and the requirements or criteria for the audit. For instance, suppose the measure of system effectiveness used in an audit is found to have less than a predetermined number of customer complaints about product quality in a three-month period. Analysis would consist of comparing customer complaint records against the criteria to determine if the system is effective. Secondly, most quantitative information is considered reliable due to the fact that by nature it should be free of emotion and bias.

Qualitative data must be unbiased and traceable, just like any observation that is used as objective evidence by the auditor. Additionally, the auditor should determine the usefulness or relevance of the information. For instance, the auditor may be informed that one customer complaint turned into a $10 million lawsuit. In this case, the data must be verified, and the auditor will seek to determine if the data have any bearing on the quality system. Once the information has been determined to have a real effect on the system, the auditor may use the data to draw conclusions about system effectiveness. Or the auditor may determine that the data represented once-in-a-lifetime event and are not relevant to current operations.

Chapter B
Basic Skills

1. TIME-MANAGEMENT TECHNIQUES

Proper preparation in the audit planning stage can eliminate many delays in the audit performance stage. To make the most efficient use of time, the auditor must plan an audit on several levels. First, the audit manager must schedule each individual audit in relation to other audits being performed so that the availability of audit team members and other resources can be assessed. Next, the lead auditor must prepare the audit plan for the individual audit. The steps involved in this audit phase were discussed in Part II of this handbook. Once a lead auditor establishes the auditing strategy, a detailed schedule must be prepared that specifies which areas are to be visited at various times throughout the day. The detailed schedule may be revised constantly during the audit, but the auditor must inform auditee management about planned activities. An auditor who makes no attempt to stick to the proposed schedule may antagonize members of the auditee's organization who have made arrangements to be available as requested.

The auditor's notification letter to the auditee should specify special arrangements, such as transportation from one audit site to another, the need for an escort, the use of special safety equipment, or the need for a conference room. At this time, the auditor should list required equipment or supplies, such as access to copy machines, printers, overhead projectors, and extension cords. By anticipating needs and making them known to the auditee in advance, an auditor communicates preparedness and a strong desire to focus on the important task of gathering information at the audit site.

To ensure the efficient use of time during the audit performance stage, the audit team should arrive promptly at the audit site at the agreed-upon time for the opening meeting. The lead auditor should retain control of the opening meeting and should not allow the auditee to take control with extended plant tours or lengthy presentations, unless such time has been scheduled into the audit.

Throughout an audit, the audit team meets daily to assess audit progress. Additionally, auditors should allow several minutes at the end of each interview to review notes, present conclusions, and reach a consensus with an auditee representative, such as the area supervisor or escort. If data indicate that certain areas need additional attention, the auditors' assignments may need to be changed. Findings that indicate severe ramifications for the quality program should be investigated thoroughly as soon as possible after they are uncovered.

Audit teams often ask to have lunch catered so that a working lunch can take place. Scheduling a small amount of time for an audit team meeting during the lunch break may aid the auditors in gathering additional information, if needed. An audit team should allow sufficient time to prepare for the exit meeting, especially when an audit lasts several days, in case additional information needs to be gathered.

An auditor should be able to recognize and overcome delay tactics. Common time-wasting techniques employed by auditees and possible solutions by auditors are discussed in Part I, chapter B.2 of this handbook. When an auditee's repeated time-wasting tactics hinder the progress of an audit and threaten to compromise the audit schedule severely, the lead auditor is responsible for notifying auditee management and the client.

2. CONFLICT RESOLUTION

The most effective method of resolving conflict is to take steps to reduce conflict occurrence. Ways to reduce conflict include eliminating misunderstandings, remaining open-minded and flexible, and avoiding surprises during the audit process.

Misunderstandings are the most common cause of conflict during an audit. Sources of misunderstanding are poor communication, poor listening, and auditor bias. The auditor must always be on the lookout for signs of misunderstanding. Indicators include a less than cooperative attitude on the part of an interviewee, repeated questions about the audit scope and purpose, and the provision of inadequate or incorrect records for review.

In these situations, the best course of action is for the auditor to repeat the information that was not fully understood before proceeding. Also, the auditor must be an active listener, meaning that he/she must not only hear what is being said but must also recognize when the message is clouded by a possible contradictory meaning. Finally, the auditor must always assume that the auditee is acting in good faith. Do not assume that a misunderstanding is on the part of the auditee. Rephrase the question in a different way. Be careful to avoid terminology that has confusing meanings. Don't assume that the auditee is familiar with specific industry jargon.

During an audit, the auditor must remain open-minded and flexible. Auditors must bear in mind that when they conduct an audit, for whatever reason or from whatever source of authority, they are disrupting the daily routine of the auditee. The auditor should consider the effect of special requests on the audited organization and ensure that the audit takes into consideration the work norms and culture of the auditee.

Unnecessary and unreasonable demands are often a source of conflict during the audit. This becomes especially true when the auditee is intimidated by the audit team and as a result is unwilling to say anything ahead of time. These kinds of issues can manifest themselves later in the form of uncooperativeness, avoidance, belligerence, or even sabotage.

A sure way to create conflict during an audit is to withhold important information about the audit's status or results and surprise the auditee at or after the exit meeting. It is therefore important that the auditor share information with the auditee on a regular basis. This is usually done during informal daily meetings or during actual audit performance. In addition, the auditor has an obligation to inform auditee personnel of the nature of the information they are recording, how it will be used, and so on. Being upfront with auditees not only helps answer some of their concerns about the audit process but also puts them at ease, thus reducing the likelihood of conflict.

If conflict should develop during an audit, the best course of action is for the auditor to temporarily stop the audit and allow a cool-down period before proceeding. If auditors don't take this action, they run the risk of getting overly involved and losing control of the audit process. The ultimate result of losing control is the premature termination of the audit or the disallowance by the auditee for the auditor to proceed. Neither of these situations is acceptable to the auditor's organization or the client. Once the conflict has diffused, the auditor can meet with the auditee to determine the source of the misunderstanding. Auditors must remain open to the possibility that they may be a direct cause of the conflict. To resolve the conflict and allow the audit to proceed, auditors must remain open-minded and listen to the auditee.

3. EFFECTIVE COMMUNICATION TECHNIQUES

Quality auditing requires effective communication with the auditee's organization, the auditor's organization, and within the audit team itself. This communication can take many forms, including written memos, notifications, and verbal conversations before and during an audit performance. Basic rules for effective communicating include (1) ensuring that the message is clear, (2) verifying that the message is received and understood, and (3) utilizing the appropriate medium for transmittal.

To ensure the message is clear, the auditor should:

- Use appropriate terminology and avoid terms that are hard to understand

- Avoid lengthy explanations that dilute the point of the message

- Ensure the accuracy of the information

- Adapt the level and approach of the communications to the audience (e.g. CEO, technicians, all engineers, etc.)

To verify that the message is received and understood, the auditor should:

- Verify that the auditee received all messages sent (e.g. via telephone, fax, e-mail, or other)

- Look for signs of understanding, such as nods of the head and words like "I see"

- Seek feedback by asking clarifying questions, and listen to the responses

- Determine when a written record of the communication is needed

To determine the appropriate medium for transmittal, the auditor should:

- Take into account the formality of the message

- Determine the technology in use by the receiver

- Use the appropriate format for transmission (e.g. notification letters, memos, electronic mail, cell phones, etc.)

In initial meetings, the auditor has a lot of work to do to establish effective communications. Possible communication techniques the auditor can use during the preaudit phase include:[121]

- Building rapport by exchanging small talk, perhaps over a cup of coffee

- Establishing trust by assuring confidentiality

- Showing empathy for the disruptions that will be inevitable, and assuring the auditee that distractions will be kept to a minimum

- Demonstrating professionalism, and working hard to be organized

- Explaining the process by reviewing the audit plan, and showing how the auditee will be kept informed

- Ensuring that the auditee "buys-in" by asking: Does this seem reasonable? Do you recommend any changes to make the process run more smoothly?

- Maintaining flexibility by considering all options, yet never relinquishing authority to conduct the audit (be firm, but flexible).

Effective communication during the performance phase of an audit involves a variety of factors, including:[122]

- Active listening

- Working with auditee escorts

- Facilitating audit teamwork

- Holding daily auditee briefings

- Accommodating auditee language requirements

- Incorporating technology that improves effectiveness

- Accommodating changes in the audit schedule, if asked

New Communication Technology

With the growing popularity and increased affordability of computers, technology can reduce audit cycle time, conserve paper, and improve audit effectiveness. For example, e-mail and faxing can reduce turnaround times and costs associated with conventional or express mailings. Digital cameras are becoming a valuable tool for auditors. A digital camera takes pictures on a disk; this disk can then be inserted into a computer to show pictures of problems uncovered during an audit. The pictures can be displayed at the closing meeting or can be printed and included in the audit report.

An auditor can use a notebook computer in conjunction with the appropriate software during the audit preparation stage to customize checklists or create flowcharts, for example. During the audit performance stage, computers can be used to consolidate observations in the audit team's daily meetings and to prepare the preliminary audit report. A computer also can be used to create the final audit report, which can be sent via e-mail if the client agrees. Additionally, if the audit is being scored, spreadsheet programs can format the checksheets and automatically compute the audit scores.[123]

Cellular phones may be useful when an auditor needs to contact a client or audit manager quickly. An auditor may also prefer to bring a cellular phone when auditing a large or remote facility where a telephone may not be accessed easily. Cellular phones can also increase productivity of those who spend large amounts of time in cars or at airports.

Video conferencing is used routinely by some auditing organizations. It is a valuable method for bringing groups of people face-to-face without incurring travel expenses. In the future, video conferencing may prove to be especially important in auditing by eliminating preaudit visits and even follow-up audits in some situations.

The use of electronic media requires that other issues be addressed, such as security, confidentiality (especially for networks), and document controls (viewing and changing documents, changing code, and backing up data).

4. PRESENTATION METHODS AND TECHNIQUES

Members of an audit team must create a favorable impression to auditee management, both in appearance and ability. Audit team members should dress appropriately for the opening meeting. Credentials of the audit team members are also presented at this time to instill confidence that the audit is being performed by competent, well-qualified individuals.

The lead auditor conducts the opening and exit meetings, as well as separate daily meetings with the auditee and the audit team. By using appropriate aids and handouts, the lead auditor ensures that the auditee is in agreement with the details outlined in the audit plan and understands the auditing methods to be used. In addition, the auditor should ensure that the auditee is able to interpret data correctly, is in accord with the information presented on the audit report, and desires to implement the needed corrective action.

The lead auditor is responsible for ensuring that a location has been set aside for presentations. The location may be a training room, conference room, or even a break area. The lead auditor should ensure that there is adequate space for expected meeting attendees. This may include determination of seating arrangements, such as classroom-style, at a conference table, or at a U-shaped table. The lead auditor must secure equipment that will be needed to make the presentation, such as flip charts, overhead projectors, data projectors, pointers, and associated support equipment and supplies (plugs, markers, pointers). Finally, the lead auditor must ensure that visual aid materials will be prepared and available at the meeting. Such materials may include copies of printed reports, copies of completed handwritten forms, (i.e. corrective action requests), overhead slides, and prepared charts.

Some auditing organizations prefer audit team members to sit together during meetings, with auditee representatives likewise grouped. They believe that such an arrangement shows cohesion and support for one another. Other auditing organizations favor a less formal atmosphere, with auditors and auditees intermingled.

The lead auditor should be certain to communicate the data analysis to the auditee both orally and visually. Using simple statistical techniques to recognize patterns and trends and evaluate their significance enables an auditor to prepare an audit report. These results must be communicated to the auditee in a timely and effective manner, and the inclusion of simple charts or graphs in the audit report or their display on an overhead projector can assist the auditee in gaining the necessary understanding of a problem.

Chapter C
Tools and Techniques

An auditor uses many types of tools to plan and perform an audit, as well as to analyze and report the results. An understanding of these tools and their application is essential for the performance of an effective quality audit. The auditor and auditee use many quality tools and techniques to define processes, identify and characterize problems, and report results. An auditor must have sufficient knowledge of these quality tools in order to evaluate whether the auditee is using these tools correctly and effectively. This chapter provides basic information on these tools, their use, and their limitations. For more in-depth information on the application of tools, readers should consult an appropriate textbook. Some general references are provided in the Recommended Readings section at the end of the book.

1. CHECKLIST, GUIDELINES, AND LOG SHEETS

Checklists are the most common tool used to collect data during an audit. Similar to check sheets, they provide an organized form for identifying information to be collected and a means for recording information once it is collected. In addition, the checklist serves as a tool to help guide the audit team during audit performance. A checklist usually contains a listing of audit questions on areas where information is needed, places for recording acceptable responses, and places for taking notes. Figures 23, 24, and 25 provide sample of checklists.

Audit guidelines are used to help focus audit activities. Typically, these consist of written attribute statements that are used to evaluate products, processes, or systems. Audit guidelines are usually not prepared by the

ISO 9001-1994 Checklist

Audit:

Ref	Question	Yes	No	Comments
4.17	**Internal Quality Audits**			
1	Are there written procedures for planning and implementing an internal quality audit?			
2	Are internal quality audits performed?			
3	Do internal audits verify whether quality activities comply with planned arrangements?			
4	Do internal audits evaluate the effectiveness of the quality system?			
5	Are audits planned and scheduled?(The schedule will depend on the basis of the status and importance of the activites to be audited.)			
6	Are audits carried out by persons independent (no vested interest) of the activity being audited?			
7	Are audits and follow up actions carried out in accordance with written procedures?			
8	Are the results of audits documented and brought to the attention of personnel having responsibility in the area studied?			
9	Is corrective action taken on any deficiencies found by the audit?			
10	Examine [a number of] audits performed within the past [year] for conformance to the above.			

Figure 23. Sample checklist, ISO 9001, clause 4.17.
Source: J.P. Russell & Assoc., ISO 123 Data Disk, 1994.

A. *Review of Customer Requirements*
  1. Is there a quality review of purchase orders to identify special or unusual requirements?
  2. Are requirements for special controls, facilities, equipment, skills preplanned to ensure they will be in place when needed?
  3. Have exceptions to customer requirements been taken?
  4. Are customer requirements available to personnel involved in the manufacture, control, and inspection of the product?
  5. Are supplier and subtier sketches, drawings, and specifications compatible with the customer's requirements?

B. *Supplier Control Practices*
  6. Is there a system for identifying qualified sources and is this system adhered to by the purchasing function?
  7. Are initial audits of major suppliers conducted?
  8. Does the system ensure that technical data (drawings, specifications, etc.) are included in purchase orders?
  9. Is the number and frequency of inspections and tests adjusted based on supplier performance?

C. *Nonconforming Material*
  10. Are nonconformances identified and documented?
  11. Are nonconformances physically segregated from conforming material where practical?
  12. Is further processing of nonconforming items restricted until an authorized disposition is received?
  13. Do suppliers know how to handle nonconformances?
  14. Are process capability studies used as a part of the nonconforming material control and process planning?

D. *Design and Process Change Control Routines*
  15. Are changes initiated by customers incorporated as specified?
  16. Are internally initiated changes in processing reviewed to see if they require customer approval?
  17. Is the introduction date of changes documented?
  18. Is there a method of notifying subtier suppliers of applicable changes?

E. *Process and Products Audits*
  19. Are process audits conducted?
  20. Are product audits used independent of normal product acceptance plans?
  21. Do the audits cover all operations, shifts, and products?
  22. Do audit results receive management review?
  23. Is the audit frequency adjusted based on observed trends?

Figure 24. Sample quality system checklist.
Source: From Charles B. Robinson, ed., *How To Plan an Audit,* (Milwaukee, WI: ASQC Quality Press, 1987), pp. 26–30.

Lab/Appraisal# _____   Date: _____   Page 1 of _____

Reference	Criteria	Results		Comments
		Sat	Unsat	
NL-QAM	1. Is monitoring and data collection equipment calibrated?			
NL-QAM	2. Is equipment calibration traceable to nationally recognized standards?			
NL-QAP-5.1	3. Is equipment calibration performed using approved instructions?			
NL-QAP-5.1	4. Are calibration records maintained for each piece of equipment?			
NL-QAP-5.1	5. Is a use log maintained?			

Figure 25. Calibration area checklist.
Source: From Hirzel, QAD Conf presentation 96 'Tools for improving Audit Proceeceses & Performance.'

auditor but rather by the auditor's organization, client, or by a regulatory authority. They are often used to ensure that specific items are evaluated during each audit when audit programs cover several locations, departments, or organizations. The primary differences between checklists and guidelines is that audit guideline items are usually written in statement form rather than as questions, and guidelines don't include provisions for recording audit results. To provide for the latter, log sheets are often used. Log sheets are simply blank columnar forms for writing down information during an audit. Used in conjunction with audit guidelines or to augment checklists, they help ensure that objective evidence collected during an audit is properly recorded. See Part II, chapter C for additional information.

2. SAMPLING THEORY, PROCEDURES, AND APPLICATIONS

Sampling is the practice of taking selected items or units from a total population of items or units. The method and reason for taking certain samples or a certain number of samples from a population should be based on sampling theory and procedures. Samples may be taken from the total population or *universe,* or the population may be separated into subgroups called *strata.* Inferences drawn from the sampling of a stratum, however, may not be valid for the total population.

To infer statistical significance from any sample, two conditions must be met. The population under consideration must be *homogeneous,* and the sample must be *random. Homogeneous* means that the population must be uniform throughout—the bad parts should not be hidden on the bottom of one load—or it could refer to the similarities that should exist when one load is checked against others from a different production setup. *Random* means that every item in the population has an equal chance of being checked. To ensure this, samples can be pulled by a random number generator or other unbiased method.

When looking at records, an auditor should take care not to pull all samples out of one file drawer or from just the front or back of drawers. Lower drawers are typically more neglected than higher drawers. If files are color-coded, the auditor should ask what the color codes mean and choose samples from each set. An auditor may choose samples on the basis of previous audit results. In addition, an auditor should verify in each audit that problems detected by previous audits have remained corrected. If any major changes have been made to a system (for example, calibration once done in-house is now done outside), the auditor may desire to pull a larger than usual sample.

It is preferable for the auditor to go to the location of the sample and select the sample for the audit. However, there are situations (long distances, convenience, files off site) where it is permissible for the auditee to provide the sample population, such as in a file, folder, or log book, to the auditor, who can then select the sample.

When sampling, auditors should record the identity of samples selected.

3. FLOWCHARTS AND PROCESS MAPPING

Process maps and flowcharts are used to depict the steps or events in a process or system that produces some output. Flowcharts are specific tools for depicting sequential activities and typically use standard drawing symbols in their creation. Process maps are flowcharting that may or may not use standard flowchart symbols. Flowcharts and process maps are effective means for understanding procedures and overall processes and are used by auditees to help define how work is performed. Flowcharts are especially helpful in understanding processes that are complicated or that appear to be in disorder. Auditors can also use flowcharts to help understand both production and service processes during audit preparation.

A flowchart can be used to describe an existing system or process or to design a new one. It can be used to:

- Develop a common understanding of an overall process, system, and sequence of operations

- Identify inspection and check points that result in a decision

- Identify personnel, by job title, performing specific steps

- Identify potential problem areas, bottlenecks, unnecessary steps or loops, and rework loops

- Discover opportunities for changes and improvements

- Guide activities for identifying problems, theorizing about root causes, developing potential corrective actions and solutions, and achieving continuous improvement

Flowcharting usually follows a sequence from top to bottom and left to right, with arrowheads used to indicate the direction of the activity sequence. Common symbols often used for quality applications are shown in Figure 26. However, there are many other types of symbols used in flowcharting, such as ANSI Y15.3, Operation and Flow Process Charts (see Figure 27a–d). Templates and computer software are available for making flowcharts, which are both easy to use and fairly inexpensive.

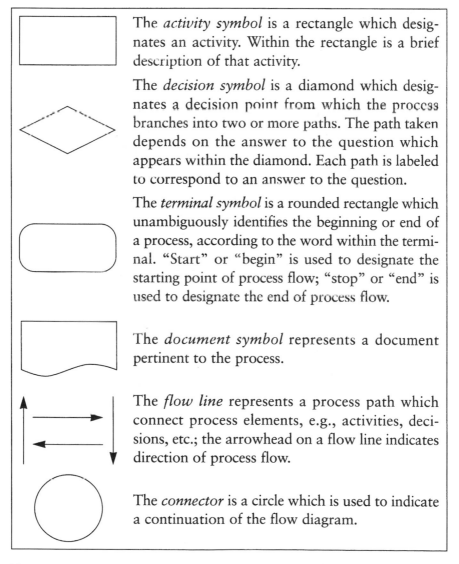

The *activity symbol* is a rectangle which designates an activity. Within the rectangle is a brief description of that activity.

The *decision symbol* is a diamond which designates a decision point from which the process branches into two or more paths. The path taken depends on the answer to the question which appears within the diamond. Each path is labeled to correspond to an answer to the question.

The *terminal symbol* is a rounded rectangle which unambiguously identifies the beginning or end of a process, according to the word within the terminal. "Start" or "begin" is used to designate the starting point of process flow; "stop" or "end" is used to designate the end of process flow.

The *document symbol* represents a document pertinent to the process.

The *flow line* represents a process path which connect process elements, e.g., activities, decisions, etc.; the arrowhead on a flow line indicates direction of process flow.

The *connector* is a circle which is used to indicate a continuation of the flow diagram.

Figure 26. Common flowchart symbols.

Source: J.M. Juran, ed., *Juran's Quality Control Handbook,* 4th ed. (New York: McGraw-Hill, 1988), p. 67. Reproduced with permission of the McGraw-Hill Companies.

(a) Activity sequence flowchart

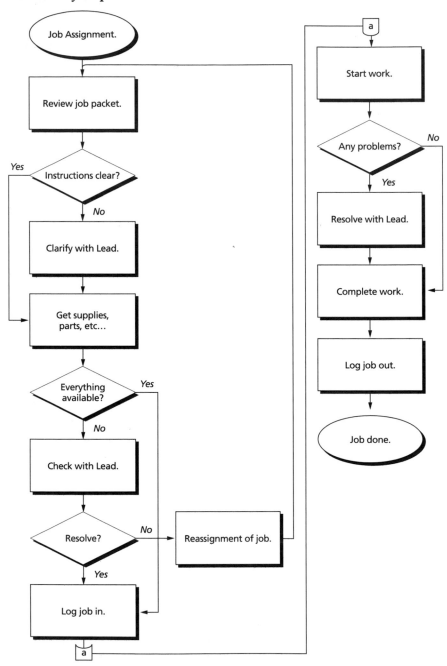

Figure 27. Types of flowcharts.
Source: From Rudolph C. Hirzel, "A Systems Approach to Auditing Systems Workshop" (presented at 28th Annual EED Conference, October 1998).

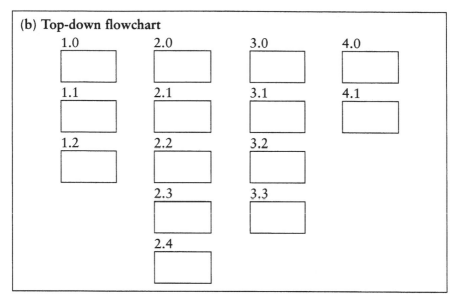

Figure 27. *Continued.*

Figures 27 (b)-(d) *Source:* Entner, Dan, "Basic Tools for Process Improvement." Delaware Community College. Used with permission.

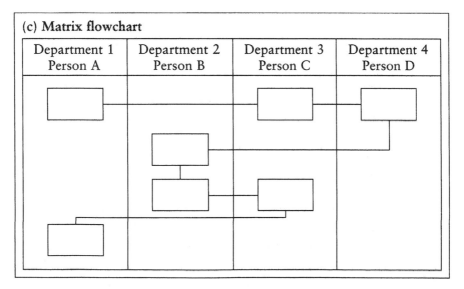

Figure 27. *Continued.*

(d) Flow process worksheet

Steps in process	OPER	TRAN	NIP	DEL	STOR
1					
2					
3					
4					
5					
6					
7					
8					

Figure 27 *Continued.*

4. PATTERN AND TREND ANALYSIS

"Pattern analysis involves the collection of data in a way that readily reveals any kind of clustering that may occur. This technique is of major value in internal quality audits, since it is so effective in making use of data from repetitive audits. It can be both location- and time-sensitive. Pattern analysis is of limited value in external quality audits owing to the lack of repetition in such audits."[124]

While no one specific single tool exists to determine patterns and trends, the following tools, matrices and data systems can help make such determinations. Patterns and trends can indicate the severity of a problem and can be used to help determine whether a problem is a systemic issue.

Line graphs connect points, which represent pairs of numeric data, to show how one variable of the pair is a function of the other. As a matter of convention, independent variables are plotted on the horizontal axis, and dependent variables are plotted on the vertical axis. Line graphs are used to show changes in data over time. A line graph is shown in Figure 28.

Bar graphs also portray the relationship or comparison between pairs of variables, but one of the variables need not be numeric. Each bar in a bar

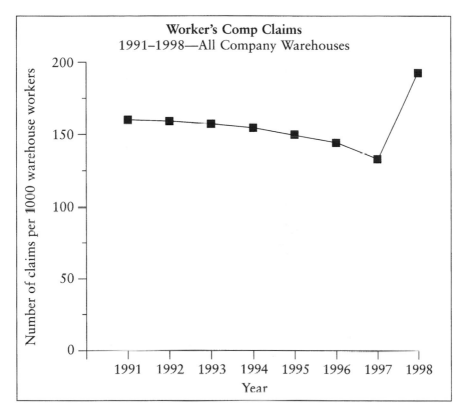

Figure 28. Line graph.

graph represents a separate or discrete value. Bar graphs can be used to identify differences between sets of data. A bar graph is shown in Figure 29.

Pie charts are used to depict proportions of data or information in order to understand how they make up the whole. The entire circle, or pie, represents 100 percent of the data. The circle is divided into slices, with each segment being proportional to the numeric quantity in each class or category. A pie chart is shown in Figure 30.

Matrices are two-dimensional tables showing the relationship between two sets of information. Matrices can be used to show the logical connecting points between performance criteria and implementing actions, or between required actions and personnel responsible for those actions. Used

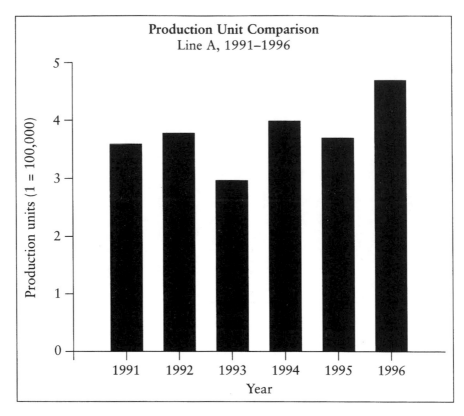

Figure 29. Bar graph.

Source: Jerry Nation, "Auditing Tools," p. 6.

this way, matrices help determine what actions and/or personnel have the greatest effect on an organization's mission. Matrices can be used by auditors as a way to focus auditing time and to organize auditing conduct. In Table 2, the matrix is used to help the auditor by identifying organizational responsibilities for the different audit areas. This particular matrix is used to maximize use of time during the site visit. Table 3, a much broader matrix, allows the auditor to do the long-range planning necessary for ensuring proper application of the audit program. In this example, the various audited areas on the Y axis are applied against the different organizations to be audited.

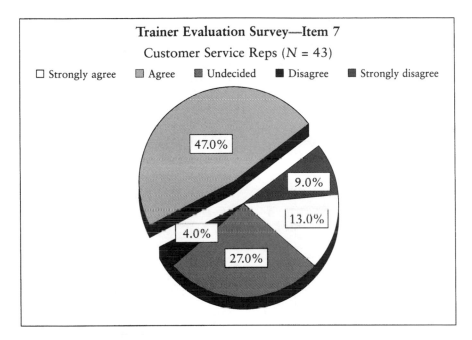

Figure 30. Pie chart.

Source: Jerry Nation, "Auditing Tools," p. 6.

Table 2.   Area of responsibilities matrix.

	Program development	Deficiency tracking	Training	Work control	Documents and records retention	Assessment
Director		X				X
Ops office			X	X	X	
Ops support	X	X	X			
Tech support		X	X	X		X
Admin.			X		X	

Source: Rudolph C. Hirzel, "Audits Making a Difference" (presented at the ASQC Fifth Annual Quality Audit Conference, 22–23 February 1996, Kansas City, Missouri).

Table 3.   Audit planning matrix.

	Administration	Chemistry	Biology	Materials	Building services	Engineering
Industrial hygiene		A		A	A	A
Radiation protection	B		B	B		
Fire protection			C	C	C	C
Industrial safety	A	A			A	
Environmental	C	C	C			C
Personnel training	B	A		B		C
Conduct of ops			C	C	C	
Quality assurance		A	C		A	C

A = First assessment   B = Second assessment   C = Third assessment

Source: Rudolph C. Hirzel, "Audits Making a Difference" (presented at the ASQC Fifth Annual Quality Audit Conference, 22–23 February 1996, Kansas City, Missouri).

Data systems exist in a wide range of forms and formats. They may include weekly and monthly reports of laboratory or organizational performance used to alert the auditing organization of potential audit areas or computerized databases that link performance to specific performance objectives or track actions to resolve programmatic weaknesses. In any case, data systems are an important tool that provides the auditor with the data needed to focus on audit activities. In Table 4, information on lost-time injuries is displayed in tabular form; the same information is displayed as a graph in Figure 31. This information can be used to focus the assessment on either the location of the injuries or the work procedures involved to identify weaknesses in the accident prevention program.

5. ROOT CAUSE ANALYSIS

Root cause analysis refers to the process of identifying the root cause for the occurrence of an unwanted effect, consequence, condition, or problem. The root cause is the most basic reason for the effect, which if eliminated or corrected would have prevented the effect from existing or occurring. Root cause has three primary characteristics:

Table 4. Lost-time accident monthly summary.

Date	Type	Area	Work procedure	Work crew	Days lost
5/3	Sprain	Bldg 12	CAP-101	Mech	4
5/5	Sprain	Bldg 5	MAP-2-12	Elec	5
5/12	Burn	Area 8	PMP-1-4	Mech	2
5/15	Abrasion	Area 10	PMP-3-7	Grnds	3
5/23	Burn	Bldg 12	CAP-103	Elec	1
5/25	Sprain	Admin bldg	N/A	N/A	1
5/29	Cut	Bldg 5	MAP-2-17	Elec	1

Source: Rudolph C. Hirzel, "Audits Making a Difference" (presented at the ASQC Fifth
Annual Quality Audit Conference, 22–23 February 1996, Kansas City, Missouri).

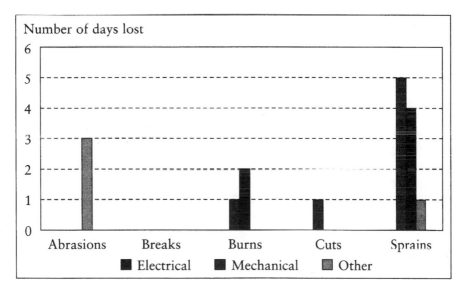

Figure 31. Lost work this month.
Source: Rudolph C. Hirzel, "Audits Making a Difference" (presented at the ASQC Fifth
Annual Quality Audit Conference, 22–23 February 1996, Kansas City, Missouri).

- It causes the effect—either directly or through a sequence of
  intermediate causes and effects.
- It is controllable—intervention would change that cause.
- Its elimination will result in the elimination or reduction of the effect.

Many methods are available for analyzing data to ultimately determine the root cause. Less-structured techniques include flowcharts, process control charts, trend analysis, Pareto diagrams, nominal group techniques, matrices, intuition based on observation, and brainstorming. More formal root cause analysis techniques include barrier analysis, change analysis, event and causal factors analysis, tree diagrams, and cause-and-effect diagrams. The method of root cause analysis is a relatively unintegrated collection of heuristics (simple methods or advice easy to use), each applicable in certain situations.[125]

6. CAUSE AND EFFECT DIAGRAMS

The *cause-and-effect diagram* (C-E diagram) is a visual method for analyzing causal factors for a given effect in order to determine their relationship. It is one of the most widely used quality tools and is also called an *Ishikawa diagram* after its inventor, or a *fishbone diagram* because of its shape.

Basic characteristics of the C-E diagram include the following:

- It represents the factors that might contribute to an observed condition or effect.

- It clearly shows interrelationships among possible causal factors.

- The interrelationships shown are usually based on known data.

C-E diagrams are an effective way to generate and organize the causes for observed events or conditions, since they help display causal information in a structured way.

C-E diagrams consist of a description of the effect written in the head of the fish and the causes of the effect identified in the major branches of the body. These main branches typically include four or more of the following six influences, but may be tailored specifically as needed:

1. People (worker)

2. Equipment (machine)

3. Method

4. Material

5. Environmental

6. Measurement

Figure 32 is a C-E diagram used to identify all the program elements that should be in place to prevent design output errors.[136]

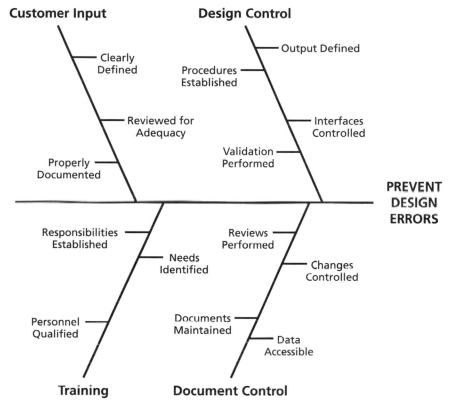

Figure 32. Cause-and-effect diagram.

Source: Rudolph C. Hirzel, "A Systems Approach to Auditing Systems" (presented at ASQ Quality Day, Motorola University, April 10, 1997).

7. PARETO CHARTS

Pareto charts, also called *Pareto diagrams* or *Pareto analysis,* are based on the Pareto principle, which suggests that most effects come from relatively few causes. As shown in Figure 33, a Pareto chart consists of a series of bars in descending order. The bars with the highest incidence, failures, costs, or other occurrences are on the left side. The miscellaneous category, an exception, always appears at the far right, regardless of size. Pareto charts display, in order of importance, the contribution of each item to the total effect and the relative rank of the items.

Pareto charts can be used to prioritize problems and to check performance of implemented solutions to problems. The Pareto chart can be a

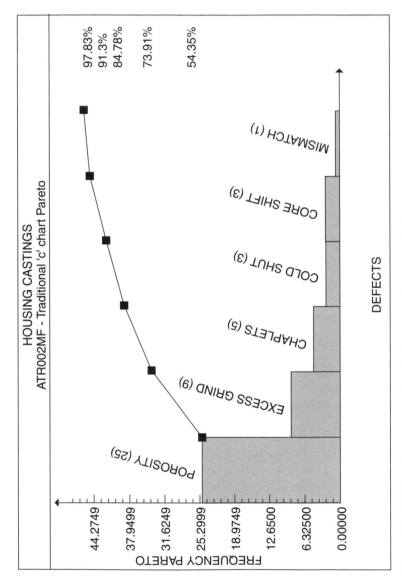

Figure 33. SQM software example of a frequency Pareto analysis.

Source: Courtesy of CIM Vision International.

powerful management tool for focusing effort on the problems and solutions that have the greatest payback.[126] Some organizations construct Pareto diagrams at year end and form corporate quality improvement teams in the areas determined to be in need of the greatest attention.

8. HISTOGRAMS

A *histogram* is a graphic summary of variation in a set of data. Histograms, such as the one shown in Figure 34, give a clearer and more complete picture of the data than would a table of numbers, since patterns may be difficult to discern in a table. Patterns of variation in data are called *distributions.* Often, identifiable patterns exist in the variation, and the correct interpretation of these patterns can help identify the cause of a problem.

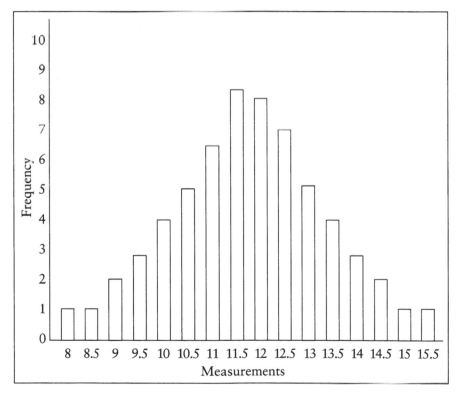

Figure 34. Histogram with normal distribution

Source: Gary K. Griffith, *Statistical Process Control Methods for Long and Short Runs,* 2d ed. (Milwaukee: ASQC Quality Press, 1995), p. 195. Used with permission.

A histogram is one of the simplest tools for organizing and summarizing data. It is used to show the number of times a given discrete piece of information occurs and is essentially a vertical bar chart of a frequency distribution. The histogram's simplicity of construction and interpretation makes it an effective tool in the quality auditor's elementary analysis of collected data.

Histograms should indicate sample size to communicate the degree of confidence in the conclusions. Once a histogram has been completed, it should be analyzed by identifying and classifying the pattern of variation, and developing a plausible and relevant explanation for the pattern. For a normal distribution, the following identifiable patterns, shown in Figure 35, are commonly observed in histograms:

a. *Bell-shaped:* A symmetrical shape with a peak in the middle of the range of data. This is the normal and natural distribution of data. Deviations from the bell shape might indicate the presence of complicating factors or outside influences. While deviations from a bell shape should be investigated, such deviations are not necessarily bad.

b. *Double-peaked (bimodal):* A distinct valley in the middle of the range of the data with peaks on either side. Usually a combination of two bell-shaped distributions, this pattern indicates that two distinct processes are causing this distribution.

c. *Plateau:* A flat top with no distinct peak and slight tails on either side. This pattern is likely to be the result of many different bell-shaped distributions with centers spread evenly throughout the range of data.

d. *Comb:* High and low values alternating in a regular fashion. This pattern typically indicates measurement error, errors in the way data were grouped to construct the histogram, or a systematic bias in the way data were rounded off. A less likely alternative is that this is a type of plateau distribution.

e. *Skewed:* An asymmetrical shape in which the peak is off-center in the range of data and the distribution tails off sharply on one side and gently on the other. If the long tail extends rightward, toward increasing values, the distribution is positively skewed; a negatively skewed distribution exists when the long tail extends leftward, toward decreasing values. The skewed pattern typically occurs when a practical limit, or a specification limit, exists on one side and is relatively close to the nominal value. In this case, there are not as many values available on the one side as on the other.

f. *Truncated:* An asymmetrical shape in which the peak is at or near the edge of the range of the data, and the distribution ends very abruptly

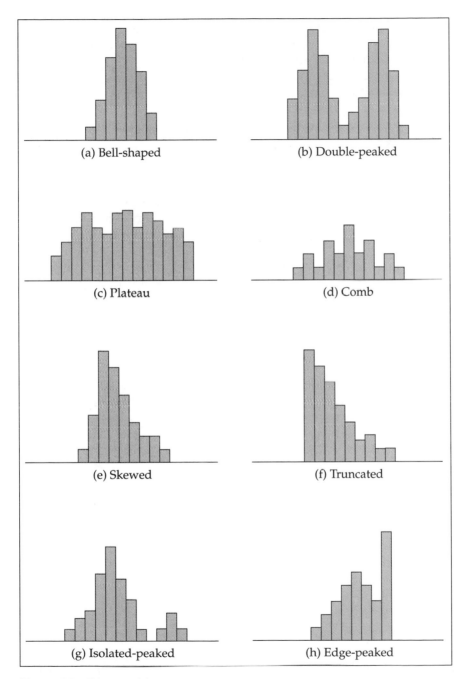

Figure 35. Common histogram patterns.

Source: Juran Institute, "The Tools of Quality Part IV: Histograms," ASQC *Quality Progress* (September 1990), p. 76. Adapted from the Juran Institute's publication, *Quality Improvement Tools.*™

on one side and tails off gently on the other. Truncated distributions are often smooth, bell-shaped distributions with a part of the distribution removed, or truncated, by some external force.

g. *Isolated-peaked:* A small, separate group of data in addition to the larger distribution. Similar to the double-peaked distribution; however, the short bell shape indicates something that doesn't happen very often.

h. *Edge-peaked:* A large peak is appended to an otherwise smooth distribution. Similar to the comb distribution in that an error was probably made in the data. All readings past a certain point may have been grouped into one value.[127]

No rules exist to explain pattern variation in every situation. The three most important characteristics are centering (central tendency), width (spread, variation, scatter, dispersion), and shape (pattern). If no discernible pattern appears to exist, the distribution may not be normal, and the data may actually be distributed according to some other distribution, such as exponential, gamma, or uniform. Analysis of distributions of these types is beyond the scope of this text, and further information should be sought from specialized statistics texts.

9. DESCRIPTIVE STATISTICS

"Descriptive statistics furnish a simple method of extracting information from what often seems at first glance to be a mass of random numbers. These characteristics of the data may relate to:

1. Typical, or central, value (mean, median, mode)
2. A measure of how much variability is present (variance, standard deviation)
3. A measure of frequency (percentiles)"[128]

Statistics is concerned with scientific methods for collecting, organizing, summarizing, presenting, and analyzing data, as well as drawing valid conclusions and making reasonable decisions on the basis of such analysis. In a narrower sense, the term *statistics* is used to denote the data themselves or numbers derived from the data, such as averages.

An auditor must look at how an auditee defines the process and necessary controls, and must establish some type of measurement system to ensure that the measurements or the process were properly defined. The auditor looks at the results of what other people have done, and if they use statistical tools, he or/she must be knowledgable enough to decide whether the information they are gathering from the data is valid. The phase of statistics that seeks only to describe and analyze a given group (sample) without drawing any conclusions or inferences about a larger group (population) is referred to as *deductive* or *descriptive statistics.* Measures of central tendency and dispersion are the two most fundamental concepts in statistical analysis.

Measures of Central Tendency

"Most frequency distributions exhibit a 'central tendency' (a shape such that the bulk of the observations pile up in the area between the two extremes)."[129] Central tendency is one of the most fundamental concepts in all statistical analysis. There are three principal measures of central tendency: mean, median, and mode.

Arithmetic Mean. The *arithmetic mean,* or *mean value,* is the sum total of all data values divided by the number of data values. It is the average of the total of the sample values. Mean is the most commonly used measure of central tendency and is the only such measure that includes every value in the data set. The arithmetic mean is used for symmetrical or near symmetrical distributions, or for distributions that lack a single clearly dominant peak.

Median. The *median* is the middle value (midpoint) of a data set arranged in numerical order, either in ascending or descending order. The median is used for reducing the effects of extreme values, or for data that can be ranked but are not economically measurable, such as shades of colors, odors, or appearances.

Mode. The *mode* is the value or number that occurs most frequently in a data set. If all the values are different, no mode exists. If two values have the most and same frequency of occurrence, then the data set or distribution has two modes and is referred to as bimodal. The mode is used for severely skewed distributions, for describing an irregular situation when two peaks are found, or for eliminating the observed effects of extreme values.

Measures of Dispersion

Dispersion is the variation in the spread of data about the mean. Dispersion is also referred to as variation, spread, and scatter. A measure of dispersion is the second of the two most fundamental measures of all statistical analyses. The dispersion within a central tendency is normally measured by one or more of several measuring principles.

Data are always scattered around the zone of central tendency, and the extent of this scatter is called dispersion or variation. There are several measures of dispersion: range, standard deviation, and coefficient of variation.

Range. The *range* is the simplest measure of dispersion. It is the difference between the maximum and minimum values in an observed data set. Since it is based on only two values from a data set, the measurement of range is most useful when the number of observations or values is small (10 or fewer).

Standard Deviation. *Standard deviation,* the most important measure of variation, measures the extent of dispersion around the zone of central tendency. For samples from a normal distribution, it is defined as the resulting value of the square root of the sum of the squares of the observed values, minus the arithmetic mean (numerator) divided by the total number of observations minus one (denominator).

Coefficient of Variation. *Coefficient of variation* is the final measure of dispersion. It is the standard deviation divided by the mean. Variance is the guaranteed existence of a difference between any two items or observations. The concept of variation states that no two observed items will ever be identical.

10. CONTROL CHART INTERPRETATIONS

Many companies use statistical process control (SPC) techniques as part of a continuing quality improvement effort. Quality auditors should be familiar with statistical techniques so that they can evaluate whether they are being properly applied by the company being audited.[130] Control charts, also called process control charts or run charts, are tools used in SPC.

Statistical process control recognizes that some random variation always exists in a process and that the goal is to control distribution rather than individual dimensions. Operators and quality control technicians use SPC to determine when to adjust a process and when to leave it alone. The ability to operate to a tight tolerance without producing defects can be a major business advantage. Control charts can tell an organization when a process is good enough so that resources can be directed to more pressing needs.[131]

A control chart, such as the one shown in Figure 36, is used to distinguish variations in a process over time. Variations can be attributed to either special or common causes. Common cause variations repeat randomly within predictable limits and can include chance causes, random

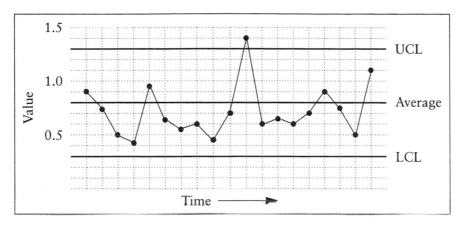

Figure 36. Control chart.

Source: Nancy R. Tague, *The Quality Toolbox* (Milwaukee: ASQC Quality Press, 1995), p. 86. Used with permssion.

causes, system causes, and inherent causes. Special cause variations indicate that some factors affecting the process need to be identified, investigated, and brought under control. Such causes include assignable causes, local causes, and specific causes. Control charts use operating data to establish limits within which future observations are expected to remain if the process remains unaffected by special causes.

> "Control charts can monitor the aim and variability, and thereby continually check the stability of a process. This check of stability in turn ensures that the statistical distribution of the product characteristic is consistent with quality requirements."[132]

> "Control charts are commonly used to:
> 1. Attain a state of statistical control
> 2. Monitor a process
> 3. Determine process capability"[133]

The type of control chart to be used in a specific situation depends on the type of data being measured or counted.

Variable data, also called *continuous data* or *measurement data,* are collected from measurements of the items being evaluated. For example, the measurement of physical characteristics such as time, length, weight, pressure, or volume through inspection, testing, or measuring equipment constitutes variable data collection. Variable data can be measured and plotted on a continuous scale and are often expressed as fractions or decimals.

The $\bar{X}$ (average) chart and the R (range) chart are the most common types of control charts for variable data. The $\bar{X}$ control chart illustrates the average measurement of samples taken over time. The R control chart illustrates the range of the measurements of the samples taken. For these charts to be accurate, it is critical that individual items comprising the sample are pulled from the same basic production process. That is, the samples should be drawn around the same time, from the same machine, from the same raw material source, and so on.[134] These charts are often used in conjunction with one another to record jointly the mean and range of samples taken from the process at fairly regular intervals. Figure 37 shows an $\bar{X}$–R chart .

Attribute data, also referred to as discrete data or counted data, provide information on number and frequency of occurrence. By counting and plotting discrete events—the number of defects or percentage of failures, for example—in integer values (1, 2, 3), an auditor is able to look at previously defined criteria and rate the product or system as pass/fail, acceptable/unacceptable, or go/no-go. Several basic types of control charts can be used for charting attribute data. Attribute data can be either a fraction nonconforming or number of defects or nonconformities observed in the sample. To chart fraction of units defective, the p chart is used. The units are classified into one of two states; go/no go, acceptable/unacceptable, conforming/nonconforming, yes/no, and so on. The sample size may be fixed or variable, which makes the technique very effective for statistically monitoring nontraditional processes such as percent of on-time delivery. Note, however, that if sample size is variable, control limits must be calculated for each sample taken.

The np chart uses the number of nonconforming units in a sample. This chart is sometimes easier for personnel who are not trained in SPC. It is easier to understand this chart when the sample size is constant, but it can be variable like the p chart.

The c chart plots the number of nonconformities per some unit of measure. For example, the total number of nonconformities could be counted at a final inspection of a product and charted on a c chart. The number of nonconformities may be made up of several distinct defects, which might then be analyzed for improvement of the process. For this chart, the sample size must be constant from or unit to unit.

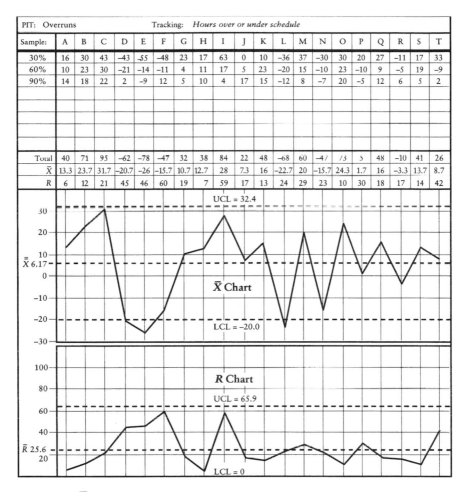

PIT: Overruns						Tracking: *Hours over or under schedule*													
Sample:	A	B	C	D	E	F	G	H	I	J	K	L	M	N	O	P	Q	R	S	T
30%	16	30	43	–43	–55	–48	23	17	63	0	10	–36	37	–30	30	20	27	–11	17	33
60%	10	23	30	–21	–14	–11	4	11	17	5	23	–20	15	–10	23	–10	9	–5	19	–9
90%	14	18	22	2	–9	12	5	10	4	17	15	–12	8	–7	20	–5	12	6	5	2
Total	40	71	95	–62	–78	–47	32	38	84	22	48	–68	60	–47	73	5	48	–10	41	26
$\bar{X}$	13.3	23.7	31.7	–20.7	–26	–15.7	10.7	12.7	28	7.3	16	–22.7	20	–15.7	24.3	1.7	16	–3.3	13.7	8.7
R	6	12	21	45	46	60	19	7	59	17	13	24	29	23	10	30	18	17	14	42

Figure 37. $\bar{X}$ and R chart example.

Source: Clive Shearer, *Practical Continuous Improvement for Professional Services* (Milwaukee: ASQC Quality Press, 1994) p. 241. Used with permisison.

The u chart is used for average number of nonconformities per some unit of measure. Sample size can be either variable or constant since it is charting an average. A classic example is the number of nonconformities in a square yard of fabric in the textile industry. Bolts of cloth may vary in size, but an average can be calculated. Figure 38 is an example of plotting attribute data using a u chart.

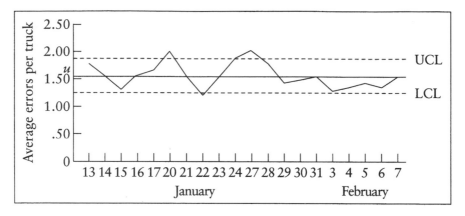

Figure 38. *u* chart for the average errors per truck for 20 days of production.

Source: John T. Burr, *SPC Tools for Everyone* (Milwaukee: ASQC Quality Press, 1993), p. 58. Used with permssion.

11. PROCESS CAPABILITY INTERPRETATION

"One of the theories most widely encountered is: 'The process can't hold the tolerances.' To test this theory, measurements from the process must be taken and analyzed to determine the amount of variability inherent in the process. This variability is then compared to the specification limits. These steps are performed in a process-capability study."[135]

Process capability provides a quantified prediction of the adequacy of a process; and it measures the capability of a process to produce products that meet specifications by measuring the inherent uniformity of the process. Generally, it is not feasible to determine process capability by direct measurement of a process under operating conditions, so capability is determined indirectly by measuring the uniformity of the product. Process capability can be used to measure process performance, monitor processes using control charts, evaluate process equipment, review tolerances based on common variation of a process, determine the effect of changes or adjustments to processes, and audit process performance.

Process capability can be determined when a predictable pattern of statistically stable behavior consisting of common causes of variation are compared to specification limits. Process capability indices numerically express the relation between the distribution and the specification limits. A process is *in a state of statistical control* when the plotted data points are within the calculated Upper Control Limit (UCL) and Lower Control

Limit (LCL) almost all the time (such as 99.73 percent) and the data do not display a particular form that would indicate an out-of-control condition (such as 7 successive data points below or above the center line of the control chart). A process is *capable* when the distribution of individual piece data is within or equal to the Upper Specification Limit (USL) and Lower Specification Limit (LSL). Histograms can be used to graphically show capability when upper and lower control limits and specification limits are added to the histogram data.

A process capability index expresses a numerical relationship between the process variability and the specification limits. The most common indices currently in use are C_p and C_{pk}. If the upper control limit and lower control limit are superimposed on the upper specification limit and lower specification limit, the C_p would equal 1. This assumes that the mean of the process is exactly centered with the specification limits. If the control limits fall outside the specification limits, the value of C_p would be less than 1. C_{pk} is a method of measuring process capability when the mean of the process is not centered with regard to the specification limits. A C_{pk} of 1 or greater means that the process is capable at a level of at least 99.73 percent conforming, which is the limit associated with an $\overline{X}$ and R chart. It is extremely important when using these capability indices that the process be in-control because the theory is based entirely on a normal distribution. If the distribution is not normal, the indices are meaningless.

> "A statistical control chart can be used to identify visible trends in the performance data measured during the audit of a quality system. It can show this information in terms of both the average error rate and the acceptable performance level."[136]

Appendix A
Audit Sampling

Chapter A
Overview

Sampling has always been a starting point for discussion among auditors. Some say that statistical sampling is the only way to perform an audit that means anything to management. Others contend that we don't need to look at a statistical sample to determine whether there is a problem. There are times when statistical sampling is a must; and there are times when judgmental sampling gives the results needed.

There are many ways of choosing the samples to be evaluated during an audit. This section explores the many ways and provides some guidance about their application.

NONSTATISTICAL SAMPLE SELECTION

Nonstatistical sampling seems to be the general rule in quality auditing. Perhaps this is because of the need to keep costs down; one way to do that is to keep the sample size small. Perhaps the system has reached near perfection, and the goal has shifted to fixing the minor or single-case problems that arise. Perhaps the auditor wants to bring these problems to management's attention, and the audit report is the only way to do this. For whatever reason, nonstatistical sampling is very popular. Nonstatistical sampling takes many forms.

Haphazard selection is where the auditor selects items with the goal to be as random as possible, yet be a representation of the total population. Here the goal is to gain insight into the population without using statistical techniques to quantify the results. The results are not statistically valid, and generalizations about the total population should be made with extreme caution.

Block selection (also called *cluster sampling*) is where consecutive items within a time frame, production run, dollar range, and so on are chosen for evaluation. For example, all purchase orders for the month of March, all purchase orders over $5000, or all XYZ product produced on swing shift from April 2 to April 9 may be reviewed. Many blocks fitting the selection category need to be examined to gain a pseudo-representative sample of the total population. Block selection is best when looking for a root cause, a possible problem with a particular machine, or a possible problem with a particular process. Statistically valid comments can be made about the blocks evaluated, but not about the total population.

Judgmental selection is just that—auditors use their knowledge or experience to select samples. Normally samples are selected based on risk to the company and potential for loss of production or data. Here the goal is to determine if the high-risk areas are being adequately controlled. One problem with judgmental sampling comes about when the auditor specifically selects samples with known problems, thus biasing the sample toward the negative. This makes the sample completely nonrepresentative of the total population. One reason for sampling this way is when a process is being done so well that the auditors are working on relatively minor or single-case problems. However, if this is the case, there may be no need for the auditor at all.

STATISTICAL SAMPLE SELECTION

For a sampling approach to be considered "statistical," the method must have random selection of items to be evaluated and use probability theory to quantitatively evaluate the results. Statistically valid sampling is necessary to quantify problems resulting from an administrative process or production line. Statistically valid sampling allows the auditor to state in the audit report that "we are 95 percent confident that the actual population deviation rate lies between 1.2 percent and 5 percent. Since this is less than the tolerable deviation rate of 6 percent, the control procedure appears to be functioning as prescribed." With a slightly different sampling technique, the auditor would be able to state, "We are 95 percent confident that the true population deviation rate is less than 4.8 percent, which is less than the tolerable deviation rate of 6 percent." These numbers and confidence levels have more meaning to upper management than saying that "we think there is a problem in document control."

There are two widely used methods of statistical sampling: simple random sampling and systematic sampling. *Simple random sampling* ensures that each item in the population has an equal chance of being selected. Random number tables and computer programs can help make the sample selections. *Systematic sampling* also ensures that each item in the population has an equal chance of being selected. The difference here is that after the sample size is determined, it is divided into the total population size to determine the sampling interval (for example, every third item). The starting point is determined using a random number table. Naturally, several computer programs are available to help determine the sample size, the sampling interval, the starting point, and the actual samples to be evaluated.

SUMMARY

Both nonstatistical and statistical sampling have their places in quality auditing. The job of the quality auditor is to know when each method is best for determining the information needed.

Chapter B

Nonstatistical Audit Sampling

The last section talked about nonstatistical types of sampling for audits: haphazard, block, and judgmental. This section examines these in more detail to try to understand the pros and cons of using each. The goal is to provide management with supportable information about the company, with the expectation that management will take action based on the results presented.

Haphazard sampling is used by auditors to try to gather information from a representative sample of a population. Items are selected without intentional bias and with the goal of representing the population as a whole. The auditor might ask to see the deficiency reports on the coordinator's desk. The deficiency reports on the coordinator's desk when the auditor comes in might be rationalized as being random and as representing the population as a whole. The auditor might ask for 10 deficiency reports, two from each line, and will ask to be the one who picks them. This might be rationalized as removing the bias from having the coordinator select the sample.

The pro side of haphazard sampling is that it is easy to select the sample, so the audit can be completed more quickly. There is less preparation time, making it possible to do more audits.

The con side of haphazard sampling could be stronger. If the coordinator is reviewing the deficiency reports for a specific department at the time the auditor walks in, the results of the audit will show that this department has a disproportionate number of deficiencies when compared to the other departments in the sample. The auditor might pick deficiency reports that catch his/her eye for some unknown reason, thus introducing an unknown bias. Haphazard sampling is the easy approach to sampling. The results do not reflect all departments, lines, items, people, problems, or a myriad of other considerations. The results are not statistically valid, and generalizations about the total population should be made with extreme caution. The results of haphazard sampling are difficult to defend objectively. Of all the nonstatistical audit sampling methods, haphazard is arguably the worst.

Block sampling or cluster sampling can be used by auditors to gain a pretty good picture of the population, if the blocks are chosen in a statistical manner. This requires that a lot of blocks be chosen before an accurate representation of the total population is obtained, and often more items are examined than if a statistical sample was selected in the beginning. Normally, auditors don't use block sampling during audits, but do use block sampling extensively after a problem has been identified. Auditors and others use block sampling when trying to determine when or how a previously identified problem began, ended, or both. For example, if a problem began in May, we might examine all items made or processed in May to try to determine when it began and whether it is still occurring. If we identified a problem with calibration of balances, we could examine every balance to determine when the problem began and whether it affected only those in one building or in one department. Some may recognize these activities as investigative actions taken subsequent to identification of a problem. Block sampling is also used in investigative actions.

The pro side of block sampling is that it allows statistically valid judgments about the block examined. With a sufficiently large number of blocks selected randomly using the same selection criteria, we can make statistically valid judgments about the total population. Single blocks allow us to narrow down the root cause of a previously identified problem by focused investigation in the area of concern. Single blocks also allow us to recognize a possible problem with a single machine or a specific process.

The con side of block sampling is that it requires sampling a large number of items before judgments about the total population can be made—larger even than statistically selected samples. Auditors often want more than just information on a particular block of time, products, or locations. Auditors want to be able to provide management with supportable statements about the entire population. For this reason, block sampling is normally not used during the audit to identify problems.

Judgmental sampling can be used by auditors to gain a pretty good picture of what is happening, although the results are not statistically valid. In the first approach, the auditor selects samples based on his/her best judgment of what is believed to give a representative picture of the population. These samples are chosen based on the auditor's past experience. Often these samples are based on those that expose the company to the greatest risk, such as high dollar orders, special orders, or critical application orders. In judgmental sampling, the auditor may look back over time and see that, historically, problems have existed in department A, activity C. Knowing this, the auditor examines that area in an audit. In judgmental sampling, the auditor may also decide to look at all orders over $2 million, or all orders destined for installation in the space shuttle. If a problem is found, the auditor examines additional samples to determine the extent of the immediate problem.

In the second approach, the quality program has reached maturity, and very few problems are identified in a general audit using random sample techniques. The company may then decide to audit all areas in which problems were identified with the intention of determining whether the activity can be improved beyond its current level. The nuclear industry and several other industries have reached this point and have begun to rely on judgmental sampling to identify areas for improvement.

The pro side of judgmental sampling is extensive. The auditor focuses on areas where previous problems have been found and corrected. High-risk areas and activities receive the most attention. These are all areas where management historically has focused attention. By doing judgmental sampling, the auditor will be providing information on areas known to be of interest to management. Judgmental sampling allows companies to focus their efforts on specific improvements rather than general assessment. It allows the auditor to more effectively use his/her time during the audit. And, finally, selection of the audit sample is relatively simple, which leaves more time to prepare for and perform the audit.

The con side of judgmental sampling is that the results are not statistically valid or objectively defensible. Judgmental sampling is open to abuse through retaliation (selecting a group for detail audit because of some previous action). Judgmental sampling causes auditors to continue to focus on areas where problems were found previously. It is a fact that an auditor focusing on an area will probably find problems that get recorded and reported. An unwritten law of auditing is that "if we look for it, we will find it." If we continue to focus only on areas where problems are found, logic would take us to the extreme where we always audit the same thing over and over. Thus, certain areas would be seen as pristine, while others would be seen as consistently incompetent. Statistical sampling is needed to provide a baseline from which further auditing using judgmental sampling may proceed.

Nonstatistical sampling has its place in auditing and in the investigation of identified problems. Haphazard sampling should be avoided if at all possible. Block sampling is effective in pinpointing problems, and statistically valid conclusions can be made about the block evaluated, but conclusions about the total population require more work. Judgmental sampling is effective in focusing the auditor's efforts and in identifying areas of improvement in a relatively mature quality program. The job of the quality auditor is to know when each method is best for determining the information needed.

Chapter C

Statistical Audit Sampling for Attributes

It's not difficult to plug numbers into a formula and calculate the results. Management likes to work with numbers that have meaning and that put boundaries around a question or an error rate. This is where statistical sampling comes in. With statistical sampling, we can state in our audit reports that "we have 95 percent confidence that the purchase orders are being correctly processed." Sample size depends on confidence level and what we want to determine.

Naturally, the larger the sample size, the more accurate the estimate. For small populations, we correct the sample size for the population. Auditing by statistical sampling is best suited for single-attribute auditing. However, once the item to be audited has been selected, many attributes can be checked during the audit. A purchase order has many attributes that can be checked simultaneously. In this way, one calculation for sample size can be used to report on many attributes.

Sample size is calculated using two formulas. The first formula is the "first estimate of the sample size" based on the binomial distribution. This formula is:

$$n_{(e)} = \frac{Z^2(p)(1-p)}{A^2}$$

where:

$n_{(e)}$ = first estimate of sample size

Z = standard deviation factor (1.96 for 95 percent confidence)

p = estimated error rate

A = desired precision

The second formula uses the first estimate of sample size and adjusts it to fit the population:

$$n_{(f)} = \frac{n_{(e)}}{1 + n_{(e)} / N}$$

where:

$n_{(f)}$ = final sample size

$n_{(e)}$ = first estimate of sample size

N = population

To use these formulas; we plug in the numbers we know or expect, and determine the sample size. Consider a known population (N) of 500. We decide that the desired precision (A) is 2 percent, the desired confidence level (Z) is 95 percent, and the estimated error rate (p) is not to exceed 5 percent. Plugging the numbers into the first equation gives:

$$n_{(e)} = \frac{1.96^2 x\ .05x\ (1-.05)}{.02^2}$$

This works out to:

$$n_{(e)} = 456$$

This obviously won't work with a total population of 500, so we need to adjust the sample size using the second equation. With $n_{(e)}$ = 456 and the population (N) of 500, the formula becomes:

$$n_{(f)} = \frac{456}{1 + 456/500}$$

This works out to:

$$n_{(f)} = 238$$

Using this sample size and finding an error rate of 5 percent, we will be able to report to management that we have 95 percent confidence that the items/processes in the population of 500 contains 475 error-free items, plus or minus 2 percent of 500 (10 items or processes).

This is a large sample size for quality auditing, but it does give the precision necessary to report good numbers to management. A little work with the formulas will show that as the population gets larger, the relative sample size gets smaller. Thus, the formulas work best with larger populations. Large populations can be found in purchasing and production and lead to better application of statistical sampling. Other ways to reduce the sample size is to reduce the precision (larger *A*) or the confidence (larger *p* and smaller *Z*).

Performing the calculations using a population *(N)* of 2000, the desired precision *(A)* is 4 percent, the desired confidence level *(Z)* is 90 percent, and the estimated error rate *(p)* is not to exceed 5 percent. Plugging the numbers into the first equation gives:

$$n_{(e)} = \frac{1.65^2 x \ .1x(1-.1)}{.04^2}$$

This works out to:

$$n_{(e)} = 153$$

Although this is fairly reasonable, we will still use the formula to correct for population. This gives:

$$n_{(f)} = \frac{153}{1 + 153/2000}$$

This works out to:

$$n_{(f)} = 142$$

As you can see from the example, large populations make the first formula accurate for determining sample size. Also note that with less precision and confidence, the sample size is reduced to a more workable number.

Using this sample size and finding an error rate of 5 percent, we will be able to report to management that we have 90 percent confidence that the items/processes in the population of 2000 contains 1800 error-free items, plus or minus 4 percent of 2000 (80 items or processes).

One caution: if, after we perform our evaluation, we find the actual error rate (p) is slightly greater than our first estimate, we must recalculate using the formulas and the new error rate to determine how many more items we would need to examine to obtain an estimate with the required confidence level and precision. If the error rate we measure is much greater than our original estimate, then it should be sufficient to indicate a real problem that needs correcting.

Chapter D
Sampling with Standards

This section examines three sampling procedures for application to quality auditing:

ANSI/ASQC Z1.4-1993 *Sampling Procedures and Tables for Inspection by Attributes*

ANSI/ASQC Z1.9-1993 *Sampling Procedures and Tables for Inspection by Variables for Percent Nonconforming*

ASQC Q3-1988 *Sampling Procedures and Tables for Inspection of Isolated Lots by Attributes*

APPLICATION

We are interested in determining conformance with procedures, instructions, and other quality program documentation. Audits for adequacy require a point-by-point comparison of the lower tier document, such as a procedure, with the upper-tier document, such as a standard. This is a 100 percent check. Thus, statistical sampling does not apply. Effectiveness and performance audits require the judgment skills of the auditor as applied to the results of the quality program. Again statistical sampling does not apply.

Conformance is determining whether an activity or document is satisfactory or not satisfactory. This, then, is attribute sampling, rather than variable sampling. In addition, we are dealing with whole numbers (1, 2, 3), so we need to deal with "discrete probability distributions." The most common of these are hypergeometric, binomial, and Poisson. For general discussion, we need to assume a large population, N. This condition is met if N is greater than or equal to $10n$, where n is the sample size. This condition is not required when the standards are used, as the sample size is corrected for small population (lot size). But what are the characteristics of the lot that we will examine during the audit?

THE MOVING LOT

Most audits are a snapshot covering a specific time period. Our snapshot is of a lot from a continuous production line. As part of the scope of the audit, we might have to examine the Deficiency Reports (DRs) for the last quarter. Obviously there were DRs written before our time period, and there will be DRs written after we are gone. This might look like this:

The population (lot size) consists of the number of DRs written during the selected time period. During a subsequent audit, the lot might be completely separate from the lot selected during this audit, or it might overlap the lot.

Thus, the lot moves for each audit performed, depending on the goals set for the audit. The process being examined can be said to have an acceptable quality level (AQL) set by the people doing the work. This is the work standard they are attempting to achieve. Now that we understand the nature of our lot, we are ready to use the standards.

ANSI/ASQC Z1.9-1993 APPLICABILITY

ANSI/ASQC Z1.9-1993 has been eliminated from consideration because it is variable sampling, and auditors need to concern themselves with attribute sampling. This leaves ANSI/ASQC Z1.4-1993 and ASQC Q3-1998 for possible use by auditors. We will consider them in turn.

ANSI/ASQC Z1.4-1993 APPLICABILITY AND USE

ANSI/ASQC Z1.4-1993 is the revised and updated version of the old MIL-STD-105. This standard assumes that isolated lots are drawn from a process and sampled separately. The process Acceptance Quality Level (AQL) is a factor in determining the sample size in this case. In auditing, we want to know the maximum error rate, which translates into a Limiting Quality Level (LQL) for the standards. Tables VI-A and VII-A of ANSI/ASQC Z1.4-1993 provide LQLs as a percent nonconforming with a probability of acceptance P_a = 10 percent and 5 percent respectively. P_a = 10 percent means that there is only a 10 percent chance that we will accept a lot with a percent nonconforming greater than our specified LQL.

As an example, let's assume that we want a 10 percent LQL for our Tot with P_a = 10 percent or less, and an AQL of 1.5 percent for a series of lots. Enter the ANSI/ASQC Z1.4-1993 standard at Table VI-A and select an LQ of 10 percent for the lot with P_a = 10 percent or less and AQL of 1.5 percent. Table VI-A shows a sample size n of 50, code letter H. This sends us to Table X-H-2 where we learn that for an AQL of 1.5 percent and a single sample size of 50, we can accept the lot with two problems noted but must reject the lot if three problems are noted. The sample size of 50 implies that our population is approximately 500 (N is greater than or equal to $10n$). If the population is very much less than 500, we need to use the calculations presented in chapter C.

Continuing with the example, we need to choose a random sample of 50 items. Computer random number generator programs or random number tables provide the selection method for our sample. When completed, assuming the results are acceptable, we will be able to say that there is a 90 percent probability that the audited attribute has a percent defective less than 10 percent. When working to very exact requirements, such as low AQL and low LQ, we need to use the operating characteristic curves to determine the discrimination desired. The operating characteristic curves are imprecise when working in this area. This brings up the second standard applicable to auditing, ASQC Q3-1998.

ASQC Q3-1998 APPLICABILITY AND USE

ASQC Q3-1998 is designed for isolated lots and uses the hypergeometric probability function. This applies even more directly to audits than ANSI/ASQC Z1.4-1993. ASQC Q3-1998 also uses the customer's specified limiting quality (LQ) as the basis for sample sizes. The goal is to have a very low probability of accepting (P_a) a lot that has a percent nonconforming equal to or worse than the LQ. ASQC Q3-1998 ties back to ANSI/ASQC Z1.4-1993 for AQLs to provide a commonality or cross-reference.

Because the process is a continuous process from which we will be pulling isolated lots, we will be working with Table B of the ASQC

Q3-1998 standard. Yes, there are cases when we will work with truly isolated lots, in which case Table A would be used, but this is the exception and the easier to use.

ASQC Q3-1998 is fairly simple to understand. Let's assume that from the DR log, we counted 239 DRs written during the period being audited. Our client isn't overly concerned with detailed compliance with the procedures, but does want each deficiency corrected. For compliance, we select an LQ of 12.5 percent, which is fairly loose. Table B8 shows our sample size to be 32. For deficiency correction, we select an LQ of 2 percent, which is fairly tight. Table B4 shows our sample size to be 200. Please note that this is almost a 100 percent sample because our population is low. From Table C3, we find that in both cases we accept the lot if we find one or zero problems in our sample.

We approach this by selecting a random sample of 200 for auditing deficiency correction. Next, we divide 200 by the 32 samples needed for the compliance portion of the audit, to get a frequency of 6. Thus for the compliance portion, we will use every sixth item from our deficiency correction sample as one of our compliance samples, beginning with item 4 (chosen because it is less than 6). The sequence looks like this:

Deficiency correction 1 2 3 4 5 6 7 8 9 10 . . . 190 191 192 193 194 195 196 197 198 199 200
Compliance   1   2   32   33

Note that because the division does not yield an even number, we end up with 33 total samples for compliance, rather than the 32 from the table. Use the extra sample as part of the audit.

We then perform the audit, and if one or fewer problems is noted for each sample (200 and 32), we can be 90 percent confident that the DRs meet the LQ specified for the attribute being checked (12.5 percent for compliance and 2 percent for deficiency correction).

SUMMARY

Although not specifically stated as being applicable to quality audits, two of the most familiar sampling plans, ANSI/ASQC Z1.4-1993 and ASQC Q3-1998, are readily applied to and used during quality audits. These allow the quality auditor to speak with authority to management about the results of the audit. There is a lot to learn about applying the standards to quality audits, but many people who have previously applied the standards to product acceptance will quickly be able to apply the standards to their auditing. Give these a try the next time you find yourself auditing a large population. You may be glad you did.

Chapter E
Proportional "Stratified" Sampling

Proportional "stratified" sampling can be used to gain an understanding of each stratum within a population, but cannot be used to make statistical inferences for each stratum. The sample size is determined by any one of the statistical methods/standards. Then the sample size is divided and applied in proportion to the population of each stratum in the total population. If the sample is not statistically determined, the statistical validity is compromised, and no statistically valid conclusions can be drawn.

For example, the population is 1000 purchase orders over the past year. Eight hundred of these are for amounts of $500 or less; 150 are for amounts of $1000 or less, and 50 are for amounts over $1000. We choose a limiting quality (LQ) of 5 percent and use ASQC Q3-1998, Table B6, to learn that the sample size is 80.

To apportion the sample to the stratum, simply set up a proportion for each:

$$\text{Under } \$500: \quad \frac{800}{1000} = \frac{X_{<500}}{80}$$

Then we solve for $X_{<500}$:

$$X_{<500} = 64$$

Similar proportions give us:

$$X_{<1000} = 12$$

and:

$$X_{>1000} = 4$$

The samples are chosen from each stratum using the random sampling techniques. If the samples are not chosen using a random sampling technique, the results will not be statistically valid.

With this knowledge, we can accept the total population with one or zero deficiencies and reject the total population with two or more deficiencies. Although we cannot make statistical inferences on each stratum, we gain some information that we can use to further investigate the stratum. If all the deficiencies are found in a particular stratum, the auditor can revise the focus of the audit to further investigate that particular stratum. If all the deficiencies are found in a particular stratum, the auditee could justifiably focus corrective action on that stratum.

This method places emphasis on the population of the strata within a population. This may not be desirable to management. For example, management may want the auditor to focus on the high-cost items, which is where their greatest risk lies.

Proportional "Stratified" Sampling is deceptive in that the auditor and auditee could be misled into drawing conclusions about each stratum instead of the total population. The method, sample size, and results allow the auditor to draw conclusions about the total population only. The results can be used by the auditor to determine where to focus further investigation. The results can be used by the auditee as a guide for where to focus corrective actions.

Chapter F
Sampling Summary

This appendix has looked at various methods of sampling that are commonly used in the performance of quality audits. Table 8 summarizes the methods, their advantages and disadvantages, and their applicability.

Statistically, random sampling must ensure that each item in the population has an equal chance of being selected. A sampling scheme is developed for selection of the samples. This scheme can use a strictly random selection based on random number tables or computerized random number generators, or a systematic sampling scheme based on the number of samples selected and the total population.

Nonstatistical sampling, although very easy and quick to perform, has many disadvantages, which include potential bias in the sample, inability to make generalizations about the total population, and indefensibility as objective sampling.

Statistically valid auditing must have random selection of items to be evaluated and use probability theory to quantitatively evaluate the results. Two methods can be applied to quality auditing to provide the ability to make statistically valid conclusions for use by management: *statistical sampling for attributes* and *sampling with standards*. These methods allow confidence levels and error estimation based on the results of the evaluation of the samples.

Auditors are encouraged to begin using statistically valid sampling when it adds value and improves the effectiveness of the audit report. When using statistical sampling techniques for the first time you may apply a single method during an audit to learn the various methods. This has the additional advantage of allowing you to educate management on

Table 8.   Sampling Methods Summary

Method	Description	Advantages	Disadvantages	Application
Statistically Random Sampling Methods				
Random Sampling	Use a random number table or generator and a sampling scheme	Ensures that each item in the population has an equal chance of being selected	Requires some time to develop scheme and select samples	Use when conclusions about a population are required
Systematic Sampling	Equally spaced samples based on the sample size	Ensures that each item in the population has an equal chance of being selected, random sample table not required	Requires some time to develop scheme and select samples	Use when conclusions about a population are required
Nonstatistical Sampling Methods				
Haphazard Selection	Auditor chooses sample using own selection method	Selection is easy, quick, and requires little planning	Cannot make generalizations about the total population	Use for system believed to have few errors, use when planning time is short
Block Selection (also called Cluster Sampling)	Auditor chooses all items within a specified time period, over a specified dollar amount, etc.	Selection is easy; can make statistically valid comments about the block evaluated	Cannot make generalizations about the total population	Use when searching for the root cause or isolating a possible problem

(continued)

Table 8.   *Continued.*

Method	Description	Advantages	Disadvantages	Application
Judgmental Selection	Auditor chooses samples based on past knowledge or experience; focus on known problem areas and areas of high risk	Selection is easy, quick, and requires little planning	Selection may take time, if past performance and experience are reviewed; possible bias in the sample; cannot make generalizations about the total population; not defensible as objective	Use for mature system believed to have few errors

Statistically Valid Sampling Methods

Method	Description	Advantages	Disadvantages	Application
Statistical Sampling for Attributes	Calculate sample size using formulas; use random or systematic sampling for selection	Can make generalizations about the total population	Requires some time to determine sample size and to develop scheme and select samples	Use when conclusions about a population are required
Sampling with Standards	Use ANSI/ASQC Z1.4 and ANSI/ASQC Q3; use random or systematic sampling for selection	Sample size easily determined; can make generalizations about the total population	Requires knowledge of the use of the standards; requires some time to develop scheme and select samples	Use when conclusions about a population are required
Proportional Stratified Sampling	Apportion a statistically valid sample among "strata" within a population	Ensures each "strata" is examined	Deceptive in that the auditor and auditee could be misled into drawing conclusions about each strata instead of about the total population	Use when there are clear "strata" within a total population and when the auditor is trying to narrow the focus of further investigation

statistical methods and the accurate results that can be obtained. Often managers have not had strong training in statistical methods (other than as applied to business applications and budget), so you will have to do some work to familiarize management with the value of statistical methods. After you and management are familiar with the methods, perform a complete audit using statistical methods and report the results to management. The company can only benefit from decisions based on the accurate information gathered through statistical quality auditing.

Appendix B
ASQ Certified Quality Auditors
Body of Knowledge
(Revised 8/97)

I. ETHICS, PROFESSIONAL CONDUCT, & LIABILITY ISSUES (5 questions)
- A. ASQ Code of Ethics
  - 1. Conflict of interest
  - 2. Confidentiality
- B. Professional Conduct and Responsibilities
  - 1. Auditor conduct
  - 2. Auditor responsibilities
  - 3. Discovery of illegal or unsafe conditions or activities
- C. Liability Issues
  - 1. Personal and corporate
  - 2. Audit record disclosure

II. AUDIT PREPARATION (32 questions)
- A. Audit Definition and Plan
  - 1. Identification of authority (internal and external)
  - 2. Determination of audit purpose
  - 3. Determination of audit type and scope
  - 4. Determination of resources required
  - 5. Team selection and identification of roles
  - 6. Requirements to audit against (e.g., standards, contracts, specifications, policy, quality award criteria)
- B. Audit Design
  - 1. Strategy (e.g., tracing, discovery)
  - 2. Data collection plan
  - 3. Sampling plan
  - 4. Logistics planning

    C. Document Review and Preparation
       1. Audit-related document review
       2. Auditee's performance history review
       3. Preparation of audit checklists, guidelines, log sheets
    D. Communication and Distribution of Audit Plan

III. AUDIT PERFORMANCE (32 questions)
    A. Audit Management
       1. Audit team management
       2. Communication of audit status to auditee
       3. Audit plan changes (e.g., schedule, priorities)
    B. Opening Meeting
       1. Presentation and review of the audit plan
       2. Confirmation of audit logistics
       3. Discussion of auditee concerns
    C. Data Collection
       1. Document/record examination
       2. Interviews
       3. Physical examination
       4. Observation of work activities
    D. Audit Working Papers
       1. Documentation of audit trail (e.g., checklists, supporting evidence)
       2. Record of observations
    E. Audit Analysis
       1. Corroboration and objectivity of evidence
       2. Data patterns and trends (e.g., repeat observations, systemic problems)
       3. Classification of observations
       4. Classification of nonconformances
       5. Conclusions
    F. Exit Meeting
       1. Presentation of audit results
       2. Discussion of follow-up actions
       3. Expectations of auditees, auditors, client

IV. AUDIT REPORTING (10 questions)
    A. Review and Finalize Audit Results
    B. Written Report Format and Content
       1. Audit details (e.g., purpose, team members)
       2. Compliance
       3. System effectiveness
       4. Conclusions to be reported
       5. Request for corrective actions

C. Issue Written Report
  1. Obtain approvals
  2. Distribute report
D. Audit Records Retention

V. CORRECTIVE ACTION FOLLOW-UP AND CLOSURE (12 questions)

A. Corrective Action Follow-up
  1. Criteria for acceptable corrective action plans
     (e.g., preventive, assigned responsibilities, timeline)
  2. Acceptability of proposed corrective action
  3. Negotiation of corrective action plans
  4. Methods for verifying corrective action
  5. Follow-up audit schedule, as required
  6. Verification of corrective action completion
  7. Effectiveness of corrective action
  8. Strategies when corrective action is not implemented
     or is not effective
B. Closure
  1. Criteria for closure
  2. Timeliness

VI. AUDIT PROGRAM MANAGEMENT (10 questions)

A. Administration
  1. Audit program objectives
  2. Identification and justification of resource requirements
  3. Management's relationship to the audit function
  4. Credibility of audit function
  5. Linkage to business performance
  6. Linkage to continuous improvement
  7. Evaluation of audit program effectiveness
  8. Summary of audit program results for review
  9. Long-term audit planning
B. Process
  1. Development and implementation of audit program procedures
  2. Development and implementation of audit program schedule
  3. Audit record keeping requirements
C. Audit Personnel
  1. Qualifications
  2. Selection
  3. Training
  4. Performance evaluation

VII. GENERAL KNOWLEDGE AND SKILLS (49 questions)
  A. Auditing Basics
       1. Quality concepts, terms, and definitions
       2. Theories and practices in quality auditing
       3. Benefits and consequences of audits
       4. Roles and responsibilities of client, auditor, auditee
       5. Characteristics of system, process, and product audits
       6. Characteristics of internal and external audits
       7. Characteristics of 1st, 2nd, and 3rd party audits
       8. Characteristics of qualitative and quantitative analysis
  B. Basic Skills
       1. Time management techniques
       2. Conflict resolution
       3. Effective communication techniques
       4. Presentation methods and techniques
  C. Tools and Techniques
       1. Checklists, guidelines, log sheets
       2. Sampling theory, procedures and applications
       3. Flow charts and process mapping
       4. Pattern and trend analysis
       5. Root cause analysis
       6. Cause and effect diagrams
       7. Pareto charts
       8. Histograms
       9. Descriptive statistics
      10. Control chart interpretation
      11. Process capability (Cp, Cpk) interpretation

Appendix C
Changes and Trends
in Auditing Practices

Although quality auditing has been in existence since the late 1940s or early 1950s, the quality audits of today bear little resemblance to those of that period. Ideally, quality auditing in the 1990s is a management tool for improvement, not an activity that management fears or resents.

No one knows for certain what changes will occur in the quality auditing field in the next decade. Trends suggest that assessment will continue to be an important management tool. Changes in the formation of audit groups, through joint audits or round robin consortiums, will ensure greater auditor independence and result in a cross-fertilization of ideas among industries. New standards, such as AS 9000 and ISO 19011, have been created and old ones revised to address societal and global needs. Advances in communications technology and the increase in the internationalization of businesses will lead to many changes in the next decade.

FORMATION OF JOINT AUDIT TEAMS
AND ROUND ROBIN CONSORTIUMS

Joint auditing is a recent trend, especially in regulated industries. Joint audits take the place of several separate audits, such as environmental, financial, and safety audits, performed at different times.

In round robin consortiums, groups of companies with similar interests each contribute one or two auditors to a group. Then, a company desiring to be audited asks this consortium for an appropriate number of auditors, depending on the size of the organization, to perform an audit. The round robin is an excellent way for a company to get independent audits performed; the auditors benefit by gaining auditing experience.

A round robin audit team must be handled the same way as a third-party registrar. Confidentiality agreements may have to be signed, and auditors should not audit a competitor or supplier. So the makeup of the audit team must be carefully contemplated. An auditee does not pay for a round robin audit, unlike a third-party registration audit. Since each organization is auditing the others, the cost of contributing the time of an auditor is involved; but the cost is absorbed by all companies that contribute an auditor or use the service.

This concept originated because companies had difficulties getting experienced auditors. The companies involved in a round robin consortium do not have to belong to the same industry; for example, a textile manufacturer and a metals manufacturer may have auditors belonging to the same team. As a result, a synergy or cross-fertilization of ideas from different industries occurs.

Round robin consortiums provide many benefits: a company gets an independent audit, and the auditors get the training and experience necessary for some types of certification. These consortiums are an excellent system for getting people qualified and getting an independent audit performed so that a company may know beforehand how it might fare in a third-party audit.

CREATION OF NEW STANDARDS

In the early days of quality auditing, very few national or international standards existed to audit against. Some regulated industries (the military, aviation, processed food, and aerospace) had standards, but most other organizations audited against self-determined, self-developed standards or requirements.

In the past 20 years, the development of numerous international, national, and industry-specific quality standards has supplemented internal (self-determined) standards, providing a common reference. The international standards in the ISO 9000 series, first issued in 1987 and revised in 1994, describe what elements quality systems should encompass but do not state how organizations should implement these elements.

Since the management system of an organization is influenced by the objectives of the organization, by its products, and by the practices specific to the organization, quality systems also vary from one organization to another. All international standards in the ISO 9000 series are independent of any specific economic sector. Collectively, they provide guidance for quality management and general requirements for quality assurance. The ISO 9001 standard and ISO 9004 guideline documents are being significantly reorganized for issuing in 2000 or 2001.

In August 1994, the Automotive Industry Action Group (AIAG) published QS-9000, a set of requirements for the automotive industry. QS-9000 is identical to the ISO 9000 series, with additional industry requirements geared specifically toward automotive quality improvement programs. However, while ISO 9001, 9002, and 9003 are strictly compliance-type documents, the addition of a TQM philosophy in QS-9000 moves the resulting document in the direction of continuous improvement. The AIAG has also published interpretations of QS-9000 requirements. While the document is criticized by some as too restrictive, it is considered by many others to be a breakthrough and a forerunner of things to come.

The next version of ANSI/ISO/ASQ 9001 is scheduled to be published in late 2000. The new version is expected to contain changes that emphasize customer satisfaction and continuous improvement.

SHIFTING FOCUS

In the 1970s, the primary purpose of auditing was compliance. Auditing in certain highly regulated fields, such as the nuclear industry, is likely to remain compliance-oriented. The current direction of the international standards groups is to make quality and environmental standards compatible and to combine quality and environmental audit standards. At this time, many are uncertain about the effects of the changes on the users of the standards and on the quality audit profession. The changes in the next issue of ISO 9001 should promote customer satisfaction and continual improvement, and the compatibility with environmental standards should result in cost savings to users of both standards. Combining the quality and environmental audit guidelines (ISO 19011) will emphasize compliance-oriented auditing.

Quality auditing is expected to focus more on effectiveness as it becomes more performance based, however. Rather than focusing just on adherence or compliance to a certain standard, companies are assessing their operations against those of world leaders by using benchmarking or by comparison with criteria such as those for the Malcolm Baldrige National Quality Award or ANSI/ISO/ASQ Q9004.

As companies try to achieve continuous improvement and reach world-class levels, they focus not just on complying with a particular standard, but rather ask, "How far can we reach, what are our goals to get there, and how do we go about that process?" As a result, a large percentage of the applications handed out for the Malcolm Baldrige National Quality Award every year are used for self-assessments within a company and are never used to apply for the award. The comprehensive criteria are based on how a system needs to be structured to attain total customer satisfaction. Benchmarking, one of the tools used during that process, is defined by the American Productivity and Quality Center as "the process of identifying, understanding, and adapting outstanding practices and processes from organizations anywhere in the world to help your organization improve its performance." Winners of the Malcolm Baldrige National Quality Award are required to share with other companies what they have learned from the process, resulting in an open invitation for others to learn from them.

References

1. ASQ Certification Department. CQA Brochure, item B0020, revised April 1999, p. 4.

2. Charles A. Mills, *The Quality Audit: A Management Evaluation Tool* (New York: McGraw-Hill, 1989), p. 87.

3. Walter Willborn, *Audit Standards: A Comparative Analysis* (Milwaukee, WI: ASQC Quality Press, 1993), p. 15.

4. *Standards for the Professional Practice of Internal Auditing* (Altamonte Springs, FL: The Institute of Internal Auditors, 1978).

5. ANSI/ISO/ASQC Q10011-2-1994, *Guidelines for Auditing Quality Systems* (Milwaukee, WI: ASQC Quality Press, 1994), p. 10, clause 10.0.

6. James W. Kolka, *ISO 9000: A Legal Perspective* (Milwaukee, WI: ASQ Quality Press; Montclair, VA: International Forum for Management Systems, Inc., 1998), p. 57.

7. American Society for Quality, *ASQ's Foundations in Quality: Certified Quality Auditor, Module 1: Ethics, Professional Conduct, and Liability Issues.* (Milwaukee, WI: ASQ Quality Press, 1998), p. 1-19.

8. Harold L. Federow, *Quality Practices and the Law* (New York: Quality Resources, 1997), p. 179.

9. Henry Campbell Black, *Black's Law Dictionary* (St. Paul, MN: West Publishing Co., 1990), p. 466.

10. Dennis R. Arter, *Quality Audits for Improved Performance,* 2d ed. (Milwaukee, WI: ASQC Quality Press, 1994), p. 18.

11. Arter, p. 12.

12. ASQC Energy Division, *Nuclear Quality Systems Auditor Training Handbook,* 2d ed. (Milwaukee, WI: ASQC Quality Press, 1986), p. 26.

13. ASQC Energy Division, p. 26.

14. ASQC Energy Division, p. 40.

15. ASQC Energy Division, p. 25.

16. J. M. Juran and Frank M. Gryna, eds., *Juran's Quality Control Handbook,* 4th ed. (New York, McGraw-Hill, 1989), p. 9.6.

17. Arter, pp. 19–20.

18. Mills, p. 89.

19. B. Scott Parsowith, *Fundamentals of Quality Auditing* (Milwaukee, WI: ASQC Quality Press, 1993), p. 24.

20. Arter, p. 41.

21. Parsowith, p. 23.

22. *Certified Quality Auditor: ASQ's Foundations in Quality, Module 2: Audit Preparation,* (Milwaukee, WI: ASQ Quality Press, 1998), pp. 2-48, 2-49.

23. J. P. Russell, *Quality Auditor Review* 1 no. 4 (1997): 3.

24. Arter, p. 35.

25. ASQC Energy Division, p. 26.

26. ASQC Energy Division, p. 26.

27. Arter, p. 23.

28. Arter, p. 26.

29. Arter, p. 37.

30. ASQC Energy Division, p. 42.

31. Mills, p. 185.

32. *Certified Quality Auditor: ASQ's Foundations in Quality, Module 3: Audit Performance* (Milwaukee, WI: ASQ Quality Press, 1998), p. 3-20.

33. *Certified Quality Auditor: Module 3,* p. 3-21.

34. Arter, pp. 39–40.

35. Arter, p. 41.

36. Arter, p. 43.

37. Arter, p. 42.

38. Arter, pp. 57–58.

39. ANSI/ISO/ASQ A8402-1994, *Quality Management and Quality Assurance—Vocabulary* (Milwaukee, WI: ASQC Quality Press, 1994), p. 5.

40. Willborn, pp. 52–53.

41. ASQC Energy Division, p. 45.

42. Parsowith, p. 30.

43. Arter, p. 62.

44. J. P. Russell and Terry Regel, *After the Quality Audit: Closing the Loop on the Audit Process* (Milwaukee, WI: ASQC Quality Press, 1996), p. 22.

45. Charles B. Robinson, *How to Make the Most of Every Audit,* (Milwaukee, WI: ASQC Quality Press, 1992), p. 94.

46. Russell and Regel, p. 11.

47. Russell and Regel, p. 104.

48. Lawrence B. Sawyer, *Sawyer's Internal Auditing,* 4th edition (Altamonte Springs, FL: Institute of Internal Auditors, 1996), p. 166.

49. Richard L. Ratliff, *Internal Auditing: Principles and techniques,* 2nd edition (Altamonte Springs, FL: Institute of Internal Auditors, 1996), p. 758.

50. Arter, p. 66.

51. ASQC Energy Division, p. 47.

52. Arter, p. 69.

53. Charles B. Robinson, *Auditing a Quality System for the Defense Industry* (Milwaukee, WI: ASQC Quality Press, 1990), p. 66.

54. Certified Quality Auditor, *ASQC Foundations in Quality, Module 5: Connective Action Follow-Up and Closure* (Milwaukee, WI: ASQC Quality Press, 1998), p. 5-9.

55. Arter, p. 73.

56. ASQC Energy Division, p. 49.

57. Robinson, *Auditing a Quality System for the Defense Industry,* p. 66.

58. Russell and Regel, pp. 119–122.

59. Russell and Regel, p. 107.

60. Russell and Regel, pp. 111–114.

61. Russell and Regel, pp. 103–107.

62. Russell and Regel, pp. 127–129.

63. ANSI/ISO/ASQC Q10011-1-1994, clause 7.0, note 15.

64. Parsowith, p. 32.

65. Arter, pp. 5–6.

66. Robinson, *How to Make the Most of Every Audit,* p. 78.

67. Arter, p. 9.

68. Allan J. Sayle, *Management Audits: The Assessment of Quality Management Systems,* 2d ed., ISBN: 0-9511739-1-X (Great Britain: Allan Sayle Associates, 1988), p. 1-8. Reproduced with permission of Allan J. Sayle.

69. Rudyard Kipling, "Elephant Child," in *Quality Quotes,* ed. Hélo Gomes (Milwaukee, WI: ASQC Quality Press, 1996), p. 94.

70. Parsowith, p. 14.

71. Russell and Regel, p. 128.

72. J. M. Juran, *Juran on Leadership for Quality: An Executive Handbook* (New York: The Free Press, 1989), p. 7.

73. David Hutton, *The Change Agents' Handbook* (Milwaukee, WI: ASQC Quality Press, 1994).

74. Russell and Regel, p. 127.

75. Russell and Regel, p. 127–146.

76. Russell and Regel, pp. 135–139.

77. ANSI/ISO/ASQ Q9004-1-1994.

78. Russell and Regel, p. 146.

79. Theodore Levitt, in *Quality Quotes,* p. 77.

80. United States Department of Commerce, Technology Administration, National Institute of Standards and Technology, National Quality Program, *Malcolm Baldrige National Quality Award, 1998 Criteria for Performance Excellence,* p. 23.

81. ANSI/ISO/ASQC Q9000-1-1994, p. 7.

82. Russell and Regel, p. 130.

83. Willborn, p. 65.

84. Parsowith, p. 33.

85. ASCQ Energy Division, p. 32.

86. Arter, p. 78.

87. Ibid.

88. Willborn, p. 13.

89. Willborn, p. 15.

90. ANSI/ISO/ASQ Q10011-2-1994.

91. Russell and Regel, p. 132.

92. Willborn, p. 13.

93. Willborn, p. 14.

94. Robinson, p. 12.

95. Don Benbow, "Distance Learning in a Cyber Classroom," ASQ *Quality Progress,* July 1998, pp. 43–45.

96. ANSI/ISO/ASQC Q10011-3-1994, p. 3.

97. J. P. Russell, *The Quality Master Plan: A Quality Strategy for Business Leadership* (Milwaukee: ASQC Quality Press, 1990; J. P. Russell & Associates), p. 7.

98. ANSI/ISO/ASQ A8402-1994, p. 5.

99. Ibid.

100. Ibid.

101. Mills, pp. 5, 6, 7.

102. Mills, pp. 2–3.

103. Mills, p. 11.

104. Sayle, p. 1-7. Reproduced with permission of Allan J. Sayle.

105. Arter, p. 3.

106. Arter, pp. 1–2.

107. ANSI/ISO/ASQ A8402-1994, p. 5.

108. Dorsey J. Talley, *Management Audits for Excellence* (Milwaukee, WI: ASQC Quality Press, 1988), p. 42.

109. Sayle, p. 1-4. Reproduced with permission of Allan J. Sayle.

110. Juran and Gryna, p. 9.4. Reproduced with permission of The McGraw-Hill Companies.

111. Willborn, p. 31.

112. Mills, pp. 36–40.

113. Mills, pp. 43–46.

114. ANSI/ISO/ASQ A8402-1994, p. 8.

115. Arter, p. 13.

116. ASQC Energy Division, p. 3.

117. ASQC Energy Division, p. 2.

118. Arter, p. 4.

119. Parsowith, pp. 4–5.

120. IIA, *Internal Auditing: Principles and Techniques;* 2d ed. (Altamonte Springs, FL, 1996), p. 671–749.

121. *Certified Quality Auditor: ASQ Foundations in Quality, Module 7,* (Milwaukee WI: ASQ Quality Press, 1998) p. 7-54.

122. *Certified Quality Auditor: ASQ Foundations in Quality, Module 7,* p. 7-55.

123. Russell and Regel, pp. 157–167.

124. Mills, p. 205.

125. Gerald F. Smith, *Quality Problem Solving,* (Milwaukee WI: ASQ Quality Press, 1998), p. 115.

126. John T. Burr, "The Tools of Quality, Part VI: Pareto Charts," ASQC *Quality Progress,* November 1990, p. 61.

127. Juran Institute, "The Tools of Quality, Part IV: Histograms," ASQC *Quality Progress* (September 1990) pp. 77–78.

128. Juran and Gryna, p. 23.15.

129. Juran and Gryna, p. 23.16.

130. Parsowith, p. xiii.

131. Peter D. Shainin, "The Tools of Quality, Part III: Control Charts," ASQC *Quality Progress,* August 1990, pp. 79–80.

132. Juran and Gryna, p. 24.8.

133. Juran and Gryna, p. 24.7.

134. Parsowith, p. 65.

135. Juran and Gryna, p. 22.41.

136. Mills, p. 214.

Recommended Readings

Reference Materials Used to Develop Exam Questions

ANSI/ISO/ASQC Q10011-1, 2, 3, *Guidelines for Auditing Quality Systems*. Milwaukee, WI: ASQC Quality Press, 1994. **T10011**

Arter, Dennis R., *Quality Audits for Improved Performance,* 2nd ed., Milwaukee, WI: ASQC Quality Press, 1994. **H0844**

ASQ Quality Audit Division, *The Quality Audit Handbook,* Milwaukee, WI: ASQ Quality Press, 1997. **H0939**

Federow, Harold L., *Quality Practices and the Law,* Quality Resources, New York, NY 1997.

Hutchins, Greg, *Standard Manual of Quality Auditing,* Englewood Cliffs, NJ: Prentice Hall, 1992.

Juran, J. M., *Quality Control Handbook,* 4th ed., 1988. **P660**

Kolka, James W., *ISO 9000: A Legal Perspective,* Milwaukee, WI: ASQ Quality Press, 1998. **H0992**

Mills, Charles A., *The Quality Audit: A Management Evaluation Tool,* Milwaukee, WI: ASQC Quality Press, 1989. **H0568**

Parsowith, B. Scott, *Fundamentals of Quality Auditing,* Milwaukee, WI: ASQC Quality Press, 1995. **H0794**

Robinson, Charles B., *How to Make the Most of Every Audit: An Etiquette Handbook for Auditing,* 2nd ed., Milwaukee, WI: ASQC Quality Press, 1992.

Russell, J. P. & Terry Regel, *After the Quality Audit: Closing the Loop on the Audit Process,* Milwaukee, WI: ASQC Quality Press. 1996. **H0927**

Sawyer, L. B., *The Practice of Modern Internal Auditing,* Altamonte Springs, FL: Institute of Internal Auditors, 1981.

Sayle, Allan J., *Management Audits,* 3rd ed., Allan J. Sayle & Assoc., 1997. **P659**

Thresh, James L., *How to Plan, Conduct, & Benefit From Effective Quality Audits,* Harrison, NY: MGI Management Institute, 1984.

Books with bolded item numbers can be purchased from ASQ.

Reference Materials Recommended by 1998 CQA's Taking the Exam

Arter, Dennis R., *Quality Audits for Improved Performance,* 2nd ed., Milwaukee, WI: ASQC Quality Press, 1994. **H0844**

ASQ Quality Management Division, *The Cerified Quality Manager Handbook,* Milwaukee, WI: ASQ Quality Press, 1999. **H0977**

Juran, J. M., *Quality Control Handbook,* 4th ed., 1988. **P660**

Mills, Charles A., *The Quality Audit: A Management Evaluation Tool,* Milwaukee, WI: ASQC Quality Press, 1989. **H0568**

Editor Selections for Additional Study

Duncan, Acheson J., *Quality Control and Industrial Statistics,* 5th ed., New York: Irwin/McGraw-Hill, 1986.

Grant, E. L., and R. S. Leavenworth, *Statistical Quality Control,* 7th ed., New York: McGraw-Hill, 1996. **P597**

Ishikawa, Kaoru, *Guide to Quality Control,* White Plains, New York: Krauss International Publications, 1982. **P104**

Mizuno, Shigeru, Edited by, *Management for Quality Improvement: The 7 New QC Tools,* Portland, OR: Productivity, Inc., 1988.

Pyzdek, Thomas, *Pocket Guide to Quality Tools,* Tucson, AZ: Quality Publishing, 1994.

Tague, Nancy R., *The Quality Tool Box,* Milwaukee, WI: ASQC Quality Press, 1995. **H0861**

Wilson, Ray and Paul Harsin, *Process Mastering,* Portland, OR: Productivity, Inc., 1998.

Glossary

DEFINITIONS TAKEN FROM
ANSI/ISO/ASQC A8402-1994*

Auditee Organization being audited

Business first party See *Contractor*

Business second party See *Purchaser*

Company-wide quality control (CWQC) See *Total quality management (TQM)*

Compatibility Ability of entities to be used together under specific conditions to fulfill relevant requirements

Concession Written authorization to use or release a product which does not conform to the specified requirements; see also *Waiver*

Contract review Systematic activities carried out by the supplier before signing the contract to ensure that requirements for quality are adequately defined, free from ambiguity, documented, and can be realized by the supplier

Contractor Supplier in a contractual situation

Correction Refers to repair, rework, or adjustment and relates to the disposition of an existing nonconformity

---

*ANSI/ISO/ASQC A8402-1994, *Quality Management and Quality Assurance—Vocabulary* (Milwaukee: ASQC, 1994). Reprinted with permission.

Corrective action Action taken to eliminate the causes of an existing nonconformity, defect, or other undesirable situation in order to prevent recurrence

Customer Recipient of a product provided by the supplier

Defect Nonfulfillment of an intended usage requirement or reasonable expectation, including one concerned with safety

Degree of demonstration Extent to which evidence is produced to provide confidence that specified requirements are fulfilled

Dependability Collective term used to describe the availability performance and its influencing factors: reliability performance, maintainability performance, and maintenance-support performance

Design review Documented, comprehensive, and systematic examination of a design to evaluate its capability to fulfill the requirements for quality, identify problems, if any, and propose the development of solutions

Deviation permit Written authorization to depart from the originally specified requirements for a product prior to its production; see also *Production permit*

Disposition of nonconformity Action to be taken to deal with an existing nonconforming entity in order to resolve the nonconformity

Entity Item which can be individually described and considered

Grade Category or rank given to entities having the same functional use but different requirements for quality

Hold point Point, defined in an appropriate document, beyond which an activity must not proceed without the approval of a designated organization or authority

Inspection Activity such as measuring, examining, testing, or gauging one or more characteristics of an entity and comparing the results with specified requirements in order to establish whether conformity is achieved for each characteristic

Interchangeability Ability of an entity to be used in place of another, without modification, to fulfill the same requirements

Item See *Entity*

Lead quality auditor A quality auditor designated to manage a quality audit

Management review Formal evaluation by top management of the status and adequacy of the quality system in relation to quality policy and objectives

Model for quality assurance Standardized or selected set of quality system requirements combined to satisfy the quality assurance needs of a given situation

Nonconformity Nonfulfillment of a specified requirement

Objective evidence Information which can be proved true, based on facts obtained through observation, measurement, test, or other means

Organization Company, corporation, firm, enterprise, or institution, or part thereof, whether incorporated or not, public or private, that has its own functions and administration

Organizational structure Responsibilities, authorities, and relationships, arranged in a pattern, through which an organization performs its functions

Preventive action Action taken to eliminate the causes of a potential nonconformity, defect, or other undesirable situation in order to prevent occurrence

Procedure Specified way to perform an activity

Process Set of interrelated resources and activities which transform inputs into outputs

Process quality audit See *Quality audit*

Process quality evaluation See *Quality evaluation*

Product Results on activities or processes

Product liability Generic term used to describe the onus on a producer or others to make restitution for loss related to personal injury, property damage, or other harm caused by a product

Product quality audit See *Quality audit*

Production permit See *Deviation permit*. A production permit is for a limited quantity or period and for a specified use

Purchaser Customer in a contractual situation

Qualification See *Qualification process*

Qualification process Process of demonstrating whether an entity is capable of fulfilling the specified requirement

Qualified Status given to an entity when the capability of fulfilling specified requirements has been demonstrated

Quality Totality of characteristics of an entity that bear on its ability to satisfy stated and implied needs

Quality appraisal See *Quality evaluation*

Quality assessment See *Quality evaluation*

Quality assurance All the planned and systematic activities implemented within the quality system, and demonstrated as needed, to provide adequate confidence that an entity will fulfill requirements for quality

Quality assurance manual See *Quality manual*

Quality assurance plan See *Quality plan*

Quality audit Systematic and independent examination to determine whether quality activities and related results comply with planned arrangements and whether these arrangements are implemented effectively and are suitable to achieve objectives

Quality audit observation Statement of fact made during a quality audit and substantiated by objective evidence

Quality auditor Person qualified to perform quality audits

Quality control Operational techniques and activities that are used to fulfill requirements for quality

Quality evaluation Systematic examination of the extent to which an entity is capable of fulfilling specified requirements

Quality improvement Actions taken throughout the organization to increase the effectiveness and efficiency of activities and processes in order to provide added benefits to both the organization and its customers

Quality loop Conceptual model of interacting activities that influence quality at the various stages ranging from the identification of needs to the assessment of whether these needs have been satisfied

Quality losses Losses caused by not realizing the potential of resources in processes and activities

Quality management All activities of the overall management function that determine the quality policy, objectives, and responsibilities, and implement them by means such as quality planning, quality control, quality assurance, and quality improvement within the quality system

Quality management manual See *Quality manual*

Quality management plan See *Quality plan*

Quality manual Document stating the quality policy and describing the quality system of an organization

Quality plan Document setting out the specific quality practices, resources, and sequence of activities relevant to a particular product, project, or contract

Quality planning Activities that establish the objectives and requirements for quality and for the application of quality system elements

Quality policy Overall intentions and direction of an organization with regard to quality, as formally expressed by top management

Quality record Document which provides objective evidence of the extent of the fulfillment of the requirements for quality or the effectiveness of the operation of a quality system element

Quality-related costs Those costs incurred in ensuring and assuring satisfactory quality, as well as the losses incurred when satisfactory quality is not achieved

Quality spiral See *Quality loop*

Quality surveillance Continual monitoring and verification of the status of an entity and analysis of records to ensure that specified requirements are being fulfilled

Quality survey See *Quality evaluation*

Quality system Organizational structure, procedures, processes, and resources needed to implement quality management

Quality system record See *Quality record*

Record Document which furnishes objective evidence of activities performed or results achieved

Repair Action taken on a nonconforming product so that it will fulfill the intended usage requirements although it may not conform to the originally specified requirements

Requirements for quality Expression of the needs or their translation into a set of quantitatively or qualitatively stated requirements for the characteristics of an entity to enable its realization and examination

Requirements of society Obligations resulting from laws, regulations, rules, codes, statutes, and other considerations

Rework Action taken on a nonconforming product so that it will fulfill the specified requirements

Safety State in which the risk of harm (to persons) or damage is limited to an acceptable level

Self-inspection Inspection of the work by the performer of that work, according to specified rules

Service Result generated by activities at the interface between the supplier and the customer and by supplier internal activities to meet the customer needs

Service delivery Those supplier activities necessary to provide the service

Service quality audit See *Quality audit*

Specification Document stating requirements

Subcontractor Organization that provides a product to the supplier

Subsupplier See *Subcontractor*

Supplier Organization that provides a product to the customer

Total quality See *Total quality management (TQM)*

Total quality control (TQC) See *Total quality management (TQM)*

Total quality management (TQM) Management approach of an organization, centered on quality, based on the participation of all its members and aiming at long-term success through customer satisfaction, and benefits to all members of the organization and to society

Traceability Ability to trace the history, application, or location of an entity by means of recorded identifications

Validation Confirmation by examination and provision of objective evidence that the particular requirements for a specified intended use are fulfilled

Verification Confirmation by examination and provision of objective evidence that specified requirements have been fulfilled

Waiver See *Concession*. A waiver is limited to the shipment of a product that has specific nonconforming characteristics within specific deviations, for a limited time or quantity

Index